Austin Morris 2200 1972-74 Au

By Kenneth Ball
Graduate, Institution of Mechanical Engineers
Associate Member, Guild of Motoring Writers
and the Autopress Team of Technical Writers.

Austin 2200 1972-74
Morris 2200 1972-74
Wolseley Six 1972-74

Autobooks

Autopress Ltd. Golden Lane Brighton BN1 2QJ England

The AUTOBOOK series of Workshop Manuals is the largest in the world and covers the majority of British and Continental motor cars, as well as all major Japanese and Australian models. For a full list see the back of this manual.

CONTENTS

ISBN 0 85147 484 5

First Edition   1973
Second Edition, fully revised   1974

© Autopress Ltd 1974

746

Printed and bound in Brighton England for Autopress Ltd by G Beard & Son Ltd

B

ACKNOWLEDGEMENT

My thanks are due to British Leyland Motor Corporation Ltd for their unstinted co-operation and also for supplying data and illustrations.

I am also grateful to a considerable number of owners who have discussed their cars at length and many of whose suggestions have been included in this manual.

Kenneth Ball
Graduate, Institution of Mechanical Engineers
Associate Member, Guild of Motoring Writers
Ditchling Sussex England.

INTRODUCTION

This do-it-yourself Workshop Manual has been specially written for the owner who wishes to maintain his car in first class condition and to carry out his own servicing and repairs. Considerable savings on garage charges can be made, and one can drive in safety and confidence knowing the work has been done properly.

Comprehensive step-by-step instructions and illustrations are given on all dismantling, overhauling and assembling operations. Certain assemblies require the use of expensive special tools, the purchase of which would be unjustified. In these cases information is included but the reader is recommended to hand the unit to the agent for attention.

Throughout the Manual hints and tips are included which will be found invaluable, and there is an easy to follow fault diagnosis at the end of each chapter.

Whilst every care has been taken to ensure correctness of information it is obviously not possible to guarantee complete freedom from errors or to accept liability arising from such errors or omissions.

Instructions may refer to the righthand or lefthand sides of the vehicle or the components. These are the same as the righthand or lefthand of an observer standing behind the car and looking forward.

CHAPTER 1

THE ENGINE

1:1 Description

The 2200 power unit incorporates a six-cylinder engine which is based on the four-cylinder version originally designed for the BLMC Maxi. That the new engine incorporates most of the Maxi features can be seen by a study of **FIG 1:1**. This shows how the transverse engine is mounted on the transmission unit, the length of the engine making it necessary to eliminate the belt-driven fan and side-mounted radiator.

Total capacity is 2227 cc, and power output 110 bhp at 5250 rev/min. Torque is 125 lbf ft (17.3 kgf m) at 2500 rev/min and compression ratio 9.0 to 1. Further details are given in **Technical Data** at the end of this manual.

At the water-pump end, the seven-bearing crankshaft carries a sprocket for the camshaft timing chain and a skew gear that drives a shaft for the oil pump and distributor. The connecting rods are split horizontally and have renewable bearing liners. The solid-skirt pistons have three compression rings and one oil control ring each. The gudgeon pin is a press fit in the small-end of the connecting rod.

The timing chain is automatically tensioned and drives an overhead camshaft that runs in an aluminium carrier secured to the detachable cylinder head. The cams operate bucket tappets that slide in bores in the carrier. These tappets enclose the top ends of the valve stems and springs, and valve clearances are adjusted by shims.

The crankshaft pulley drives two belts, one for the alternator and water-pump and the other for the power steering pump (if fitted). The oil pump circulates oil through a fullflow filter with a renewable element. The oil relief valve is non-adjustable.

1:2 Overhauling methods and information

Owners who are not trained mechanics will find much useful information in **'Hints on Maintenance and Overhaul'** at the end of this manual. This will ensure that work is carried out efficiently and with maximum safety.

References to the righthand and lefthand of the car will be those seen from the rear when looking forward. No. 1 cylinder and No. 1 valve are at the water-pump end of the engine. When the engine is removed, the water-pump end will be called the front.

Special tools are needed for some operations and most of these will be illustrated and given the makers part numbers.

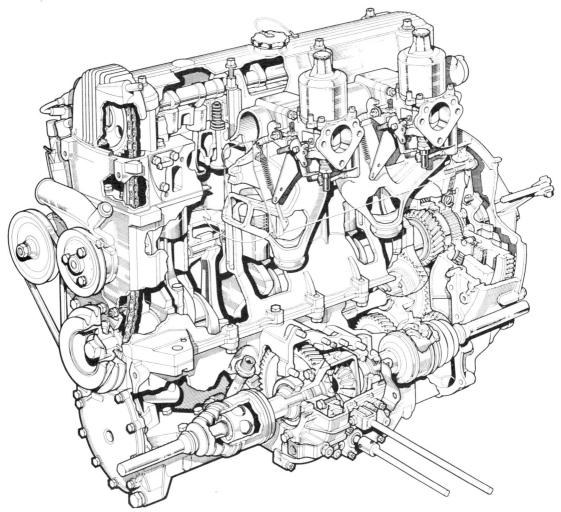

FIG 1:1 Cut-away view of the 2200 engine and transmission, showing the chain drive to the overhead camshaft (left). Note the absence of a belt driven fan

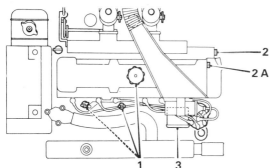

FIG 1:2 Locations of the parts needed when carrying out routine maintenance on the engine

Key to Fig 1:2 1 Oil filler cap and dipstick   2 Drain plug (manual gearchange)   2A Drain plug (automatic) 3 Oil filter

1:3 Routine maintenance

Refer to **FIG 1:2**. With car standing level, check oil at dipstick 1 and top-up if necessary, keeping the oil at MAX mark. 1 5 pt (1.7 US pt, .9 litre) will span the MIN to MAX marks.

Every 6000 miles (10,000 km or six months) drain off the old oil and refill with fresh. Drain plug is 2 (manual) and 2A (automatic) At the same mileage fit a new oil filter element 3 (see **Section 1:9**).

1:4 Adjusting valve tappet clearances

Refer to **FIG 1:3**. Check the clearances every 12,000 miles (20,000 km or 12 months). Do the following:
1 Remove air cleaner. Disconnect hose 2 and distributor vacuum pipe 3. Disconnect oil pipe 4. Remove screws 5 and lift off cover and gasket 6.

2 Remove sparking plugs. Turn camshaft **against normal direction of rotation** using tool 18G.1153 (see 4). Check with feeler gauges as at 12, working in the following sequence (No. 1 tappet is at the sprocket end).

3 Check tappet No. 1 with valve No. 12 fully open:

,,	,,	,,	7	,,	,,	,,	6	,,	,,
,,	,,	,,	9	,,	,,	,,	4	,,	,,
,,	,,	,,	2	,,	,,	,,	11	,,	,,
,,	,,	,,	5	,,	,,	,,	8	,,	,,
,,	,,	,,	10	,,	,,	,,	3	,,	,,
,,	,,	,,	12	,,	,,	,,	1	,,	,,
,,	,,	,,	6	,,	,,	,,	7	,,	,,
,,	,,	,,	4	,,	,,	,,	9	,,	,,
,,	,,	,,	11	,,	,,	,,	2	,,	,,
,,	,,	,,	8	,,	,,	,,	5	,,	,,
,,	,,	,,	3	,,	,,	,,	10	,,	,,

4 Adjustment is necessary only if the clearance (inlet and exhaust) is less than .012 inch (.31 mm). Correct clearances are .016 to .018 inch (.41 to .46 mm) for inlet valves and .020 to .022 inch (.51 to .56 mm) for exhaust when cold. If new parts have been fitted or valves reground, set the clearances to the correct figures just given.

Adjustment:

1 Turn engine until cylinder No. 1 (nearest to water-pump) is on compression stroke. Align crankshaft pulley mark with TDC indicator (see 1 in **FIG 1 : 7**). Align sprocket and carrier marks (see 4).

2 Remove chain tensioner screw 5. Insert $\frac{1}{8}$ inch Allen key 6 and turn 90 deg. clockwise to retract tensioner. Remove sprocket and let chain hang on guides (7).

3 Slacken bolts 8 evenly to release valve spring tension. Fit clips 9 (Part No. 18G.1218) to hold each pair of tappets in place. Lift off carrier 10.

4 Remove tappets needing adjustment in turn. Check thickness stamped on shim inside tappet (see 11). The correct shim thickness will be given by adding together the clearance as checked to the thickness of the shim removed and taking away the dimension for the correct clearance. Shims are available as follows:

5 97 .097 inch (2.47 mm)	13 .113 inch (2.87 mm)
99 .099 inch (2.52 mm)	15 .115 inch (2.93 mm)
01 .101 inch (2.56 mm)	17 .117 inch (2.98 mm)
03 .103 inch (2.62 mm)	19 .119 inch (3.03 mm)
05 .105 inch (2.67 mm)	21 .121 inch (3.08 mm)
07 .107 inch (2.72 mm)	23 .123 inch (3.13 mm)
09 .109 inch (2.77 mm)	25 .125 inch (3.18 mm)
11 .111 inch (2.83 mm)	27 .127 inch (3.23 mm)

6 Smear shim with petroleum jelly and insert into tappet. Refit tappets into correct bores and hold in place with clips. Refit carrier and tighten bolts in diagonal sequence evenly to 20 lbf ft (2.8 kgf m).

7 Set crankshaft to TDC with No. 1 cylinder on the compression stroke. Temporarily fit camshaft sprocket and align marks. Remove sprocket, fit to chain with alignment mark at top and lift chain to engage crankshaft sprocket. Fit camshaft sprocket and tighten bolt to 35 lbf ft (4.8 kgf m). Turn Allen key anticlockwise to release chain tensioner and refit screw. Refit plugs and cylinder head cover. Use new O-ring seals if necessary. Tighten bolts to 6 lbf ft (.8 kgf m). Refit remaining parts in reverse order to dismantling.

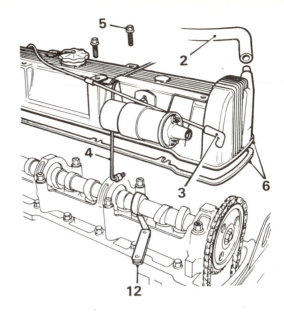

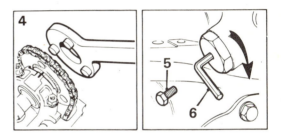

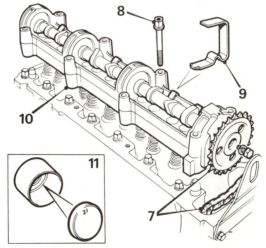

FIG 1 : 3 Sequence of operations when adjusting tappet clearances. The numbers are used in the text

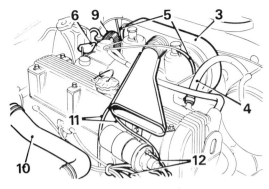

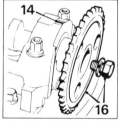

FIG 1:4 Operations involved when removing the cylinder head. The numbers are used in the text

1:5 Servicing cylinder head and camshaft

This work can be done with the engine in the car. Refer to **FIG 1:4**.

Removing head:

1 Disconnect battery, drain cooling system and remove air cleaner 3. Disconnect hose 4 and mixture control cables 5. Release progressive throttle assembly 6 from manifold (see **Chapter 2**). Disconnect heater hoses 7.
2 Remove exhaust pipe clamps 8. Disconnect fuel pipe 9. Disconnect top hose 10 at thermostat housing and bleed hose at radiator (see **Chapter 4**).
3 Disconnect oil pipe from block and vacuum pipe from distributor 11. Disconnect all wiring to head. Remove distributor cap and plug leads. Remove cover as in **Section 1:4** (see 13). Repeat operations 1 and 2 in **Section 1:4** under 'Adjustment'.
4 Slacken head bolts evenly in diagonal sequence, then lift off head and gasket.

Dismantling and servicing head:

Refer to **FIG 1:5** and remove manifolds 2 and heater rail. Remove housing and lifting bracket 3. Slacken bolts

4 evenly. Fit clips 5 (Tool No. 18G.1218) to hold pairs of tappets in place. Lift off carrier 6. Clean carbon from combustion chambers.

Compress valve springs (7) and remove parts 8 and 9. Remove oil seal rings from inlet valve stems and remove valves, keeping them in correct order.

Check valve seats and stems for wear. Have pitted valve seats recut and then grind in the valves until seats are a smooth matt grey. Check valve springs against **Technical Data**. Seats in the head may be cut back if too wide or inserts may be fitted by a garage if too far gone. Clean off all traces of carbon and valve grinding compound.

Reassembling and refitting head:

Reverse the dismantling procedure, using new seals on the inlet valve stems. Dip the seals in oil before refitting. Use new gaskets throughout. Check and adjust the valve clearances (see **Section 1:4**) after refitting the head. The head bolts must be tightened progressively in the sequence shown in **FIG 1:6** to a torque of 60 lbf ft (8.3 kgf m).

Follow operations 6 and 7 at the end of **Section 1:4** when reassembling the camshaft drive and cover.

Servicing the camshaft:

Remove the head cover and gasket (see beginning of **Section 1:4**). Repeat operations 1 and 2 under 'Adjustment' in the same Section, but do not remove the sprocket. Check end float between sprocket and camshaft locating plate (see inset, bottom right in **FIG 1:5**). Renew plate if necessary. End float is given in **Technical Data**.

Remove sprocket and let chain hang on guides. Repeat operation 3 under 'Adjustment' in **Section 1:4**. Withdraw camshaft rearwards after removing tappets.

Check journal diameters against figures in **Technical Data**. Check tappet and camshaft bores in carrier for wear or pick-up. Check cams and tappet faces for excessive wear.

When reassembling, oil the camshaft and fit into the carrier. Fit tappets in original bores after oiling. Fit carrier and tighten bolts evenly in diagonal sequence to 20 lbf ft (2.8 kgf m). Temporarily fit sprocket and chain. Check tappet clearances and adjust if necessary (see **Section 1:4**). Complete the assembling as in operation 7 at the end of **Section 1:4**.

1:6 Servicing the timing gear

The timing chain tensioner:

Refer to **FIG 1:7**. Turn crankshaft pulley notch to TDC with No. 1 cylinder at firing point (see 1 in illustration). No. 1 cylinder is nearest the water pump. Firing point is at top of compression stroke with both valves closed. Remove crankshaft pulley (see **Section 1:7**). Remove cylinder head cover (see operation 1 at start of **Section 1:4**). Align sprocket and carrier marks 5.

Remove tensioner screw 6, insert $\frac{1}{8}$ inch Allen key 7 and turn it clockwise to retract tensioner. Slacken locknut and turn chain guide adjuster to back of cam

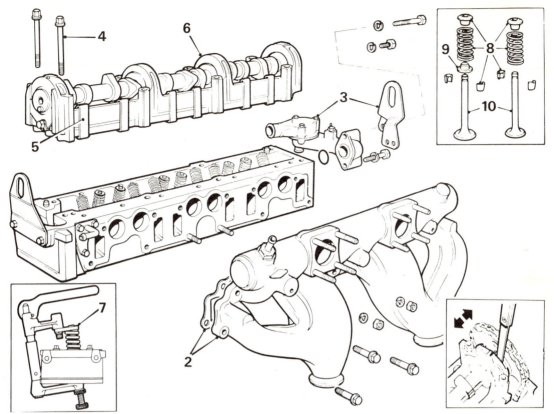

FIG 1:5 Components of the cylinder head and valve gear. Inset (bottom right) shows method of checking camshaft end float

(see 8). Wire chain to sprocket. Pull sprocket off camshaft (9). Remove front cover (10). Top bolt illustrated is a dowel bolt and locates the fixed chain guide. It has a sealing washer. Remove tensioner adaptor 11 and tensioner 12.

Turn Allen key to dismantle tensioner (13). Check for wear. Clean the parts, oil them and reassemble, fully retracting the head. Refit the tensioner.

Refit cover, locating lower end of fixed guide on dowel bolt. Tighten to 20 lbf ft (2.8 kgf m). Fit camshaft sprocket. Align marks and tighten bolt to 35 lbf ft (4.8 kgf m). Turn adjuster (8) until chain is tight but not taut. Tighten adjuster locknut.

Turn Allen key anticlockwise to release tensioner and refit adaptor screw 6. Reverse remaining dismantling procedures, tightening the pulley bolt to 60 to 70 lbf ft (8.3 to 9.7 kgf m).

Timing chain guides:

To remove and refit these, repeat the preceding dismantling instructions and retract, but do not remove, the chain tensioner. From top, remove bolts securing guides (see 19, 20 and 28 in **FIG 1:9**). Remove fixed guide 20. Disengage lower end of adjustable guide 19, turn adjuster 18 through 90 deg. and remove guide.

To reassemble, engage lower end of adjustable guide with adjuster cam. Set adjuster so that guide is vertically aligned with chain sprockets. Repeat the preceding instructions for the tensioner, starting with 'Refit cover —', after fitting the fixed guide.

Timing chain and sprockets:

The timing chain must be parted in situ, using tool No. 18G.1151 (see **FIG 1:24**). If the tool is not available the work must be entrusted to an agent. To remove and refit a chain proceed as follows:

Remove cylinder head cover (operation 1 at start of **Section 1:4**). Remove crankshaft pulley and oil seal (see **Section 1:7**). Repeat operations 1 and 2 under 'Adjustment' in **Section 1:4**.

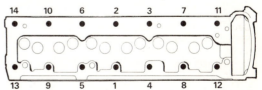

FIG 1:6 Correct sequence for tightening cylinder head bolts

Refer to **FIG 1:8** and remove oil thrower 7 and crankshaft sprocket 8. **Note that rounded shoulder of sprocket faces oil thrower.**

Find bright link in chain and fit bridge piece of tool 18G.1151 into link. Use pointed pins of extractor, inserting them in depressions in link pins. Tighten press until pins are forced out of link plate. Remove chain.

Fit new chain and then fit locating bridge legs so that they centralize link in press anvil. Depressions in pins must face moving head of press. Fit link with chamfered face away from chain. Press link home. Fit rivet adaptor

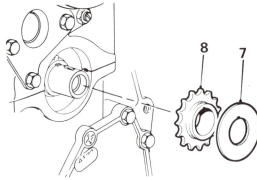

FIG 1:8 Removing the oil thrower 7 and camshaft drive sprocket 8 from the crankshaft

so that chisel ends bear on link pins. Tighten press by hand, using tommy bar provided. Check that there is slight play in the link, with no tight spots.

Refit the dismantled parts in the reverse order of dismantling, making sure that the crankshaft is still at TDC on the firing point of No. 1 cylinder and the camshaft sprocket marks are aligned.

1:7 Servicing crankshaft oil seals and housing

Servicing front oil seal (water pump end):

Refer to **FIG 1:10**. Proceed as follows:

1 On cars with automatic transmission, remove the power unit (see **Section 1:10**).

2 Slacken alternator mountings and remove belt 2 (see **Chapter 4**). If power steering pump is fitted, remove drive belt (see **Chapter 8**). Flatten lock tab 4 and remove pulley bolt 5 (tool 18G.98A). Lever pulley 6 off crankshaft.

3 On cars with manual gearchange take the weight of the power unit under the transmission casing or by lifting at the front bracket. Remove nut 8 from front righthand engine mounting and nut 9 from front lefthand mounting.

4 Remove alternator (10). Remove mounting plate (11). Extract seal using tool 18G.1087 (12).

5 Clean seal housing and cut sealing plugs flush if necessary (13). Oil flange and lip of new seal and drive into place with tool 18G.1162 (14).

6 Reverse dismantling procedure, tightening bolts 11 to 18 lbf ft (2.5 kgf m). Lubricate pulley boss before fitting. Tighten mounting nuts to 30 lbf ft (4.1 kgf m). Tighten pulley bolt to 60 to 70 lbf ft (8.3 to 9.7 kgf m). Adjust belts.

Rear oil seal (manual gearchange):

Refer to **FIG 1:11**. To renew seal proceed as follows:

1 Remove clutch with engine in car (see **Chapter 5**). Screw centre piece of tool 18G.1152 into cage. Locate cage over primary gear and bolt centre to crankshaft with thin-headed bolts (2). Screw cage inwards until it contacts seal (3).

2 Set slot 4 uppermost and pull primary gear 5 as far away from the engine as possible. Insert collets 6 through slot. Locate them in groove in gear (6). Position them opposite each other, away from the slot.

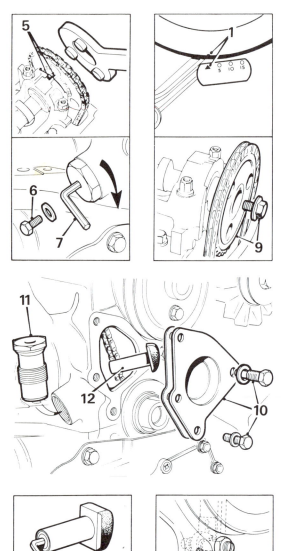

FIG 1:7 How to service the camshaft chain tensioner. The numbers are used in the text

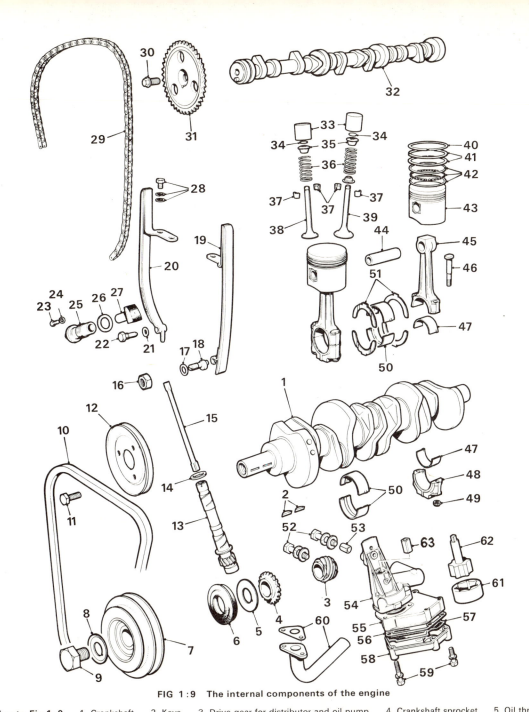

FIG 1:9 The internal components of the engine

Key to Fig 1:9 1 Crankshaft 2 Keys 3 Drive gear for distributor and oil pump 4 Crankshaft sprocket 5 Oil thrower 6 Crankshaft front oil seal 7 Crankshaft pulley 8 Lock washer 9 Bolt 10 Drive belt 11 Screw 12 Water pump pulley 13 Distributor drive shaft 14 Thrust washer 15 Oil pump drive shaft 16 Locknut for adjuster 17 Sealing washer 18 Adjuster 19 Chain guide—tight side 20 Chain guide—tensioner side 21 Sealing washer 22 Dowel bolt 23 Screw 24 Sealing washer 25 Adaptor 26 Washer 27 Chain tensioner assembly 28 Screw—chain guides 29 Chain 30 Bolt 31 Camshaft sprocket 32 Camshaft 33 Tappets 34 Shim 35 Valve spring cap 36 Valve spring 37 Valve cotters 38 Exhaust valve 39 Inlet valve 40 Top compression ring 41 Tapered compression rings 42 Oil control ring 43 Piston 44 Gudgeon pin 45 Connecting rod 46 Big-end bolt 47 Big-end bearing shells 48 Big-end cap 49 Nut 50 Main bearing shells 51 Thrust washers 52 Bolts—oil pump to casing 53 Ring dowel 54 Oil pump body 55 Oil strainer body 56 Gasket 57 Oil strainer 58 Cover 59 Bolts 60 Oil suction pipe 61 Oil pump outer ring 62 Oil pump rotor 63 Oil pump drive coupling

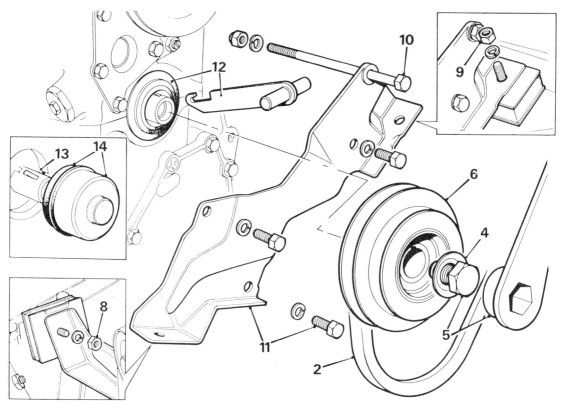

FIG 1:10   Operations required to remove and refit the crankshaft front oil seal

3 Unscrew nut 7 to withdraw gear and seal.

4 To fit a new seal, fit primary gear to crankshaft. Fit sleeve 9 over clutch splines to protect seal lip. Oil seal and sleeve with EP.90 oil and push seal 10 up to its housing.

5 Refit tool (11), screwing clockwise until seal is fully home. Remove tool and refit clutch.

Rear oil seal (automatic transmission):

Refer to **FIG 1:12**. To renew seal do the following:

1 With power unit out of car, remove transmission assembly (see **Chapter 6a**).

2 Release locking tabs and remove parts 4. Prise out the oil seal 5.

3 To fit the new seal, first check the seal housing. Cut the oil seal plugs flush if necessary (see 13 in **FIG 1:10**) and flange with EP.90 oil and press the seal into place with tool 18G.1108 (see 7).

4 Reassemble in reverse order of dismantling, tightening drive plate bolts (4) to 60 lbf ft (8.3 kgf m).

Flywheel and housing:

To remove the flywheel, remove the cover as in **Chapter 5,** after taking away the battery and battery tray. Remove the clutch as described in the same chapter. Remove the four bolts and retaining plate and drift the flywheel off the crankshaft with a hide mallet.

To renew the starter ring gear, sawcut the ring and split it with a cold chisel. **Remove all burrs from mating surfaces.** Heat the new ring to a light blue colour (300 to 400°C or 572 to 752°F). Fit to flywheel with rounded teeth away from flange.

To remove the flywheel housing, remove the battery and tray, and the clutch release bearing and cover assembly (see **Chapter 5**). Remove the starter motor (see **Chapter 10**). Remove the clutch thrust plate (3 setscrews). Remove the flywheel without removing the clutch from it.

Fit sleeve over primary gear splines (see **FIG 1:11**). Support power unit and remove screw securing rear lefthand mounting to housing. Unlock and remove six bolts and three nuts inside housing. Remove two external bolts at top and six nuts from lower edge. Withdraw housing and gasket.

Reverse dismantling to refit housing, using a new gasket. Lubricate oil seal with EP.90 oil. Tighten housing fixings progressively to 18 lbf ft (2.5 kgf m). Tighten clutch and flywheel assembly bolts to 60 lbf ft (8.3 kgf m) and clutch thrust plate screws to 10 lbf ft (1.4 kgf m).

1 : 8 Primary gear end float

Refer to **FIG 1 : 13** to check end float. The engine can remain in the car. If the flywheel housing is removed (see **Section 1 : 7**), check the end float by fitting the thrust washer, primary gear and the clutch and flywheel assembly to the crankshaft (see inset top left in illustration). Check the end float clearance at C (7).

To check with housing in situ, remove the housing oil seal (see **Section 1 : 7**) and then remove the primary gear and thrust washer (4). Wipe parts clean. Refit washer and gear hard against shoulder. Measure protrusion of crankshaft at A (5). Measure depth of flywheel recess at B (6). Differences between measurements is end float.

To adjust, remove gear and select washer to give correct float of .003 to .005 inch (.08 to .13 mm). Four washers are available in thicknesses of .153 to .155 inch (3.89 to 3.94 mm), .156 to .158 inch (3.96 to 4.01 mm), .159 to .161 inch (4.04 to 4.09 mm) and .162 to .164 inch (4.11 to 4.17 mm).

Reassemble in the reverse order to dismantling.

1 : 9 Servicing the lubricating system

Renewing filter element:

Refer to **FIG 1 : 14**. On cars with automatic transmission, drain the engine oil, clean the magnet and refit the drain plug. Unscrew bolt 2. Be ready to catch draining oil and remove bowl, but leave head 6 behind if only operation is renewal of element. Discard element and seal 3. Remove circlip 4 and withdraw parts 5. If necessary, remove head and gasket (6).

Renew rubber washers if deteriorated. Clean bowl and other parts and dry thoroughly. If head was removed, clean the faces and fit a new gasket (6A), aligning it correctly as shown in the inset. Assemble internal parts in correct order, fitting the new element and sealing ring (3). Tighten centre bolt to 20 lbf ft (2.8 kgf m). Start engine and check for leaks. Stop engine and check oil level after a few minutes.

Servicing oil pump (manual gearchange):

Refer to **FIGS 1 : 15** and **1 : 16**. To remove pump, do the following:

1 Drain engine oil, wipe magnet and refit drain plug. Turn crankshaft pulley notch to TDC with No. 1 cylinder firing (2). Remove distributor (see **Chapter 3**).

2 Push split tube or tool 18G.1147 over pump shaft and withdraw it (4). Raise and support front of car. Remove crankshaft pulley (see **Section 1 : 7**). Remove gearbox cover 7 (8 setscrews and one countersunk screw with lockwasher).

3 Remove filter and head, catching draining oil (see **Section 1 : 9**). Fit tool 18G.1149 to rachet wrench 9, apply pressure as shown and unscrew pump outlet. Remove pump pick-up pipe 10. Remove pump bolts with sealing and spring washers (11). Free the pump and extract dowel 12, using a $\frac{5}{16}$ inch (8 mm) tap.

4 Manoeuvre the pump down, tilt it back and withdraw it (13).

Dismantle pump as shown in **FIG 1 : 16**. Although serviced as an assembly it may be inspected for wear.

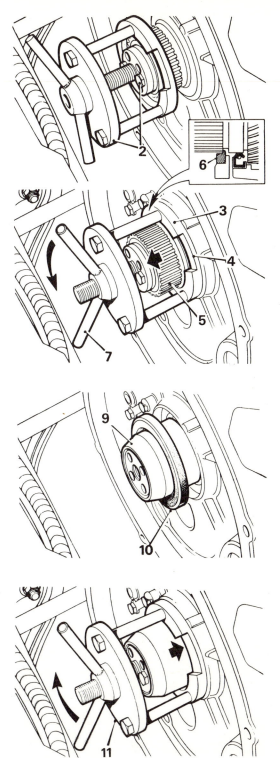

FIG 1 : 11 Operations required to remove and refit the crankshaft oil seal in the flywheel housing (manual gearchange). The seal is part 10

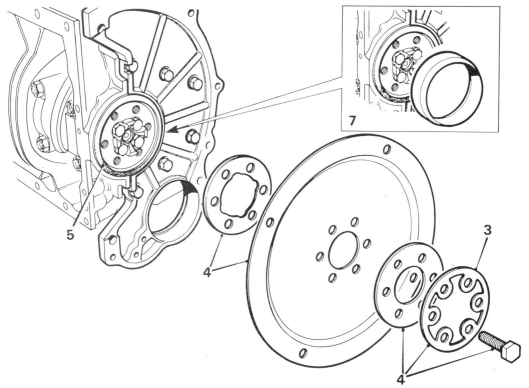

FIG 1:12   Removing and refitting the crankshaft rear oil seal on cars with automatic transmission

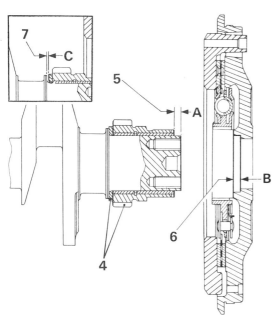

FIG 1:13   Checking end float of crankshaft primary gear (manual gearchange). Inset (top left) shows clearance between thrust washer and crankshaft flange

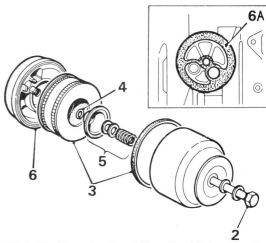

FIG 1:14   Removing the oil filter. Head 6 should not be disturbed if operation is renewal of element only. Fit head gasket 6A correctly

Key to Fig 1:14   2 Centre bolt   3 Element and sealing ring   4 Circlip for bolt   5 Plate, seal and spring for centre bolt   6 Filter head   6A Gasket for head

Note that O-ring seals are fitted in the main oil feed as follows:

Manual gearchange cars: between transmission case and crankcase.

Cars with automatic transmission: between transmission case and crankcase lower extension. Also between lower extension and crankcase.

After cleaning, check end float of outer ring and rotor using a straightedge and feelers (6). Outer ring end float .004 to .005 inch (.10 to .12 mm). Inner rotor end float .0045 to .0055 inch (.11 to .14 mm). Outer ring clearance in body (7) .011 inch (.28 mm). Rotor lobe clearance (8) .0035 inch (.089 mm). **Renew pump if worn beyond limits.** Reassemble pump after oiling internal parts.

When refitting pump, locate it in position and loosely fit bottom bolt ($2\frac{1}{4}$ inch or 57 mm long) and pump outlet connection. Fit dowel and top bolt leaving fixings $\frac{1}{4}$ inch (6 mm) slack. Fit suction pipe with long central bolt.

Tighten pump bolts to 20 lbf ft (2.8 kg m). Tighten pump outlet to 25 lbf ft (3.4 kg m). Reverse rest of dismantling procedure and refill with oil. Tighten front cover setscrews to 10 lbf ft (1.4 kgf m) and pulley bolt to 60 to 70 lbf ft (8.3 to 9.7 kgf m).

Servicing oil pressure relief valve:

Refer to **FIG 1:17**. Remove valve as follows:

On cars with automatic transmission, drain the engine oil. Remove oil filter and head, catching draining oil (see earlier in this Section). Withdraw valve. **This is not adjustable and must be serviced as an assembly.**

Refit valve 3 with relief hole downwards. Mark 4 is in line with the hole. Refit filter. Refill with oil (automatic), run engine and check for leaks. Check oil level.

Oil pump drive:

Details of this are given in **Section 1:13**. See also **FIG 1:9**.

1:10 Removing and refitting power unit

Removing (manual gearchange):

Refer to **FIG 1:18** and do the following:

1 Remove bonnet. Drain oil, clean magnet and refit plug 3. Drain cooling system and remove cylinder block drain plug (see **Chapter 4**). Lift expansion tank 4 to one side.

2 Remove battery and tray 5 and carrier 6. Disconnect fan leads 7. Remove radiator assembly after disconnecting hoses 8. Disconnect all wiring to engine (9).

3 Disconnect power steering pump 10 (when fitted) and tie back to towing bracket. Remove air cleaner 11 and disconnect cables 12. Release throttle bracket 13. Disconnect fuel pipe 14 and servo hose 15. Release oil pipe from block and clip (16). Disconnect heater hoses 17.

4 Release clutch slave cylinder and move it aside (18). Release exhaust pipe 19. Remove top starter motor bolt 20. Lift front of car and fit stands. Remove starter motor (22).

5 Extract pin 23 and detach steady rod (24). Release exhaust pipe and support it (25). Detach lower tie

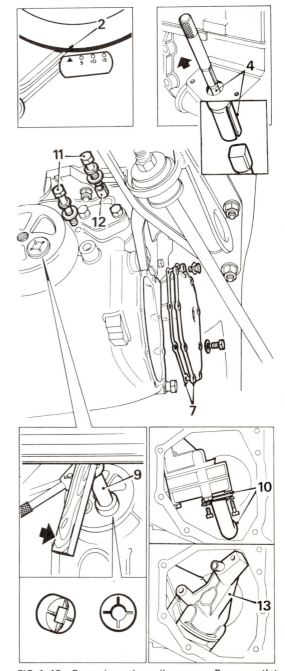

FIG 1:15 Removing the oil pump. Pump outlet connector is unscrewed with tool 18G. 1149 (bottom left). Timing notch in crankshaft pulley is shown at 2

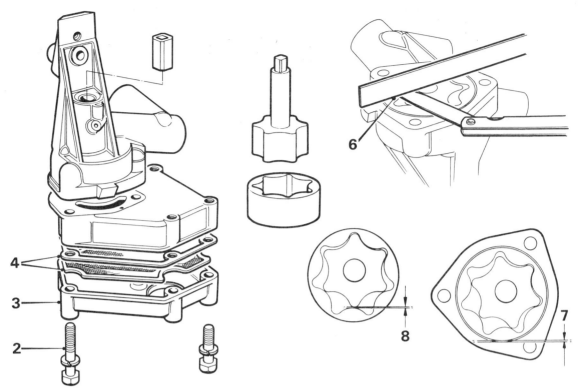

FIG 1:16 Components of the oil pump. Checking end float of rotors (top right). Checking clearance of rotors and lobes (7 and 8)

rod (26). Disconnect speedometer cable 27. Release drive shafts, fit tool 18G.1146 (see **FIG 1:24**) between housing and shaft and strike with a mallet (28). Remove each front hub and shaft assembly (see **Chapter 7**).

6 Take the weight of the power unit and remove nut 30 (front righthand engine mounting). Remove nut 31 (rear righthand mounting). Remove bolts 32 and 34.

7 Slacken alternator 33 and secure it against cylinder block. Disengage engine mounting brackets, lift power unit and disconnect alternator plug 36. Continue lifting, making things easier by removing the righthand adaptor bracket from flywheel housing.

FIG 1:17 Removal of oil pump relief valve 3. Hole in side is located by aligning mark 4

Refitting (manual gearchange):

Lower the unit into place in reverse order, locating the righthand studs and fitting nuts and spring washers. Locate lefthand mountings in body brackets and tighten fixings to 30 lbf ft (4.1 kgf m). Tighten righthand mountings to same torque. Continue in reverse order of dismantling.

Removing (automatic transmission):

Refer to **FIG 1:19** and follow the preceding instructions for cars with manual gearchange with the following additions:

1 Release the bonnet lockplate. Drain the automatic transmission (4) or plug the drive shaft apertures if the transmission is not being dismantled.

2 Remove both horns (12). Disconnect the kickdown cable from throttle control and brackets (16). Disconnect manual control (top) and parking cables from their selector rods and bracket (18). **Slacken adjusting nuts on selector side only.**

3 Disconnect earth cable 24. Pull manual control cable through from below (29).

Refitting (automatic transmission):

Reverse the dismantling procedure. After installation check transmission selection and parking engagement (see **Chapter 6a**).

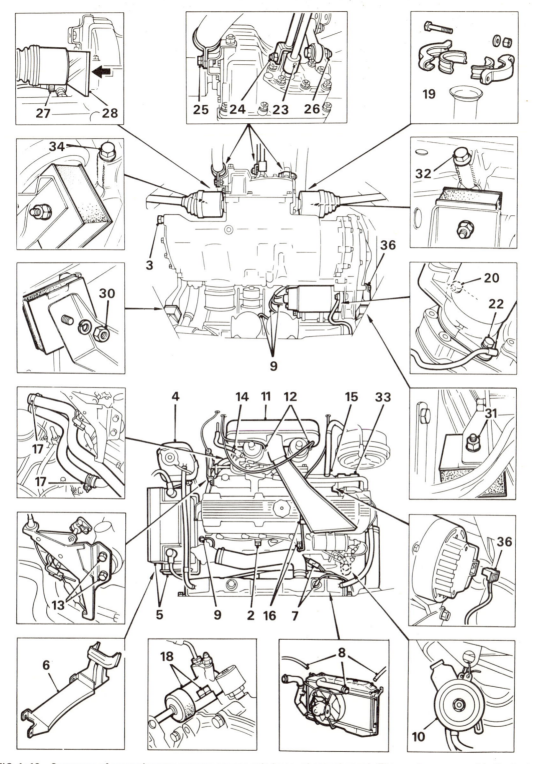

FIG 1:18 Sequence of operations to remove power unit (manual gearchange). The numbers are used in the text

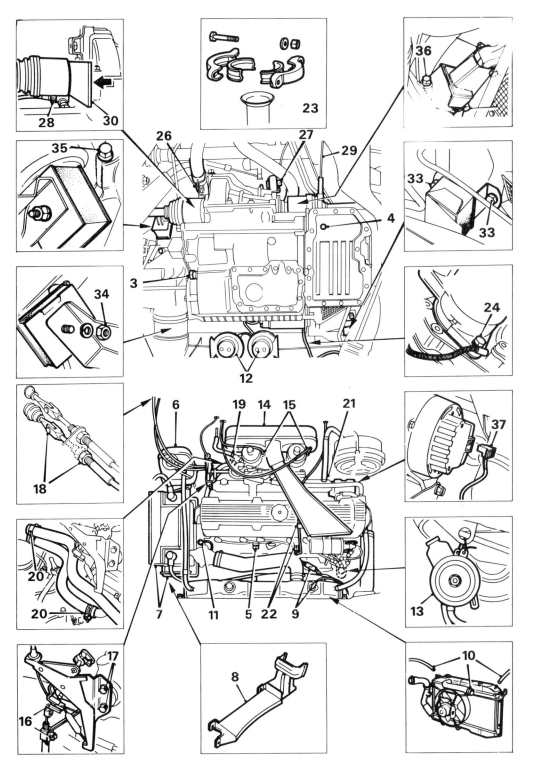

FIG 1:19 Sequence of operations to remove power unit (automatic transmission). The numbers are used in the text

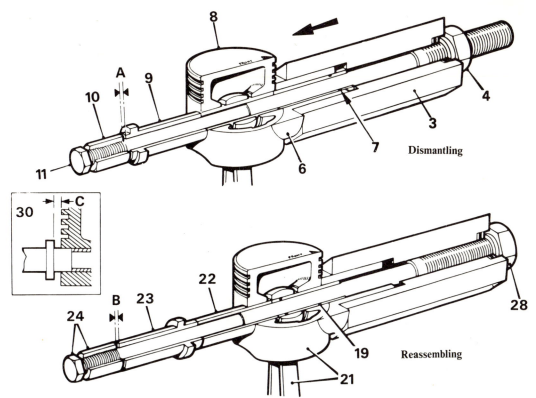

FIG 1:20 Service tool 18G.1150 and 1150B is needed when removing and refitting the press-fit gudgeon pin. The numbers are used in the text

1:11 Servicing pistons and connecting rods

Removing:

For this operation remove the power unit as in the preceding Section. Remove the transmission assembly (see **Chapter 6** or **6a**). Remove cylinder head and gasket (see **Section 1:5**).

Lay cylinder block on distributor side. Refer to **FIG 1:9** and check that rods 45 and caps 48 are marked consecutively from the water pump end. **Rods and caps must be kept together and returned to their correct journals.**

Remove big-end nuts 49. Withdraw caps and bottom liners or shells 47. Push rod and piston out from top of block after removing ring of carbon at top of bore.

Check bolts 46. Nut 49 should run freely down threads. Fit new parts if there is pick-up or permanent stretch. Renew bearing shells if worn. Diametrical clearance may be checked with 'Plastigage'. It must not exceed .0015 to .003 inch (.038 to .076 mm). Refer to 'Big-end bearing shells'.

Refitting:

Fit bearing shells, making sure tags locate in notches in rod and cap. Lubricate piston with graphited oil (Acheson's Colloids 'Oildag'). Fit assemblies to their original bores, taking care that piston crown marking 'FRONT' or a stamped triangle faces to the front or water pump end of the engine. The big-end markings must run consecutively from the front.

Use a compressor tool on the piston rings and after fitting the assemblies, oil the crankpins and fit the big-end caps, tightening the nuts to 33 lbf ft (4.6 kgf m). Reverse rest of dismantling procedure, refill with engine oil and refill the cooling system.

Overhauling:

Refer to **FIG 1:20**. This shows the tools 18G.1150 and 1150B that are needed to remove and refit the gudgeon pins. Torque wrench 18G.537 is also required.

Dismantling:

Remove the rings upwards and hold body 3 in a vice. Retract nut 4 until flush with end of screw. Push screw forward until nut contacts thrust race. Fit adaptor 18G.1150B with piston ring cut-away uppermost (6). With grooved end first, slide parallel sleeve 7 onto screw.

Fit piston with mark 'FRONT' or triangle on crown towards adaptor (8). **This is important because the gudgeon pin is offset.** Fit remover/replacer bush 9 with flange away from gudgeon pin. Screw on stopnut 10 to give about .032 inch (.8 mm) end play at A. Lock stopnut securely with screw 11.

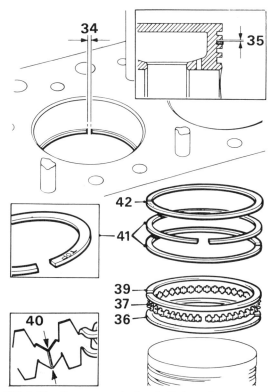

FIG 1:21 Correct methods of fitting piston rings. Ring gap and side clearance are checked as shown at 34 and 35. Note butting ends of expander ring at 40

Check that bush 9 and sleeve 7 are positioned in bores on both sides of piston. Set piston in clean curved face of adaptor 6. Screw nut 4 up to thrust race, hold screw 11 and turn nut 4 until gudgeon pin is withdrawn.

Reassembling:

Remove large nut 28 and pull screw out of body a few inches. Threads of nut and screw must be oiled and adaptor in place. Fit parallel sleeve 19 up to shoulder with grooved end last. Lubricate gudgeon pin and bores in piston and connecting rod with graphited oil (Acheson's Colloids 'Oildag').

Fit rod and piston on tool with rod entering the sleeve up to the groove (21). Make sure that the piston and rod face correctly, with piston crown marking 'FRONT' (or a triangle) to the front or water pump end of the engine and the markings on the rod and big-end cap facing the distributor side of the engine.

Fit gudgeon pin 22 up to connecting rod. Fit remover/replacer bush 23 with flange nearest gudgeon pin. Fit stop-nut to give .032 inch (.8 mm) play at B and lock securely with screw (24). Set piston in clean curved face of adaptor with adaptor cut-away uppermost. Screw nut 28 up to thrust race. Set torque wrench 18G.537 to 12 lbf ft (1.7 kgf m) **which is the minimum figure for an acceptable fit.** Hold the lockscrew (24) and use the torque wrench on the large nut. Pull the

gudgeon pin into place until the flange on bush 23 is .04 inch (1 mm) from the piston skirt (see C in inset 30). **Never let the flange contact the piston.**

If the torque wrench does not break throughout the pull, the gudgeon pin fit is not acceptable. The components must be renewed. Keep the large nut and the screw well oiled.

Remove the tool and check that piston pivots and slides freely. If tight, wash assembly in fuel or paraffin (kerosene), lubricate with graphited oil and recheck. If still tight, dismantle and check for dirt or damage. Check piston and connecting rod for alignment.

Piston rings:

Refer to **FIG 1:21.** When fitting new rings, check gap in cylinder bore (34). Push ring about one inch down bore with a piston. Measured gap should be .011 to .022 inch (.28 to .55 mm) for compression rings 41 and 42 and .015 to .045 inch (.38 to 1.14 mm) for the oil control ring pair, 36 and 39. Check side clearance 35. It should not exceed .0015 to .0035 inch (.03 to .08 mm) for compression rings.

To fit rings, position bottom oil control ring 36 below lowest groove in piston. Fit expander 37 in groove. Move bottom ring into groove. Fit upper oil control ring 39. Ends of expander must butt (see 40). Set ring gaps and expander gap at 90 deg. to each other. Fit tapered compression rings 41 in second and third grooves with mark 'TOP' uppermost. The thicker ring 42 goes in the top groove. Set ring gaps at 90 deg. to each other and away from thrust side of piston.

Big-end bearing shells:

The correct clearance for big-end bearings is given early in this Section. If the bearing metal of the shells is scored or pitted, renew the shells. Check the crankpins for wear or ovality. If excessive, have the crankshaft reground to one of the undersizes mentioned in **Technical Data** and fit the appropriate size of shells. **Never try to rectify excessive clearance by filing the rods or caps and do not scrape the bearings in an attempt to correct the fit.** If a big-end is tight when reassembled, dismantle it and check for dirt behind the shells.

1:12 Servicing the crankshaft

Removing:

Remove power unit (see **Section 1:10**). Remove transmission assembly (see **Chapter 6** or **6a**). Remove cylinder head cover (see **Section 1:4**). Remove camshaft sprocket (see **Section 1:5**). Remove front oil seal, oil thrower, and crankshaft sprocket (see **Section 1:6**). Remove distributor drive gear and drive shaft (see **Section 1:13**).

Lay cylinder block on distributor side. Remove crankcase lower extension from automatic transmission (ten fixings inside and four outside).

Check crankshaft end float at No. 3 bearing by levering shaft fully in one direction. Use feelers between crankshaft face and face of thrust washers 12 in **FIG 1:22**. Correct float is .002 to .003 inch (.05 to .07 mm). To rectify, remove No. 3 cap and push on one end of each half-washer in crankcase to release them. Remove

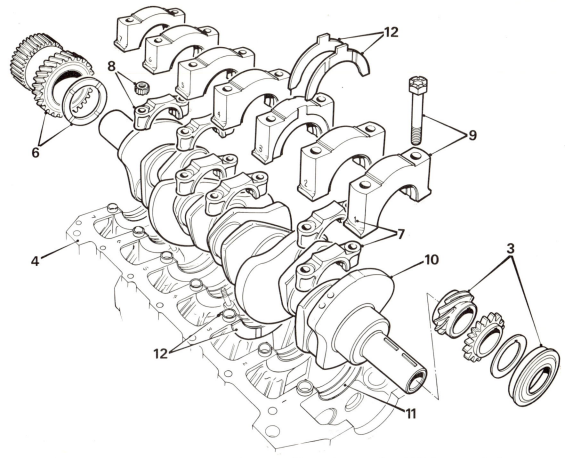

FIG 1:22 Removing the crankshaft. Note how tags of lower thrust washers 12 fit in grooves in the cap

tagged half-washers from cap. From the selection of thrust washer thicknesses available, select a set that will give the correct end float (see later). Push crankcase half-washers (without tag) into place round the crank-shaft with oil grooves facing outwards.

To remove the shaft, remove the primary gear and thrust washer (see 3). Check that big-end and main bearing caps are numbered from the water pump end. Remove all caps and lift out the shaft. If original bearing shells are to be refitted, store them in their correct order.

Refitting:

Check bearings against figures given in **Technical Data**. Wear and excessive clearance may be corrected by regrinding the crankshaft to one of four undersizes and fitting new shells. **Never try to adjust clearances by filing caps.** Fit new shells if the journals are satis-factory, but the bearing surfaces in the shells are scored or pitted. The clearance should be correct without the need for adjustment.

Flush out the crankshaft oilways under pressure particularly if a bearing has 'run'. Inject fresh oil. Fit top shells and thrust washers to crankcase, oil liberally and

fit crankshaft. Fit thrust washers to No. 3 cap with tags correctly located. Fit and tighten this cap and check the end float with feelers or a dial gauge. Selective thrust washers are available as follows:

.089 to .091 inch (2.26 to 2.29 mm)
.091 to .093 inch (2.29 to 2.36 mm)
.093 to .095 inch (2.36 to 2.41 mm)

Continue fitting the main bearing caps, tightening to 70 lbf ft (9.7 kgf m). Check shaft for free rotation after each tightening. If it suddenly becomes tight, remove cap and check for dirt behind shells. Fit the big-ends, tightening to 33 lbf ft (4.6 kgf m).

Reverse the rest of the dismantling procedure and refill with oil.

1:13 The drive shaft for the oil pump and distributor

Details of the shaft are given in **FIGS 1:9** and **1:23**.

Removing:

With automatic transmission only, remove the trans-mission assembly (see **Chapter 6a**) and lay the block on its carburetter side with supports. Remove cylinder head

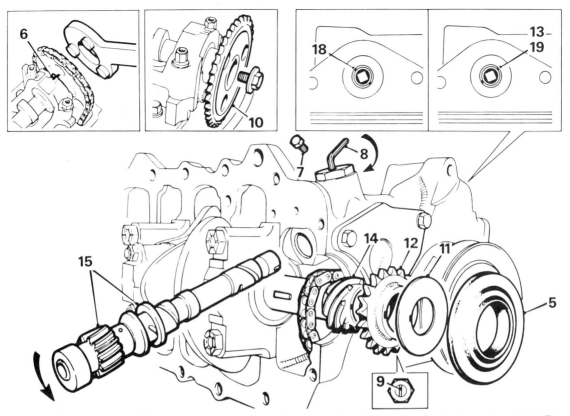

FIG 1:23 Removing and refitting the distributor drive shaft. Correct location of drive slot is shown (top right). The numbers are used in the text

cover (see **Section 1:4**). Remove the oil pump drive shaft (see **Section 1:9**). Remove the oil pump on cars with manual gearchange (see **Section 1:9**). Remove front oil seal (see **Section 1:7**).

Align camshaft marks (see 6). Remove screw 7, turn Allen key 8 clockwise to retract tensioner. Slacken locknut 9 and turn chain guide adjuster to back of cam. Remove sprocket 10, oil thrower 11 and small sprocket 12. Note that rounded sprocket shoulder faces the thrower. Note position of drive shaft slot (see 13). It should be at 2 o'clock with large segment uppermost. Withdraw shaft 15 from gear 14. Note thrust washer (see 15).

Check parts for wear after cleaning. Note how oil pump is driven (see **FIG 1:9**).

Refitting:

Fit thrust washer. Check that No. 1 piston (nearest water pump) is at TDC (see 1 in **FIG 1:7**). Enter drive shaft and position slot as shown at 18, with slot at 10 o'clock and large segment uppermost. Fit gear 14. As the teeth mesh the shaft will turn anticlockwise through 90 deg., bringing the slot back to position 19.

Fit distributor and check that rotor arm is set to fire No. 1 cylinder with contact points just opening (see **Chapter 3**). Reverse the rest of the dismantling procedure. Check the ignition timing.

1:14 Engine mountings

Front lefthand:

When removing, take the weight of the power unit, lowering it again slightly after releasing the mounting. When refitting, note that the mounting flange fits over the crossmember. Tighten bolt and nut to 30 lbf ft (4.1 kgf m).

Front righthand (manual gearchange):

To remove, set handbrake, raise front of car with wheels supported and fit a wedge between front tyre and bottom rear edge of wheel arch. Take weight of power unit. Remove mounting nut from crossmember. Slacken tie-rod fixing to lower suspension arm. Release tie-rod bracket from body, pull down and turn it sideways. Lift power unit slightly and release rear mounting from bracket. Remove front righthand mounting.

Refit mounting as for front lefthand. Tighten tie-rod bracket bolts (two long ones at front end). Tighten tie-rod to suspension arm bolt to 40 to 50 lbf ft (5.5 to 6.9 kgf m).

Rear lefthand (manual gearchange):

Support power unit. Lift expansion tank and set aside. Remove mounting nut at engine bracket. Release mounting from body bracket and withdraw downwards. Refit as for front lefthand mounting.

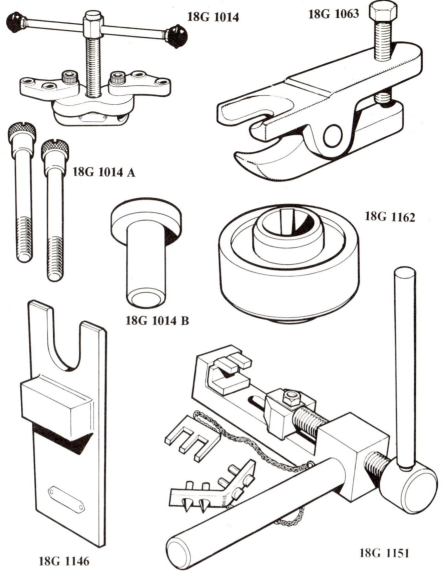

FIG 1 : 24   Some of the service tools used when working on the engine

Key to Fig 1 : 24   Basic gear and pulley remover, 18G.1014   Adaptor screws for basic remover, 18G.1014A   Crankshaft thrust pad, 18G.1014B   Steering arm and swivel hub ball pin remover, 18G.1063   Replacer for crankshaft front oil seal, 18G.1162 Drive shaft remover, 18G.1146   Remover and replacer for timing chain link, 18G1151

Rear lefthand (automatic):

To remove, apply handbrake, lift front of car and support power unit. Disconnect lower engine tie-rod at transmission bracket. Remove bolt from mounting to body bracket. Release rear righthand mounting bracket from torque converter housing. Lower power unit and remove mounting and bracket.

To refit, reverse dismantling procedure, ensuring that mounting bracket fits easily over torque converter housing. Distance between faces 1.68 inch (43 mm). Flanges on mounting fit over top of brackets. Tighten to

30 lbf ft (4.1 kgf m). Position mounting assembly, engage body bracket and torque converter and pull up into position.

Rear righthand (automatic):

Repeat the instructions for the front righthand mounting (manual gearchange) but note that two screws secure the mounting bracket to the torque converter.

When refitting, secure the mounting bracket to the torque converter housing before the tie-rod bracket bolts are fitted.

1:15 Reassembling a stripped engine

Provide a new set of gaskets, make sure all parts are clean and oil bearing surfaces liberally. Fit the crankshaft (see **Section 1:12**). Check that all camshaft and distributor drive parts are in position. Refit pistons and connecting rods (see **Section 1:11**). Fit head and camshaft drive and remaining parts in reverse order of dismantling. Use the torque wrench figures given in **Technical Data**.

When the power unit is in the car and all connections have been checked, fill with fresh oil to the correct level and refill the cooling system. Once the engine has started, check all round for leaks. Check the ignition timing (see **Chapter 3**). After a hundred miles on the road, check all bolts and fixings for tightness.

1:16 Fault diagnosis

(a) Engine will not start

1 Defective coil
2 Faulty distributor capacitor (condenser)
3 Dirty, pitted or incorrectly set contact breaker points
4 Ignition wiring loose or insulation faulty
5 Water on plug leads, damp distributor
6 Battery discharged, terminals corroded
7 Faulty or jammed starter. Switch defective
8 Plug leads wrongly connected
9 Vapour lock in fuel pipes due to heat
10 Defective fuel pump or float mechanism
11 Overchoking or underchoking, sticking carburetter piston
12 Blocked petrol filter or carburetter jet
13 Leaking valves, broken springs
14 Sticking valves
15 Valve timing incorrect
16 Ignition timing incorrect

(b) Engine stalls

1 Check 1, 2, 3, 4, 5, 10, 11, 12, 13 and 14 in (a)
2 Sparking plugs defective or gaps incorrect
3 Retarded ignition
4 Mixture too weak
5 Water in fuel system
6 Petrol tank vent blocked
7 Incorrect valve clearances

(c) Engine idles badly

1 Check 2, 4 and 7 in (b)
2 Air leak at manifold joints
3 Carburetter jet wrongly positioned
4 Air leak in carburetter
5 Over-rich mixture
6 Worn piston rings
7 Worn valve stems or guides
8 Weak exhaust valve springs

(d) Engine misfires

1 Check 1, 2, 3, 4, 5, 8, 10, 12, 13, 14, 15 and 16 in (a); 2, 3, 4 and 7 in (b)
2 Weak or broken valve springs

(e) Engine overheats (see **Chapter 4**)

(f) Compression low

1 Check 13 and 14 in (a), 6 and 7 in (c) and 2 in (d)
2 Worn piston ring grooves
3 Scored or worn cylinder bores
4 Breakdown of head gasket

(g) Engine lacks power

1 Check 3, 10, 11, 12, 13, 14, 15 and 16 in (a); 2, 3, 4 and 7 in (b); 6 and 7 in (c) and 2 in (d)
2 Leaking joint washers
3 Fouled sparking plugs
4 Automatic ignition advance not operating

(h) Burnt valves or head seats

1 Check 13 and 14 in (a); 7 in (b); 2 in (d) and also check (e)
2 Excessive carbon build-up round valve seats and head

(j) Sticking valves

1 Check 2 in (d)
2 Bent valve stem
3 Scored valve stem or guide
4 Incorrect valve clearance

(k) Excessive cylinder wear

1 Check 11 in (a) and see **Chapter 4**
2 Lack of oil
3 Dirty oil
4 Piston rings gummed up or broken
5 Badly fitting piston rings, gaps too small
6 Bent connecting rod

(l) Excessive oil consumption

1 Check 6 and 7 in (c) and check (k)
2 Ring gaps too wide
3 Oil control rings defective
4 Scored cylinders
5 Oil level too high
6 Leaking oil seals, filter, joints
7 Ineffective inlet valve stem oil seals

(m) Crankshaft or connecting rod bearing failure

1 Check 2 in (k)
2 Restricted oilways
3 Worn journals or crankpins
4 Loose bearing caps
5 Very low oil pressure
6 Bent connecting rod

(n) Internal water leakage (see **Chapter 4**)

(o) Poor water circulation (see **Chapter 4**)

(p) Corrosion (see **Chapter 4**)

(q) High fuel consumption (see **Chapter 2**)

(r) Engine vibration

1 Loose alternator bolts
2 Mounting rubbers loose or ineffective
3 Exhaust pipe mountings defective
4 Engine steady loose or faulty
5 Misfiring due to mixture, ignition or mechanical faults

CHAPTER 2

THE FUEL SYSTEM

2:1 Description

Fuel pump:

This is an SU electric pump mounted in a bracket secured to the flange of the fuel tank. When the ignition is switched on, a solenoid in the pump is energized. This deflects a diaphragm to draw fuel into the pump through an inlet valve. This action breaks the electrical circuit at a contact breaker and the spring-loaded diaphrgam forces fuel along pipelines to the carburetter through an outlet valve. At the end of the diaphragm stroke the contact points close, the solenoid is re-energized and the sequence is repeated so long as the carburetter demands fuel.

The carburetters:

These are SU type HS6. Refer to **FIG 2:6**.

The air intake bore through body 1 is fitted with a butterfly valve 34 in throttle spindle 33 to control the volume of mixture passing to the engine. Piston 9 rises and falls inside chamber 7 and when at rest virtually blocks the air intake. Its movement is due to the depression in the air intake system associated with engine load and throttle opening. This depression affects the space above the piston, causing the piston to rise and fall, thus producing a variable choke aperture in the body. This constantly changing volume of air which is drawn into the engine demands a variable quantity of fuel to produce the correct mixture. Tapered needle 11 is attached to the underside of the piston so that it also rises and falls inside a jet 42. The smallest diameter of the needle is in the jet when the piston is fully raised, so that there is maximum air and fuel when required. Rapid fluctuations of the piston and needle are damped out by hydraulic damper 15.

Rich mixture for starting from cold is obtained by pulling the jet down to a smaller diameter of the tapered needle. Fuel is supplied to the jet by the usual system of a float-controlled needle valve in chamber 21. The cam on lever 59 comes into play when the choke control is pulled out. It provides for a small throttle opening at the same time as the rich mixture needed for easy starting from cold.

2:2 Routine maintenance

Refer to inset, bottom right, in **FIG 2:6**. Every 6000 miles (10,000 km or six months) remove the dampers 15 and add engine oil until the level is $\frac{1}{2}$ inch (13 mm) above the top of the hollow rod of piston 9. At the same time oil the throttle linkages and pedal fulcrum.

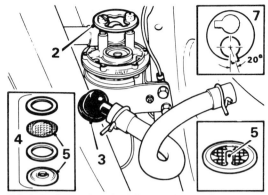

FIG 2:1 Removing the inlet nozzle and filter on the fuel pump. The numbers are used in the text

Every 12,000 miles (20,000 km or 12 months) renew the air cleaner elements. Change more frequently if conditions are very dusty.

Unscrew the two square-headed nuts. Remove the cleaner assembly, unscrew the wing nut and discard the old elements. Clean all surfaces and fit the new elements, making sure the seals are in place and are serviceable.

Every 6000 miles (10,000 km or six months) make a visual check of all fuel pipes and connections. At the same mileage check the carburetter idling speed and mixture settings (see **Section 2:4**).

2:3 Servicing the fuel pump

Cleaning filter:

Refer to **FIG 2:1**, drain the fuel tank and refit the plug (see **Section 2:9**). Slacken clamp plate screws 2, noting angle of inlet nozzle 3. Detach nozzle and catch draining fuel. Extract filter, washers and inlet valve (4).

Wash filter in fuel and blow dry. Renew defective parts. Check valve (5) by sucking and blowing with the mouth. Valve tongue should allow .06 inch (1.6 mm) of movement (5 in righthand inset).

Refit valve, tongue side inwards. Fit filter domed side out, with washer each side. Refit nozzle as shown at 7, tighten screws, put fuel in the tank and check for leaks and pump operation.

Removing and refitting:

Drain tank and refit plug. Disconnect inlet hose from tank (see **FIG 2:1**). Squeeze ends of clip with pliers. Release mounting bracket from tank flange. Note that earth tag fits on inner screw between bracket and flange. Disconnect outlet hose, cables and breather tube.

When refitting, check that inlet and outlet nozzles face correctly (see 7 in **FIG 2:1**). Make sure the breather tube is clear and fitted correctly.

Overhauling:

Before removing the pump for overhaul it is wise to do some simple tests if the pump is inoperative. First disconnect the outlet hose. If the pump then operates

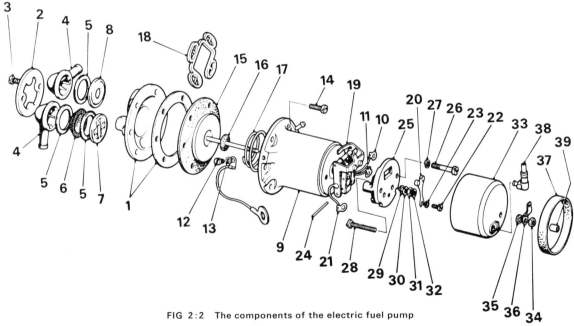

FIG 2:2 The components of the electric fuel pump

Key to Fig 2:2 1 Pump body and gasket   2 Spring clamp plate   3 Screw   4 Inlet/outlet nozzle   5 Sealing washer
6 Filter   7 Inlet valve   8 Outlet valve   9 Coil housing   10 5 B.A. terminal tag   11 2 B.A. terminal tag   12 Earth screw
13 Spring washer   14 Screw-housing to body   15 Diaphragm assembly   16 Impact washer   17 Spring   18 Armature
guide plate   19 Rocker   20 Blade   21 2 B.A. terminal tag   22 Screw for blade   23 Dished washer   24 Spindle for
contact breaker   25 Pedestal   26 Pedestal to housing screw   27 Spring washer   28 Screw for terminal   29 Spring washer
30 Lead washer for screw   31 Nut for screw   32 Spacer—nut to cover   33 End cover   34 Nut for cover   35 Shakeproof
washer   36 Lucas connector   37 Sealing band   38 Non-return valve   39 Insulating sleeve

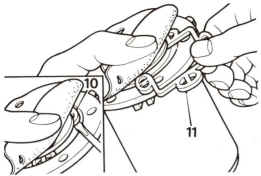

FIG 2:3 Prising out the lobes 10 when removing the armature guide plate 11 from the fuel pump housing

with ignition switched on, check for a sticking float needle in the carburetter (see **Section 2:6**). If the pump still does not operate, check all electrical connections and earthing. If current is present, remove the pump cover, clean the contact points and try again. If not satisfactory, dismantle and inspect the pump.

Refer to **FIG 2:2**. Remove sealing tape from cover 33, then remove band 37 and parts 34, 35, 36 and 39. The cover may now be removed. Release contact blade 20, noting that long coil lead fits between dished washer and blade. Separate body 1 from housing 9 (six screws). Remove clamp plate 2, the nozzles 4, filter 6, sealing washers 5 and valves 7 and 8.

Refer to **FIG 2:3**, turn back edge of diaphragm and prise both ends of armature guide plate 10 free from recess. The diaphragm will now be free to turn. Unscrew it anticlockwise. Remove spring 17 (**FIG 2:3**). Note impact washer 16.

Refer to **FIG 2:4**. Remove parts 13, noting that coned face of nut faces the lead washer. Cut this washer free from thread. Hold pedestal firmly and remove parts 14.

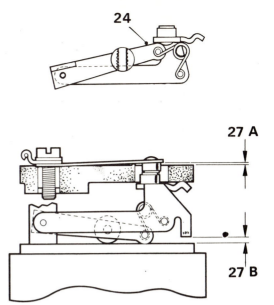

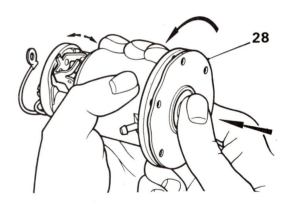

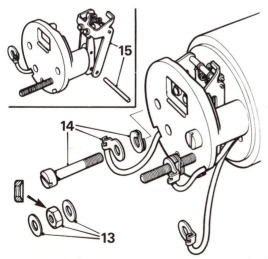

FIG 2:4 Remove parts 13 and 14 and the second pedestal screw to release the fuel pump contact breaker. The rockers and hinge pin are shown at 15 (top left)

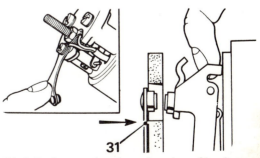

FIG 2:5 Correct location of rockers 24 when reassembling (top). Setting blade and rocker finger clearances (second view). Turning and pressing the diaphragm 28 for rocker 'throw-over' (third view). Bending contact blade until it just rests on pedestal rib 31 (bottom view)

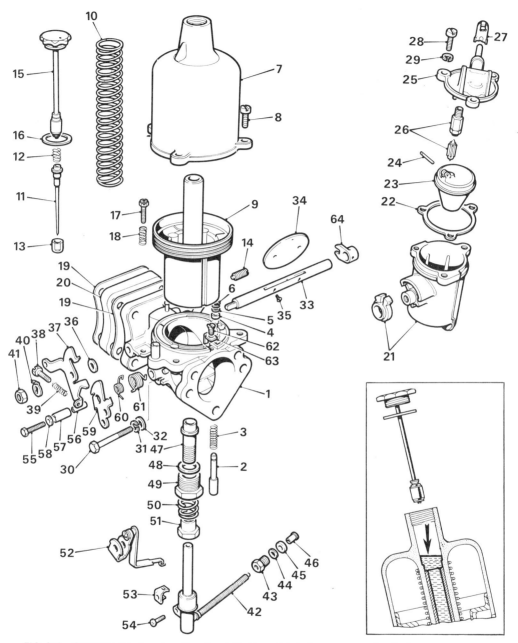

FIG 2:6 Components of carburetter. Inset (bottom right) shows correct level of piston damper oil

Key to Fig 2:6 1 Body   2 Piston lifting pin   3 Spring for pin   4 Sealing washer   5 Plain washer   6 Circlip   7 Piston chamber   8 Screw   9 Piston   10 Spring   11 Needle   12 Spring   13 Support guide   14 Locking screw   15 Piston damper   16 Sealing washer   17 Throttle adjusting screw   18 Spring   19 Joint washers   20 Insulator block   21 Float-chamber and spacer   22 Joint washer   23 Float   24 Hinge pin—float   25 Lid   26 Needle and seat   27 Baffle plate   28 Screw   29 Spring washer   30 Bolt—securing float-chamber   31 Spring washer   32 Plain washer   33 Throttle spindle   34 Throttle disc   35 Screw   36 Washer   37 Throttle return lever   38 Fast-idle screw   39 Spring   40 Lock washer   41 Nut   42 Jet assembly   43 Sleeve nut—jet flexible pipe   44 Washer   45 Gland   46 Ferrule   47 Jet bearing   48 Sealing washer   49 Jet locating nut   50 Spring   51 Jet adjusting nut   52 Pick-up lever   53 Link   54 Screw—securing link   55 Pivot bolt   56 Tube—inner   57 Tube—outer   58 Distance washer   59 Cam lever   60 Spring—cam lever   61 Spring—pick-up lever   62 Screw   63 Guide   64 Lost motion lever

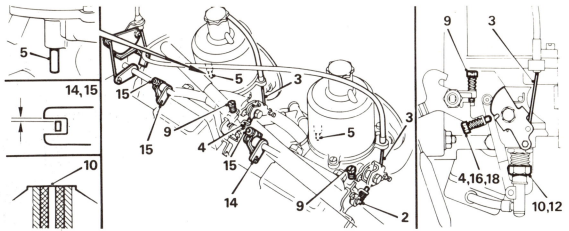

FIG 2:7 Relevant details when tuning and adjusting carburetters. The numbers are used in the text

Note position of terminal and spring washer. Tip pedestal and push out rocker pin (see 15). **This pin is hardened and must be renewed with a genuine SU part.**

Clean all parts in fuel, but remove gum formation with methylated spirit. Renew all sealing washers and the lead washer. Suck and blow on valves to check action. Tongue on valve should allow a lift of about .06 inch (1.6 mm) (see 5 in **FIG 2:1**). Wash filter and blow dry. Check action of non-return valve 38 and ensure that the vent tube is clear (see **FIG 2:2**).

Check diaphragm 15 for deterioration. Check coil leads and security of tags. If points on rocker 19 and blade 20 are burned or pitted renew both assemblies. Check pedestal 25 for damage.

Reassemble in the reverse order. Refer to **FIG 2:5**. Refit rocker after setting it to position shown at 24. Do not overtighten the pedestal screws and do not strain the earthing wire.

Screw the diaphragm into place without the guide plate. Screw it in until the rocker assembly will not 'throw over' when the centre of the diaphragm is pressed, but make sure nothing is jammed.

Check the rocker setting after fitting the contact blade and coil lead.

The setting is shown at 27A and 27B. The lift of the blade above the pedestal at 27A must be .035 ± .005 inch (.9 ± .13 mm). Bend the stop on the rocker behind the pedestal if necessary. Check gap at 27B. It should be .070 ± .005 inch (1.8 ± .13 mm). Bend the stop-finger if necessary.

Set diaphragm 28. Hold pump as shown and unscrew diaphragm, pressing and releasing thumb until rocker just 'throws over'. Unscrew a fraction until diaphragm holes line up with holes in housing. Unscrew a further four holes or two-thirds of a turn. Insert guide plate into recess, pressing centre lobes in first, followed by the two end lobes (see **FIG 2:3**).

Assemble the valves correctly (see **FIG 2:1**). Inlet valve has tongue inwards and outlet valve outwards. Check the contact points (see 31 in **FIG 2:5**). The blade must rest on the rib on the pedestal face. If necessary, bend blade as shown. Adjust blade so that points are slightly offset, with blade points a little above rocker points when they are closed. After fitting end cover and band, seal with tape.

Check operation of pump as suggested at the start of 'Overhauling'. If pump operates rapidly without much flow, suspect an air leak on the suction side, or defective valves. **Never pass compressed air through the pump.**

2:4 Tuning carburetters

Setting idling speed:

Refer to **FIG 2:7**. Do the following:
1 Provide a reliable tachometer (revolution indicator) and a twin-carburetter balancing device. If system must conform to laws governing exhaust emission it will also be necessary to use an exhaust gas analyser.
2 Remove air cleaners and top up dampers (see **Section 2:2**). Check that throttle operates correctly and that mixture control (choke) cables 3 return fully and have $\frac{1}{16}$ inch (2 mm) free play. Also check for slight clearance between fast-idle screws 2 and 4 and their cams.
3 Raise lifting pins 5, release them and check that pistons fall freely (see **Section 2:6**). Connect the tachometer and select P on cars with automatic transmission. Run engine up to working temperature and then for five more minutes. Run engine up to 2500 rev/min for thirty seconds. If adjustments cannot be completed in three minutes, increase engine speed to 2500 rev/min for thirty seconds and then recommence tuning. Repeat this procedure every three minutes if necessary.
4 Set idling speed to 600 rev/min, turning adjusting screws 9 equally as required. Set up the balancing meter. If balance is incorrect, adjust by turning one screw 9 as required. Reset the idling speed by turning both screws equally and again check the balance. Check fork clearance (see 14 and 15). Slacken clamping bolts and use feeler gauge to set clearance to .012 inch (.31 mm) between link pin and fork as shown by arrows in inset on left. Tighten clamp bolts.

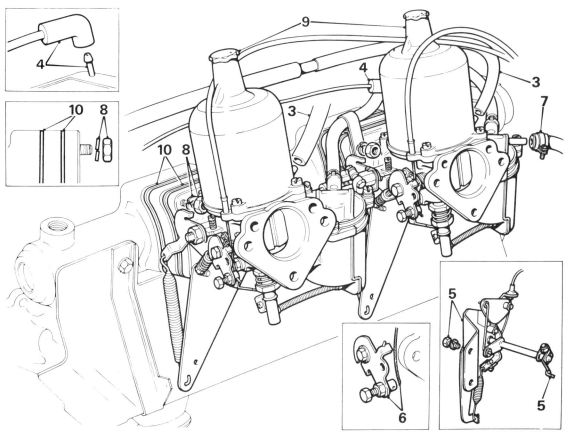

FIG 2:8 Parts affected when removing carburetters. The numbers are used in the text. Inset (bottom right) shows the progressive throttle assembly that is bolted to the inlet manifold

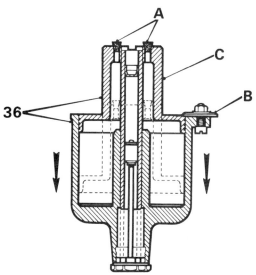

FIG 2:9 Timing the drop of the carburetter suction chamber. Piston and chamber 36, plugs at A, large washer at B and piston at C

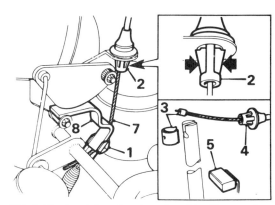

FIG 2:10 Servicing the throttle cable. The numbers are used in the text

5 If a smooth idle is not obtainable, adjust mixture as follows:

6 Stop engine and remove suction chambers and pistons (see **Section 2:6**). Turn adjusting nuts (see 10 and 12) until jets are flush, but not above, bridge in intake bore (see 10, lower left). If just below bridge, make sure both jets are in same position. Turn nuts down by two complete turns. Refit pistons and suction chambers and top up damper oil (see **Section 2:2**).

7 Run engine at idling speed. Achieve fastest speed on tachometer by turning nuts up or down. Turning up will weaken mixture and turning down will enrich it. Now turn nuts up slowly and evenly until speed just starts to fall and then turn them equally downwards by the minimum amount until the maximum speed is regained. Recheck the idling speed and balance, adjusting at screws 9 as required.

8 Check the fork clearance as described in operation 4. Make sure the mixture control cables 3 have the necessary free movement (see operation 2). Slacken screws 2 and 4 until well clear of cams (see 16 and 18). Pull out mixture (choke) control knob until jets are about to move (see part 42 in **FIG 2:6**). Lock the control in this position.

9 Turn each fast-idle screw (2, 4, 16 or 18) until it just touches the cam and then turn each screw equally to obtain a fast-idle speed of 1100 rev/min. This completes the tuning.

2:5 Removing and refitting carburetters

Disconnect the battery and remove the air cleaners. Disconnect the hoses 3 (see **FIG 2:8**). Pull off the distributor vacuum pipe elbow 4. Release the progressive throttle assembly (see 5). Disconnect choke cables 6. Disconnect fuel pipe 7. Release the carburetters (8 nuts).

When refitting, renew joint washers 10, fitting one on each side of distance pieces. Reverse dismantling procedure. Check and adjust settings (see preceding Section). Fit air cleaners.

2:6 Overhauling carburetters

Dismantling:

Refer to **FIG 2:6**. Clean outside of carburetter. Mark rim of suction chamber 7 and body 1 to ensure correct replacement. Remove damper 15. Remove screws 8 and lift off chamber 7. Remove spring 10, lift piston 9 straight out and pour off oil inside rod. Remove screw 14 and withdraw needle assembly 11, 12 and 13. Do not bend the needle.

Release hooked end of spring 61. Support head of jet 42 and remove screw 54. Unscrew nut 43 from float chamber 21, withdraw the jet downwards and take care of parts 44, 45 and 46.

Remove nut 51 and spring 50, unscrew locating nut 49 and remove jet bearing 47. Remove pivot bolt 55 to release cam lever 59. Make a note of the location of the associated parts 56, 57, 58, 60 and 61.

Release float chamber (bolt 21). Mark lid 25 for correct reassembly and detach it. Pull out pin 24 by the serrated end to release float 23. Withdraw needle (26). Unless worn, there is no point in removing throttle butterfly disc 34. If it must be removed, mark its position

in relation to the intake bore, squeeze the split ends of screws 35 together, unscrew them and push disc out of spindle 33. Note location of lever 37 before removing nut 41. When refitting disc, snap throttle shut to centralize it in bore and then fit the screws, spreading the split ends just enough to stop them turning.

Inspecting:

Clean the parts in fuel. Check fit of spindle 33 in body and renew if slack. Check float needle and seat 26. Flooding of the carburetter may have been due to a worn needle (look for groove on needle seating). Renew both parts if suspect. Renew all other worn parts. Clean inside of float chamber. Check needle and spring against **Technical Data**.

Check the piston and suction chamber without fitting the spring. The parts must be clean and dry. **Do not use abrasives on piston and suction chamber surfaces.** Refer to **FIG 2:9** and test as follows:

1 Refit damper. Plug holes at A with rubber plugs or Plasticene. Insert piston fully.

2 Fix large washer to one lug of chamber so that it overlaps bore (see B). Turn assembly upside down as shown, hold the piston and time the fall of the chamber.

3 Total fall of the chamber should take between 5 and 7 seconds. If longer, check piston and chamber surfaces for dirt or damage. Renew assembly if time is still outside the limits.

Reassembling:

Fit needle, guide and spring into piston, with guide flush with face of piston. Tighten screw 14 against flat on guide. Refit jet bearing 47, tightening nut 49. Fit parts 50 51, screwing the nut on as far as possible. Insert jet 42. Fit gland parts with flexible tube projecting a minimum of $\frac{3}{16}$ inch (4.8 mm) beyond gland 45.

Reassemble the float chamber. Do not overtighten needle seat (part of 26). Fit needle, coned end first. Refit float 23, inserting pin 24 serrated end last. Refit lid on new joint washer 22. Secure assembly to body with bolt 30.

Fit jet tube to float chamber, tightening sleeve nut 43 just enough to compress the gland. This may leak if overtightened. Refit the piston and suction chamber. Do not forget the spring and align the marks made when dismantling. Tighten screws 8 evenly. Reconnect the jet link by holding up lever 59, supporting the jet head and fitting screw 54.

Screw down adjusting nut 51 by two turns (12 flats) to give an initial setting and then refit the carburetters (see **Section 2:5**). Tune and adjust them as described in **Section 2:4** after topping-up the damper oil (see **Section 2:2**).

2:7 Removing and refitting cables

Throttle cable:

Refer to **FIG 2:10**. To remove, slacken clamp screw 1. Press in plastic retainers (2) and ease outer cable through (RED end). Release cable from throttle pedal lever by removing clip (see 3). Press in plastic retainers 4 and ease outer cable through bulkhead (BLACK end).

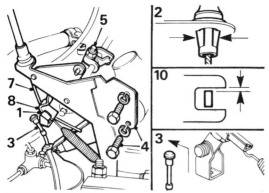

FIG 2:11 Servicing the throttle linkage. The numbers are used in the text

To refit cable, reverse the procedure. Check condition of pedal stop rubber 5. Its contact face should be .75 inch (19 mm) from bulkhead. Pull down on the inner cable 7 to take up all free movement of the pedal. Raise lever 8 until it just touches the cam above it. Tighten the cable clamp screw. Press the pedal and check that the cable allows the cam to return fully. On cars with automatic transmission, check the down-shift cable adjustment (see **Chapter 6a**).

Mixture control (choke) cables:

These can be seen in front of the suction chambers in **FIG 2:8**. To renew the cables, release the clamp screws at 6. Pull out the control knob and note the angle of the twin cables and location of the long cable. Release the instrument panel and pull it forward and down. Unscrew the large nut securing the choke control behind the panel. Note spring washer. Pull cables through bulkhead.

Reassemble by introducing the long cable into the control housing to pick up the long outer cable. Enter the short cable to pick up its outer cable. Push in the control knob and reassemble to the panel. Refix the panel. Connect the cables to the carburetter levers so that there is $\frac{1}{16}$ inch (2 mm) free movement before pulling on the cables starts to move the levers. Make sure the fast-idle screws are clear of their cams (see **Section 2:4**).

2:8 The throttle linkage

Refer to **FIG 2:11**. To remove the assembly, slacken the inner cable clamp screw at 1. Press in plastic retainers and ease outer cable through bracket (see 2). On cars with automatic transmission, disconnect the down-shift cable from the lever (see 3). Remove screws to release assembly (see 4).

When refitting, pull down on the inner cable as described under 'Throttle cable' in **Section 2:7**, and follow those instructions to the end, but also set the

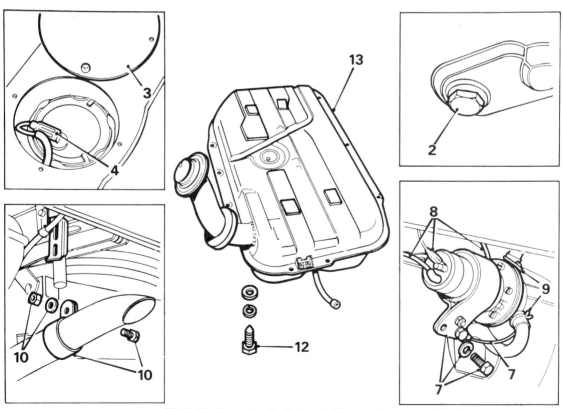

FIG 2:12 Removing the fuel tank. The numbers are used in the text

progressive throttle lever so that the pin is .012 inch (.31 mm) away from the top edge of the fork as at 10. This operation is described in operation 4 in **Section 2:4**. The lever can be seen at 15 in **FIG 2:7**.

When automatic transmission is fitted, reconnect the down-shift cable and check the adjustment (see **Chapter 6a**).

2:9 Removing and refitting fuel tank

Refer to **FIG 2:12**. Disconnect battery, open filler lid and drain tank at plug 2. Refit plug. Remove access lid 3 from floor of luggage compartment. Disconnect gauge cable 4 and tape to access hole. Raise and support rear of car. Remove rear bumper.

Disconnect fuel pump bracket from tank (7). Disconnect cables and breather tube 8 and hoses 9. Release exhaust pipe (10) and lower it for clearance. Support tank 13, remove screws 12, lower the tank, clean the fuel pipe, withdraw filler pipe from body and remove tank.

When refitting, renew grommets and spacing rubbers if necessary. Renewal of the gauge unit is accomplished with tool No. 18G.1001, giving the unit part of a turn until the lugs are clear. Reverse the dismantling procedure, noting that the fuel pump earth terminal fits on the inside bracket screw, between the bracket and the tank flange.

2:10 Fault diagnosis

(a) Restricted flow or no fuel from pump

1 Air vent in tank restricted
2 Fuel pipes blocked
3 Air leaks at pipe connections
4 Pump filter blocked
5 Pump diaphragm defective
6 Pump spring broken
7 Faulty valve assembly in pump
8 Fuel vapourizing in pipelines due to heat

(b) Float chamber lacks fuel

1 Check (a)
2 Sticking float needle valve
3 Float level set too low

(c) Float chamber floods

1 Defective float needle valve
2 Float level set too high
3 Punctured float

(d) Excessive fuel consumption

1 Carburetters need adjusting
2 Fuel leakage
3 Sticking mixture control
4 Dirty air cleaner
5 Wrong carburetter needles
6 Engine running too hot
7 Brakes binding
8 Tyres too soft
9 Idling speed too high
10 Car overloaded

(e) Idling speed too high

1 Rich fuel mixture
2 Throttle or mixture controls sticking
3 Idling screws wrongly adjusted
4 Worn throttle butterfly valves or spindles

(f) Poor idling

1 Check (c)
2 Vacuum pipe to distributor faulty
3 Vacuum pipe to brake servo faulty
4 Sticking piston
5 Worn throttle spindle and bushes
6 Air leaks at manifold joints

(g) Difficult starting

1 Check most of preceding Sections
2 Faulty ignition
3 Mechanical defects in engine
4 Air leaks at manifold joints

(h) Noisy fuel pump

1 Loose mountings
2 Air leaks on suction side or at diaphragm
3 Obstruction in fuel pipe
4 Clogged pump filter

NOTES

CHAPTER 3

THE IGNITION SYSTEM

3:1 Description

The Lucas distributor, type 25.D6, incorporates two automatic ignition timing controls. The first operates centrifugally and the second by vacuum. These controls may be seen in **FIG 3:3**. In the centrifugal device (16 and 17), weights fly outwards against the tension of small springs as engine speed rises. This movement advances the contact breaker cams (top 17) relative to the distributor driving shaft 19. The contact points then break earlier to give advanced ignition timing.

The vacuum unit 11 is connected to the carburetter intake system by a pipe. Depression in this system operates on a diaphragm in the unit, the suction varying with the load on the engine. Diaphragm movement turns contact breaker plate (top 12).

The distributor shaft is driven anticlockwise, as shown by the arrow in the inset (top left) in **FIG 3:2**.

3:2 Routine maintenance

The following operations should be carried out every 6000 miles (10,000 km or six months). Refer to **FIG 3:1**.

Lubrication:

1 Release clips 1 (bottom right) and lift off the distributor cap. Lightly smear cams 13 with grease.

2 Using 20W engine oil, apply one drop to moving contact pivot (lowest 14).
3 Inject two or three drops of oil into the space indicated (top 14).
4 Apply two or three drops of oil to recess in shaft (central 14). **Do not remove the screw.**

Make sure that oil and grease do not contaminate the points 4. Be sparing with lubricating oil at all times.

Checking:

With rotor arm fitted, turn the shaft in the direction of the arrow (anticlockwise) and release it. It should return freely to its original position. Check the contact points 4 for dirt and pitting.

Adjusting contact breaker gap:

1 Remove the cap (clips 1). Disconnect central and No. 1 high-tension leads (1) from cap. The lead positions are marked in **FIG 3:2** (inset, top left).
2 Disconnect lead and place water shield to one side (2). Remove the rotor arm and turn the engine until the contact points are fully open (3). Turn the engine by operating the starter motor carefully. Alternatively, remove the sparking plugs, engage top gear and push the car forwards (not backwards).

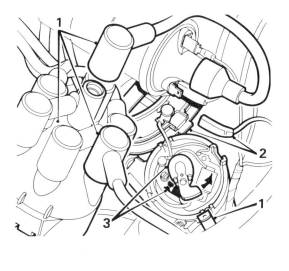

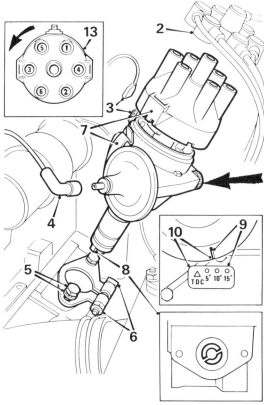

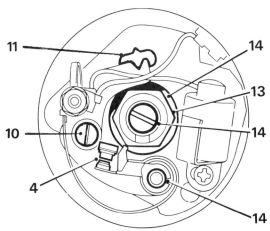

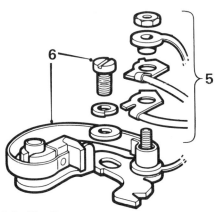

FIG 3:1 Distributor with cap removed (top), details of contact breaker platform (centre) and one-piece contact breaker parts (bottom). The numbers are used in the text

FIG 3:2 Operations involved when removing the distributor. Inset (top left) shows plug lead connections to cap for correct firing order. All numbers are used in the text

3 With points fully open as at 4, use feelers to check the gap. Correct opening should be .014 to .016 inch (.36 to .41 mm). Make sure that the feeler blades are free from oil or grease.

4 Adjust gap if necessary. Slacken screw 10 a little and insert a screwdriver blade in notches 11. Turn as required and then tighten screw. Turn the engine for a further check. If new points are fitted, increase the gap to .019 inch (.48 mm) to allow for bedding-in of the heel.

Cleaning or renewing the contact points:

If inspection shows that the points are dirty or pitted, they must be cleaned or removed for attention. Do the following, referring to the lower view in **FIG 3:1**.

1 To clean the points without removal, use fine emery paper and then wipe clean with a fuel-moistened cloth.

2 To remove the contact set, remove the nut and both leads from the stud (part of 5). Remove screw 6 (see 10 in central view). Lift off the contact set.

3 The contact assembly is available as a one-piece set, and badly eroded points are best serviced by fitting a

new set. If the points may be cleaned up satisfactorily, use fine emery paper or a smooth carborundum stone, keeping the faces flat and square. Wipe clean afterwards.

4 When renewing a contact set, note how the bottom half of the insulating bush assembly locates the spring on the stud (see lower right in the bottom view of **FIG 3:1**). The top bush is fitted above the lead terminals and the nut tightened moderately (see assembly 5). Set the gap. Check the ignition timing (see **Section 3:4**).

The distributor cap and rotor arm:

Clean the inner surfaces of the cap. Note that slight spark erosion of the brass segments is normal. Press on the carbon brush in the centre of the cap (see 3 in **FIG 3:3**). It should spring out again quite freely and protrude about $\frac{3}{16}$ inch. Renew the cap if it is cracked or damaged.

The rotor arm is a push fit (see 4 in **FIG 3:3**). Slight spark erosion of the brass plate is normal. Renew the arm if erosion is excessive, if the arm is cracked or damaged or if it is loose on the shaft. When refitting it, make sure the key engages fully in the slot in the shaft.

Cleaning and adjusting the sparking plugs:

Refer to **FIG 3:4**. Remove lead 1 and partly unscrew plug 4. Brush the seating 3 free from dirt. Unscrew the plug. Mark leads for correct replacement.

Plugs are best cleaned on a sand-blasting machine. If this is not available, wash oily plugs in a solvent and dry thoroughly. Remove all carbon with a sliver of wood and wire-brush the threads. **Do not use a wire brush on the firing points.** Use a thin flat file to clean up the central tip till it is square with the side electrode and then restore the sparking surfaces of the side electrode until they are clean and bright (see 7). Check the gap between the electrodes, using feeler gauges. Set to .025 inch (.63 mm) by bending the side electrode only. **Do not attempt to bend the central electrode.**

Refit the plugs by hand, screwing them down onto their gaskets. Tighten them a further quarter of a turn only. Refit the leads correctly. If there is any doubt about their location, refer to the inset, top left in **FIG 3:2** and connect the numbered sockets to the plugs, starting with plug No. 1 at the water pump end of the engine. This will give the correct fitting order of 1, 5, 3, 6, 2, 4.

3:3 Removing and refitting distributor

Refer to **FIG 3:2** and do the following:
1 Disconnect the battery. Withdraw plug leads 2 from cap. Detach low-tension lead 3 from side of distributor. Disconnect vacuum pipe 4.
2 Slacken **one** clamping plate securing bolt 5. Slacken clamp bolt 6 and withdraw distributor. **Do not turn the engine.**
3 Refit the distributor by releasing clips and removing cap 7. Offer the distributor to the engine with the vacuum timing control facing towards the righthand side of the car. Turn the distributor shaft by means of the rotor arm until the driving dogs engage (8) Note that the dogs and driving slot are offset and can only engage in one position (see inset of slot, bottom right).

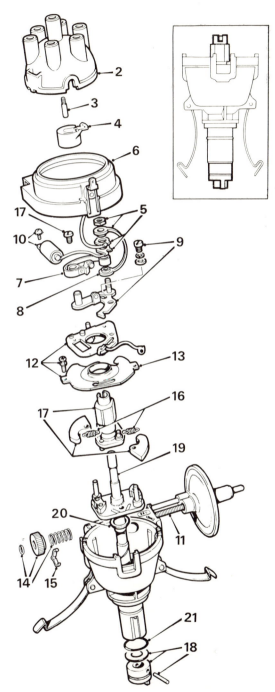

FIG 3:3 Components of the distributor. The numbers are used in the text. Inset (top right) shows the relative positions of rotor arm slot and driving dog offset

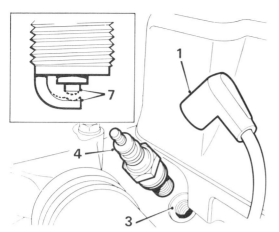

FIG 3:4 Sparking plug lead 1, seating 3, plug 4 and electrodes 7. Dotted lines show erosions of electrodes

4 Turn the engine until the mark on the crankshaft pulley is at 10 deg. BTDC as indicated at 9 and 10 in the upper inset on the right. Turn the distributor body until the contact points are just beginning to open and then lightly tighten the clamp bolt. Refit the cap.

5 Refit the plug leads in the order shown (top left). No. 1 plug is at the water pump end of the engine.

6 Connect a stroboscopic timing light. Start the engine and keep the speed no higher than 1000 rev/min. Check the position of the pulley timing mark, turning the distributor body until it is at approximately 12 deg. BTDC. This will be a little to the right of the 10 deg. mark shown at 9 and 10. When satisfied, tighten the clamp plate bolt and the bolt securing the plate to the block. Set the timing accurately to 12 deg. BTDC by turning the milled nut indicated by the arrow on the right. Finally, connect up the vacuum pipe 4.

3:4 Ignition timing

The correct setting is 12 deg. BTDC (before top dead centre) at 1000 rev/min with the vacuum pipe disconnected (see 4 in **FIG 3:2**).

Check the timing by following operation 6 in the preceding Section. If the distributor has not been disturbed, adjustment may be effected by turning the milled nut indicated by the arrow on the right. The position of the pulley timing mark will lie a little to the left of the central position between marks 10° and 15° (see 9 in inset on right). Do not forget to reconnect the vacuum pipe.

3:5 Servicing the distributor

Refer to **FIG 3:3** and do the following, after removing the distributor as in **Section 3:3**:

1 Unclip and remove cap 2. Pull off rotor arm 4. Remove the contact set (5, 7, 8 and 9) as described in **Section 3:2**, withdrawing shield 6 when the terminal is clear.

2 Detach link 11 of vacuum unit from moving plate for contact breaker (see upper item of parts 12). Remove the two screws and lift off the plate assembly 12 and 13. Turn the bottom plate clockwise to release it from the moving plate.

3 Vacuum unit 11 may be removed by prising off the circlip, unscrewing the milled nut and taking off the spring (see 14). Note the ratchet spring 15.

4 Lift off springs 16. Remove the screw in the top end of shaft 19 and pull off the cams and weights 17. Drive out pin 18 to remove the driving dog. Note the washers 18 and 20. 21 is an O-ring on the body.

Check parts for wear or damage. Excessive clearance of shaft in body will lead to erratic ignition. Inspect cap for cracks or tracking. The latter is seen as a black line between adjacent brass segments. Renew cap if either fault is evident.

Reassembling distributor:

Reverse the dismantling procedure, lubricating the shaft and body bearings with engine oil. Lubricate the bearing surfaces of contact plates 12 and 13 with Ragosine molybdenized non-creep oil.

Refer to the inset (top right) when refitting the driving dog 18. Note how the large offset of the dog is to the left when rotor arm slot at the top is facing the operator as shown.

Adjust the contact breaker gap. If a new set of points is fitted, it is recommended that the gap be increased to .019 inch (.48 mm) to allow for bedding-in of the operating heel. Turn the micrometer adjustment nut (14) until it is in a midway position. Refit the distributor and check the timing as described in **Sections 3:3** and **3:4**.

If it is necessary to renew the capacitor (condenser), remove the screw, unship the cable tag from the contact breaker stud and lift the capacitor away (see 5 and 10 in **FIG 3:3**). Difficult starting may be attributable to a faulty capacitor.

3:6 Sparking plug leads and plug condition

The leads are readily removable by pulling them off the sparking plugs and the distributor cap. If renewal is attempted, change the leads one at a time to avoid mistakes in the firing order (see end of **Section 3:2**).

The condition of the firing end of sparking plugs will give some indication of engine tune as follows:

A normal deposit should be brown to greyish tan in colour, this being the result of correct carburation and a mixture of high-speed and low-speed driving. If the deposits are white or yellowish they indicate greater heat due to long periods of constant speed driving, probably rather fast. Black, wet deposits are caused by oil entering the combustion chamber past worn pistons and bores or down valve stems. If the black deposits are dry and fluffy they usually indicate running with a rich mixture, but they may also be due to incomplete combustion through defective ignition or excessive idling.

Overheated sparking plugs have a white, blistered look about the centre electrode and the side electrode may be badly eroded. The cause may be poor cooling, wrong ignition timing or sustained high speeds with heavy loads.

3:7 Fault diagnosis

(a) Engine will not fire

1 Battery discharged
2 Distributor contact points dirty, pitted or badly adjusted.
3 Distributor cap dirty, cracked or 'tracking'
4 Carbon brush inside cap not touching rotor
5 Faulty cable, switch, or loose connections in low-tension circuit
6 Distributor rotor arm cracked
7 Faulty coil
8 Broken contact breaker spring
9 Contact points stuck open
10 High-tension lead from coil to distributor detached or broken

(b) Engine misfires

1 Check 2, 3, 5 and 7 in (a)
2 Weak contact breaker spring
3 High-tension plug or coil leads cracked or damaged
4 Loose sparking plug(s)
5 Sparking plug insulation cracked
6 Sparking plug gap incorrectly set
7 Ignition timing too far advanced

NOTES

CHAPTER 4

THE COOLING SYSTEM

4:1 Description

The system is pressurized to raise the boiling point of the coolant. The rise in pressure is, however, restricted to 15 lb/sq in (1.05 kg/sq cm) by a spring-loaded valve in the expansion tank filler cap.

The natural thermo-system action of heated water tending to rise to the top tank of the radiator, and falling down through the core to be cooled, is augmented by a centrifugal impeller pump which is mounted on the left-hand end of the cylinder block. The outer end of the pump spindle carries a pulley, the drive being by V-belt from a pulley on the crankshaft.

A thermostatically-controlled electric fan is mounted behind the forward-facing radiator (see **FIG 4:3**).

To secure a rapid warm-up from cold, there is a thermostat valve in a housing attached to the head. This is closed when the coolant is cold, thus preventing circulation through the top hose to the radiator. When the coolant heats up, the thermostat valve opens and coolant is then free to pass through the radiator.

An expansion tank is mounted low down behind the battery (see **FIG 4:1**). It is connected by a hose to the top tank of the radiator, and as the coolant expands with heat it escapes down the pipe into the expansion tank.

When the engine stops and the coolant temperature drops, the partial vacuum created in the radiator top tank causes coolant to be drawn back up the hose.

4:2 Routine maintenance

Topping-up radiator:

Refer to **FIG 4:1**. **Note that there is pressure in the system when it is hot. In these circumstances, never remove filler plug 1 before releasing the expansion cap 12. Remove the expansion tank cap slowly to release the pressure and take precautions against scalding from steam by protecting the hand with a cloth.** Check every 6000 miles (10,000 km or six months).

Having removed the expansion tank cap, check the coolant level inside with a dipstick. If it is below $2\frac{1}{4}$ inch (60 mm), add fresh coolant. Use antifreeze mixture if it is in use in the system.

Remove filler plug 1 and top-up with coolant to the top of filler neck and refit the plug. Use antifreeze mixture if required. Remember that topping-up with water will dilute the strength of antifreeze.

Check the system for leaks if there is a persistent need for topping-up.

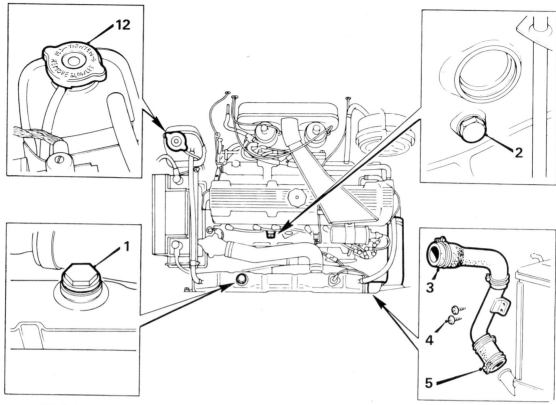

FIG 4:1   Radiator filler plug 1, cylinder block drain plug 2, bottom hose 3 and expansion tank cap 12

Adjusting belt tension:

Refer to **FIG 4:2**. Every 6000 miles (10,000 km or six months), check belt tension midway between the top pulleys (see arrow at 1). Deflection under moderate hand pressure should be approximately $\frac{1}{2}$ inch (13 mm). On cars with automatic transmission, remove access panel (see start of **Section 4:5**).

Adjust if necessary by slackening bolts 2 and 3. To tighten the belt, push the alternator 5 away from the engine and retighten the bolts. It is best to press on the alternator by the bracket at the drive end. **Do not over-tension the belt as it will lead to bearing wear.**

4:3 Draining and refilling system

Draining:

Take note of the warning at the start of the preceding Section. Refer to **FIG 4:1** and do the following:
1 Remove filler plug 1. Remove drain plug 2 from front of cylinder block. On cars with automatic transmission and power steering, disconnect the radiator hose 3 at the water pump end.
2 Release the connecting hose from the radiator baffle (two screws 4). Disconnect bottom end of hose at 5.

Refilling:

1 Connect bottom of hose to radiator and refit the connecting hose. On cars with automatic transmission and power steering, reconnect the hose to the water pump at 3.
2 Refit cylinder block drain plug. Fill system with coolant to top of filler neck and refit filler plug 1. See **Section 4:9** for details of antifreeze mixtures.
3 Run engine at a fast idle for 30 seconds. Stop the engine and release and retighten the expansion tank filler cap 12 to release any pressure. Top-up at the radiator filler plug. Top-up coolant in the expansion tank to a level of $2\frac{1}{4}$ inch (60 mm) from bottom of tank.

4:4 Servicing fan and radiator

Removal:

Refer to **FIG 4:3** and do the following:
1 If system is hot, read the warning at the start of **Section 4:2**. Remove radiator filler plug 2 and expansion tank cap. Disconnect battery at 1.
2 Remove cylinder block plug 3 to drain the system. Disconnect cable 4 from thermostatic switch. Disconnect wiring plug and socket at 5.

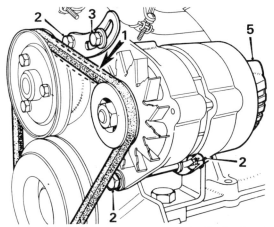

FIG 4:2 Adjusting water pump belt. Deflection is indicated at 1. Pivot bolts 2, link bolt 3 and alternator 5

3 Disconnect top hose 6. Disconnect bottom hose from water pump at 7 and release pipe from radiator baffle (screws 8). Disconnect air bleed hose at 9. Disconnect expansion hose at 10.

4 Remove bolts 11. Release radiator from plastic clips 12 on front crossmember and withdraw it.

Servicing fan motor:

Remove the two bolts on each side of the radiator to release the motor carrier. Remove fan by unscrewing the grub screw securing it to the motor shaft. Release motor from carrier (3 screws and nuts).

Test motor by connecting it (without fan) to a 13.5 volt battery supply with a moving coil ammeter in series. Meter should read 3 amp (maximum) after 60 seconds from cold. The running speed should lie between 3500 and 4000 rev/min after 60 seconds from cold.

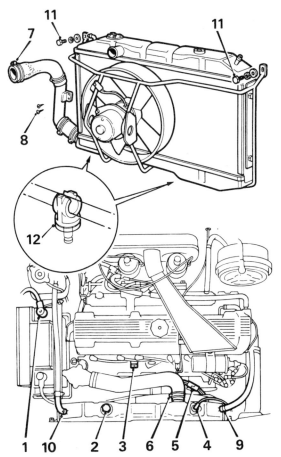

FIG 4:3 Details for removing the radiator. Note how bar underneath radiator fits in plastic clips 12. The numbers are used in the text

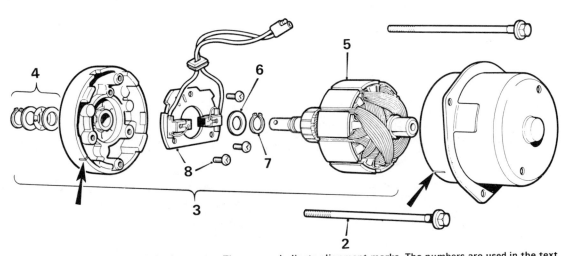

FIG 4:4 The components of the fan motor. The arrows indicate alignment marks. The numbers are used in the text

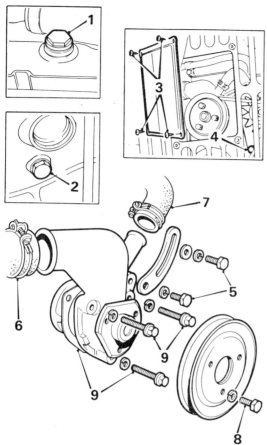

FIG 4:5 Removing the water pump. The numbers are used in the text

Dismantling motor:

If repairs are indicated, dismantle the motor. Refer to **FIG 4:4**. Remove bolts 2 and withdraw end cover assembly 3 complete. Remove circlip and washers 4. Withdraw armature 5, washer 6 and circlip 7. Release brush carrier (8).

Check that brushes are not less than 3/16 inch (4.76 mm) long. Renew brush gear set if necessary. Clean commutator (copper segments at lefthand end of armature 5). Polish with fine glasspaper (not emery cloth). A badly worn commutator may be skimmed in a lathe. Clean swarf from between the segments **but do not undercut the insulation.**

Reassembling:

Reverse the dismantling procedure. Lubricate shaft and bearing bushes with Shell Turbo 41 oil. Line up marks arrowed, when refitting cover. Fit spring washer between shim washers at 4. Tighten through-bolts to 14 lbf in (.17 kgf m). Test the motor as described earlier. If it still does not operate it will be necessary to have the windings checked at a Service station.

Refitting motor:

Reverse the dismantling procedure, making sure that the fan grubscrew engages the dimple in the motor shaft.

Refitting radiator assembly:

This is a simple reversal of the dismantling procedure. When finished, refill with coolant as described in **Section 4:3**.

4:5 Servicing water pump

Refer to **FIG 4:5**. Do the following:
1 If system is hot, follow the instruction at the start of **Section 4:2**. Remove the radiator filler plug 1 and lower the coolant level by removing cylinder block plug 2.
2 On cars with automatic transmission, remove panel from lefthand wing valance (screws 3). On all cars, slacken alternator pivot bolt and nut 4. Remove bolts 5.
3 Disconnect radiator hose 6 and heater hose 7. Remove pulley (3 bolts 8). Remove bolts 9 to release water pump from block. The pump is best serviced as an assembly.

Refitting pump:

Reverse the dismantling procedure. Fit dished side of pulley inwards. Tighten pump securing bolts to 20 lbf ft (2.77 kgf m). Tighten pulley bolts to 8 lbf ft (1.11 kgf m). Adjust belt tension (see **Section 4:2**). Refill colling system (see **Section 4:3**).

4:6 Servicing thermostat

Refer to **FIG 4:6**. If system is hot, drain it after referring to the start of **Section 4:2**. It is only necessary to remove the cylinder block drain plug to lower the coolant level. Remove bolts to release outlet and gasket (3). Withdraw thermostat 4.

If valve is stuck open, thermostat must be renewed. To check operation, immerse thermostat in water, heat the water and note the temperature at which the valve opens. The thermostat and thermometer must not touch the container. The standard thermostat should open at 74°C (165°F). This temperature is stamped on the base of the thermostat.

Refit the thermostat on a new gasket and refill the system (see **Section 4:3**).

To remove the thermostat housing, partially drain the system as described in the preceding instructions. Remove the battery. Disconnect the wiring from the thermal transmitter. Disconnect the top hose and the heater hose on the underside. Remove the engine lifting bracket and then the remaining bolt and hose clip. There is a sealing ring between the housing and the cylinder head.

Refit in the reverse order and then refill the system (see **Section 4:3**).

4:7 Fan motor relay and switch

The relay is mounted in front of the battery on the righthand wing valance. There are three cable connections. Make a note of these so that they may be reconnected correctly.

The motor thermostatic switch is mounted in the radiator header tank at the opposite end to the filler cap (see 4 in **FIG 4:3**). To remove it, disconnect the battery. Disconnect the cable from the switch. Lift out the switch and joint washer after removing the three nuts and spring washers. Renew the switch if it is faulty.

4:8 Cylinder block plugs

These blank off manufacturing holes and one of them is readily identified slightly above the cylinder block drain plug (see 2 in **FIG 4:1**). To renew a leaking plug, drain the system (see **Section 4:3**). Remove the radiator (see **Section 4:4**). Remove the engine intake and exhaust manifolds.

. Drill a hole in the faulty plug, insert a steel bar or screwdriver and prise out the plug.

Before fitting the new plug, clean out the recess and dry it thoroughly. Coat the plug periphery with sealing compound and drive it into place with a round drift that is almost the inside diameter of the plug. Reverse the dismantling procedure and refill the system.

4:9 Antifreeze solution

For protection in freezing conditions, add an approved antifreeze to the cooling water. This may be Unipart Frostbeat, Bluecol antifreeze or one conforming to BS.3151 or BS. 3152.

The addition of $4\frac{1}{4}$ pints ($5\frac{1}{4}$ US pints or 2.4 litres) gives a 25% solution that will start freezing at —13°C (9°F) and will be frozen solid at —26°C (—15°F).

$5\frac{3}{4}$ pints (7 US pints or 3.2 litres) will make a $33\frac{1}{3}$% solution that starts freezing at —19°C (—2°F) and will be frozen solid at —36°C (—33°F).

Double the volume for 25% solution gives a 50% solution that starts freezing at —36°C (—33°F) and is solid at —48°C (—53°F).

When antifreeze is used, topping-up with plain water will dilute the solution and reduce the protection. Use antifreeze solution for topping-up.

4:10 Fault diagnosis

(a) Poor coolant circulation

1 Radiator core blocked
2 Engine water passages restricted
3 Coolant level too low
4 Loose belt
5 Defective thermostat
6 Collapsed radiator hoses

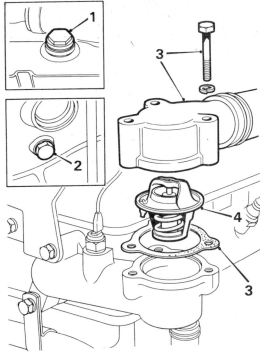

FIG 4:6   Removing thermostat 4. 1 is the radiator filler plug, 2 is the cylinder block plug and 3 is the outlet with its bolts and gasket

(b) Overheating

1 Check (a)
2 Faulty ignition or carburation
3 Tight engine
4 Binding brakes, slipping clutch
5 Defective fan motor or thermostatic switch

(c) Internal water leakage

1 Cracked cylinder wall or head
2 Loose cylinder head bolts
3 Faulty head gasket

(d) Corrosion

1 Impurities in water
2 Infrequent draining and flushing

NOTES

CHAPTER 5

THE CLUTCH

5:1 Description

FIG 5:2 shows the external operating mechanism and FIG 5:3 shows the internal parts. Flywheel 8 is bolted to the crankshaft. Inside the flywheel is a pressure plate 7 and a driven plate 9. The driven plate is splined to the primary gear in the transmission, and is provided with friction linings. Lugs on the pressure plate pass through clearance holes in the flywheel and these are bolted to flexible drive straps 11.

Diaphragm assembly 7 is also bolted to the same ends of the straps, so that pressure on the assembly can be made to force pressure plate 7 away from the flywheel against powerful spring pressure inside assembly 7.

This spring pressure, when the clutch is engaged, nips the driven plate between the pressure plate and the flywheel so that the whole assembly will rotate as one unit, transmitting drive from the engine to the gearbox.

When the clutch pedal is depressed, lever 14 presses on release bearing 15 (see FIG 5:2). This bearing in turn presses on plate 2 which is bolted to the diaphragm spring assembly 7 (see FIG 5:3). The spring is compressed and the pressure plate is pushed away from the flywheel, thus relieving the nip on the driven plate. In consequence, the plate slows down and the drive from the engine to the gearbox is disconnected. The drive is restored when the clutch pedal is released, the engagement being smoothly taken up by the friction linings on the driven plate.

5:2 Routine maintenance

Refer to FIG 5:1. Every 6000 miles (10,000 km or six months) check the fluid level in the clutch master cylinder reservoir 2. Note that this is the smaller of the two reservoirs. If necessary, top-up to the level indicated on the outside. It is essential to use the correct fluid. This is Unipart 550 Brake Fluid or a brake fluid conforming to Specification SAE.J.1703a. **Do not use any other type of fluid.**

Check that the vent hole 3 is clear. **Take care not to let the fluid drip onto the body paintwork as it is a solvent.** Wipe the cap before unscrewing it so that dirt cannot fall inside.

At the same mileage, check the condition of the pipe and hose in the clutch hydraulic system.

5:3 Bleeding the clutch system

This will be necessary if the clutch hydraulic system has been dismantled or if there is a 'spongy' feel to clutch pedal operation, with the possibility of the clutch not fully disengaging.

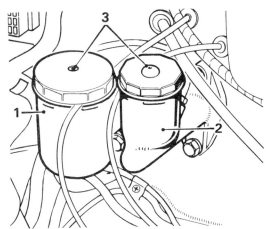

FIG 5:1 Location of master cylinder reservoirs in engine compartment. Clutch reservoir 2 is the small one, reservoir 1 being for the brake system. Keep vent holes 3 clear

The bleed screw is on the clutch slave cylinder (see arrow in inset, top right in **FIG 5:2**). Remove the dust cap and attach a rubber or plastic tube to the nipple. Immerse the free end of the tube in a small quantity of clean brake fluid in a glass jar. Make sure that the reservoir is topped-up with the correct fluid (see **Section 5:2**). Check this level during the operation to make sure that it has not fallen too low.

Open the bleed screw about three-quarters of a turn, get a second operator to depress the clutch pedal fully, and while it is held down, close the bleed screw. The pedal may then be released. Continue with this sequence, watching the immersed end of the tube for air bubbles. When they cease, tighten the bleed screw during a down stroke of the pedal. Check the fluid level in the reservoir. Restore the dust cap.

5:4 Servicing the release bearing

Refer to **FIG 5:2**. Note how lever 14 is operated by the slave cylinder (top right). The lower ball-end presses release bearing 15 inwards to disengage the clutch. A worn bearing is renewed as follows:

1 Lift expansion tank out of bracket and place to one side. Remove battery and tray. Release slave cylinder (bolts 3), pulling it off the pushrod.
2 Attach lifting gear to bracket at same end of engine. Release righthand rear engine mounting bracket from rubber mounting and clutch cover (nuts 5). Remove lefthand rear engine mounting bolt 6.
3 Lift engine to remove bracket. Lower again to remove the lower stud 8 from between the body and the suspension tie-rod. Locking two nuts together on the stud 9 will enable it to be turned. Remove the studs 10 in the same way. Remove bolts 11.
4 Lift engine to normal position and remove clutch cover 12. Remove pin 13 to release lever 14. Lift out bearing and shaft 15 and press the bearing off the shaft.
5 Press new bearing into place, then reverse the dismantling procedure.

5:5 Servicing the clutch assembly

Removing:

Refer to **FIG 5:3** and proceed as follows:

1 Remove cover and release bearing as in preceding Section. Remove thrust plate 2 and retaining plate 3. Remove starter motor (see **Chapter 12**).
2 Use a soft-faced hammer through the starter hole to drive the flywheel assembly 5 off the primary gear, working evenly all round.

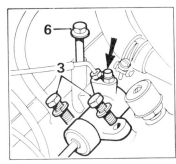

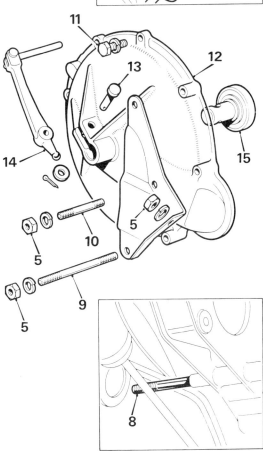

FIG 5:2 Operations for removing the clutch cover and release bearing. The numbers are used in the text. Arrow (top right) points to the slave cylinder bleed screw

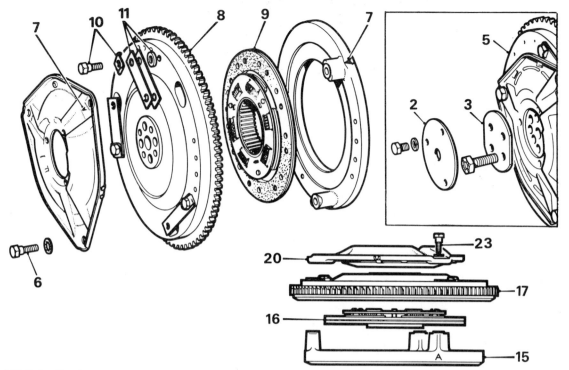

FIG 5:3 Clutch components. Inset (top right) shows release bearing thrust plate and flywheel retainer. The numbers are used in the text

Dismantling:

1 Slacken bolts 6 evenly. Note alignment marks **A** and remove the diaphragm (see 7).
2 Lift flywheel 8 off pressure plate. Remove driven plate 9. Unlock bolts 10 and remove the driving straps 11, noting the spacing washer between the straps and the flywheel.

Inspecting:

Clean the parts and check for wear or damage. Check the pressure plate for cracks or scoring. Examine diaphragm spring assembly 20 for wear or broken parts. Check the driving straps for elongated holes and the securing bolts for wear.

Check the linings on driven plate 9. They should be smooth and polished and light in colour. Renew the plate if they are worn thin or are uneven in thickness, or if they have been contaminated with oil. A very dark opaque colour is a sign of burning and oil contamination.

Check for loose or broken springs in the shock-absorbing hub and for worn spring apertures in the clutch centre. Look for wear of the hub splines. It is always a good plan to renew the plate if there is any doubt about its condition.

Reassembling:

Check, and if necessary, adjust the primary gear end float (see **Section 1:8**). Place pressure plate 15 on a flat surface (see bottom right). Fit the driven plate 16 with springs uppermost. This side is also marked 'FLYWHEEL SIDE'.

Drop flywheel 17 into place and refit the driving straps to the flywheel with the spacers in between. Use new lockwashers and make bolts finger tight. Fit diaphragm 20 with **A** marks aligned. Do not tighten bolts 23.

Tighten driving strap-to-flywheel bolts to 18 lbf ft (2.5 kgf m) and turn up the locking tabs.

Refitting:

1 Fit assembly to crankshaft and tighten flywheel bolts to 60 lbf ft (8.3 kgf m).
2 Tighten diaphragm bolts 23 to 15 to 18 lbf ft (2.1 to 2.5 kgf m). Refit bearing plate 2 and tighten the bolts to 10 lbf ft (1.4 kgf m).
3 Refit the release bearing and cover (see preceding Section).

5:6 Servicing the master cylinder

Refer to **FIGS 5:4** and **5:5** and proceed as follows:

Removing:

1 Release clutch pedal from operating fork (see **FIG 5:4**). Disconnect pipe 2 from master cylinder 4 and plug hole and pipe end to exclude dirt.
2 Unscrew nut 3 and bolt 3. Withdraw cylinder from bulkhead, noting the adjustment shims for pedal travel that are fitted under the flange.

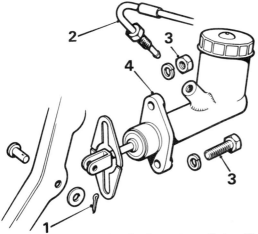

FIG 5:4 Removing the clutch master cylinder. The numbers are used in the text. Note packing pieces for flange

Overhauling:

1 Remove dust cover 2 (see **FIG 5:5**). Extract circlip 3 and remove pushrod 4.
2 Withdraw piston assembly 5. Lift leaf 6 in thimble 9 and pull piston 7 out of thimble. Remove seal from piston.
3 Compress spring and release stem of valve 8 from the elongated hole in the thimble. Remove spacer and curved washer 10 from valve stem. Remove seal 11.

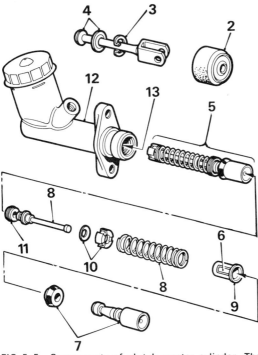

FIG 5:5 Components of clutch master cylinder. The numbers are used in the text

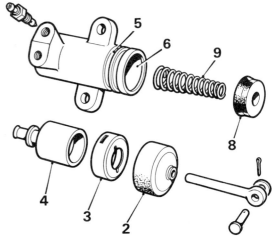

FIG 5:6 The components of the clutch slave cylinder. The numbers are used in the text

Inspecting:

Clean the cylinder in methylated spirit and all the internal parts in clean brake fluid. **Use no other solvents.** The cylinder bore must be smooth. If it is scored or pitted the cylinder must be renewed. Check that all ports are clear of obstructions. Always renew the seals. These are available in kit sets. The bore diameter of the cylinder is $\frac{5}{8}$ inch (15.87 mm).

Reassembling:

1 Immerse all parts in the correct brake fluid and assemble wet. Fit seal 11 with its flat face against the valve shoulder. Fit washer and spacer 10. The washer must have its domed side against the valve head. The legs of the spacer must face the valve head.
2 Fit spring centrally on spacer. Insert thimble in spring and compress spring until valve stem engages with elongated hole in thimble. Centralize the parts.
3 Fit a new seal to the piston with its flat face against the large piston shoulder. Insert piston stem into thimble and press home until the spring leaf engages behind the small shoulder.
4 Insert the piston assembly into the bore, taking care not to trap or turn back the lip of the seal. Press the assembly down the bore and refit the circlip.
5 Smear pushrod and sealing areas of dust cover with Girling Rubber Grease and fit the cover.

Refitting:

Reverse the removal procedure, then bleed the system as described in **Section 5:3**.

5:7 Servicing the slave cylinder

Refer to **FIG 5:6** and remove the cylinder as instructed in **Section 5:4**, disconnecting and plugging the flexible pipe. Remove dust cover 2 then release the crimping and pull off cap 3. Blow out piston assembly 4 with gentle air pressure at the inlet port. Drape the parts in a cloth to avoid loss or damage.

Wash the body 5 in methylated spirit and use brake fluid to clean the internal parts. Renew the body if the bore 6 is pitted or scored. Renew the seal 8. The correct bore of the cylinder is $\frac{7}{8}$ inch (22.22 mm) diameter.

Reassemble the internal parts after wetting them with the correct brake fluid (see **Section 5:2**). Fit the new seal with its flat face against the piston shoulder. Refit small end of spring 9 over piston stem.

Insert the piston assembly into the bore, taking care not to trap or turn back the lip of the seal. Refit cap if serviceable, otherwise renew it. Crimp retaining slots to retain cap on body. Smear sealing areas of dust cover with Girling Rubber Grease and refit it.

Refit the slave cylinder and bleed the system as described in **Section 5:3**.

The slave cylinder flexible pipe:

If it is necessary to remove this pipe in situ, drain the fluid by attaching a tube to the bleed nipple on the slave cylinder and pump it into a container by operating the clutch pedal. Unscrew the pipe connections at the master and slave cylinder bosses. When a flexible pipe has been refitted it is necessary to bleed the system (see **Section 5:3**).

5:8 Fault diagnosis

(a) Drag or spin

1 Oil on driven plate linings
2 Leaking hydraulic system
3 Driven plate distorted
4 Warped or damaged pressure plate
5 Broken driven plate linings
6 Air in the hydraulic system

(b) Fierceness or snatch

1 Check 1, 2, 3 and 4 in (a)
2 Worn linings
3 Worn release mechanism

(c) Slip

1 Check 1 in (a) and 2 in (b)
2 Weak spring
3 Seized slave cylinder piston
4 Release bearing shaft tight in housing

(d) Judder

1 Check 1 and 3 in (a)
2 Warped pressure plate
3 Broken drive straps
4 Contact area of linings not evenly distributed
5 Faulty rubber mountings and steady

(e) Tick or knock

1 Worn driven plate splines
2 Worn release bearing
3 Faulty starter pinion drive
4 Defective drive straps
5 Broken shock-absorber springs in driven plate hub
6 Flywheel loose on crankshaft

NOTES

CHAPTER 6

SYNCHROMESH TRANSMISSION

6:1 Description

This transmission has a manual gearchange with synchromesh engagement for each of the four forward gears. It is housed beneath the engine to form the power unit (see **FIG 1:1**). Integral with this unit is a pair of final drive gears and a differential assembly, the crownwheel and casing being shown in **FIG 6:15**. The output shafts from the differential are coupled by drive shafts and universal joints to the front wheels.

The gearshift mechanism in the gearbox is coupled to a remote gearchange control by long rods, as can be seen by the inset in **FIG 6:2**.

FIG 6:14 shows the drive down to the gearbox, primary gear 8 taking the drive from the clutch driven plate through the straight splines at the righthand end. Gear 10 is splined to the first motion shaft shown in the central view of **FIG 6:8** where the same gear is shown as part of assembly 34. The first motion shaft drives the laygear shown at the top of **FIG 6:11** and this in turn drives the third motion shaft shown in **FIG 6:12** according to the gear selected, with the exception of top gear. Direct coupling between the first and third motion shafts gives top gear.

The action of baulk ring female cones on male cones integral with the gear dogs to be engaged, causes the necessary speeding up or slowing down that will give synchronized speeds and silent engagement. The parts can be see in **FIG 6:12**, the synchronizer and baulk ring assembly being items 5 and 9. One of the gear cones is clearly shown in assembly 8.

Reverse gear is obtained by sliding gear 57 (see **FIG 6:11**) into engagement with the lefthand gear of assembly 11 in **FIG 6:12**. As this sliding gear is driven by the laygear, the introduction of a third gear gives reversed rotation. A pinion on the end of the third motion shaft engages with the final drive crownwheel (see 17 in **FIG 6:6**).

6:2 Routine maintenance

As the synchromesh transmission shares the same lubricating system as the engine, routine maintenance is confined to following the instructions in **Section 1:3**.

6:3 Servicing the remote control
Removing:

Work inside the car and remove the front carpet. Release the flange of the rubber gaiter (ring and 4 screws). Press and turn the cap shown at the top of **FIG 6:2** after pulling the gaiter clear. The gearlever may then be lifted out.

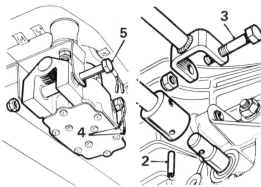

FIG 6:1 Detaching the gearbox remote control assembly. 2 is the extension rod roll pin, 3 is the steady rod bolt, 4 are the reversing light switch connections and 5 is the housing-to-bracket bolt

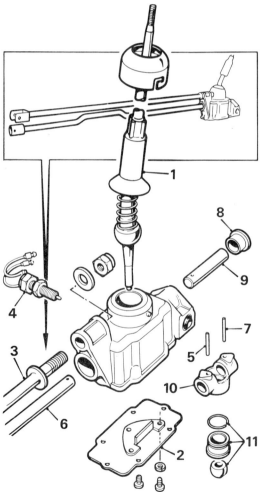

FIG 6:2 Dismantling the remote control assembly. The numbers are used in the text

Refer to **FIG 6:1** and drive out pin 2 from underneath the car. Remove nut and bolt 3. Remove connections 4 from reversing light switch. Release remote control housing from bracket (bolt 5).

Dismantling:

Refer to **FIG 6:2**. Do the following:
1 Remove bottom plate 2. Remove steady rod 3. Remove reversing light switch 4 (if fitted).
2 Pull extension rod 6 rearwards, drive out pin 5 to release the rod from eye 10. Push the eye forward and release it from support rod 9 by driving out pin 7.
3 Lever out plug 8 and drive out support rod 9. Remove eye 10. It may be dismantled by driving out bearing assembly (see 11). The circlip will be displaced from the nylon bearing seat.

Reassembling:

After checking all parts for undue wear and renewing if necessary, proceed as follows:
1 Use $\frac{1}{2}$ oz (14 g) of Duckhams Laminoid 'O' Grease and apply it with a brush to the hemispherical surface in the housing, into the selector rod eye, into the two selector rod bearing locations and to the upper surface of the bottom cover, particularly on the reverse lift plate (see **FIG 6:3**).
2 Insert the ball-end bearing into the nylon seat and retain with the circlip. Refit the extension rod eye.
3 Fit support rod and plastic plug. Reassemble the support and extension rods to the eye, making sure that the cranked part of the extension rod is uppermost to clear the exhaust system.
4 Continue in the reverse order of dismantling, finally refitting the gearlever.

Adjusting:

Refer to **FIG 6:3**. Slacken screws 20. Engage third or fourth gear and push reverse lift plate 21 into contact with the lower end of the gearlever. A screwdriver in a screw head will enable the plate to be moved within the limits of the slotted holes in the cover.

Tighten the cover screws and check that third and fourth gears can be selected freely.

Refitting to car:

Reverse the sequence of instructions given under 'Removal'.

6:4 Servicing the gear selector mechanism

The external connections are shown on the right in **FIG 6:1** and the internal parts in **FIG 6:4**.

Removing:

Drain the engine/gearbox assembly and remove the extension and steady rods (see last part of 'Removing' in preceding Section). Do not release the remote control housing. Remove the six nuts and pull the selector housing off the studs.

Overhauling:

Refer to **FIG 6 : 4**. Do the following:
1 Remove circlip 2 and pivot pin 3 (right). Remove bell-crank levers (3 left), noting the washers on each side.
2 Push out selector shaft 4. Push out locating pin 5. Pull out interlock spool 6.
3 If necessary, lever out oil seal 7 and drive out Silent-bloc bush 8. Clean and check the parts for wear and renew if required.

Reassembling:

1 Fit the new Silentbloc (if necessary) and if the oil seal needed renewal, drive it in with tool 18G.1190 (see 11). Refit the interlock spool and the locating pin.
2 Insert selector shaft into spool. Assemble the bell-crank levers and washers, refit in the housing and fit the pivot pin. Retain the pin with the circlip.

Refitting:

Clean the joint faces, remove all burrs and fit a new joint washer. Reverse the removal procedure.

6:5 Removing and refitting gearbox

Removing:

Refer to **FIG 6 : 5** and do the following:
1 Remove the power unit (see **Chapter 1**). Remove starter motor (bolts 2). Remove clutch cover and mounting bracket (nuts and bolts 3). Remove clutch thrust plate 4 and flywheel plate 5. Use soft-faced hammer in starter motor hole to drive off flywheel 6.
2 Remove flywheel housing (see fixings at 7). Remove dipstick and guide 8. Mark its position and then remove distributor 9 (see **Chapter 3**). Extract oil pump drive shaft with tool 10 (18G.1147).
3 Remove lower bolt and bracket from alternator (see 11). Remove rear engine mounting and bracket 12. Unlock and remove crankshaft pulley bolt 13 and pull off pulley 14.
4 Remove mounting bracket 15. Remove 16 bolts 16. One bolt enters downwards near the final drive housing and has a UNC thread (see top arrow). Lift the engine off the gearbox (see 17).

Refitting:

Check that joint faces are clean and free from burrs. Fit new joint washers. Check the oil feed O-ring 20 and renew it necessary. Check the oil seal 19 and renew it if there has been leakage. Examine sealing plugs 21 and renew if defective.

Lower engine into place and tighten bolts evenly. $\frac{5}{16}$ inch UNF bolts should be tightened to 25 lbf ft (3.5 kgf m). $\frac{3}{8}$ inch UNF bolts should be tightened to 30 lbf ft (4.1 kgf m) and the $\frac{5}{16}$ inch UNC bolts should be tightened to 12 lbf ft (1.7 kgf m).

Trim off excess from ends of sealing plugs 21. Fit crankshaft pulley oil seal. Reverse dismantling procedure, tightening the fixings as follows: Flywheel housing studs 6 lbf ft (.8 kgf m). Flywheel housing nuts and bolts 18 lbf ft (2.5 kgf m). Flywheel bolts 60 lbf ft (8.3 kgf m).

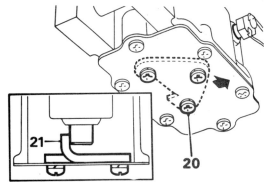

FIG 6 : 3 Adjusting the reverse lift plate 21. It is secured to the bottom cover of the remote control housing by screws 20

Clutch thrust plate bolts 10 lbf ft (1.4 kgf m) and clutch cover bolts 15 lbf ft (2.1 kgf m). Crankshaft pulley bolt 60 to 70 lbf ft (8.3 to 9.7 kgf m).

Turn up all locking tabs. Refit distributor, aligning marks made before removal. Tension alternator driving belt correctly (see **Chapter 4**).

Refit the power unit as described in **Chapter 1**.

6:6 Dismantling gearbox

Refer to **FIG 6 : 6** and do the following:
1 Pull off idler gear and thrust washers (see 9 in **FIG 6 : 14**). Remove oil filter (see **Chapter 1**). Remove oil pump connector 5 (see tool 18G.1149 top right). Remove front cover 6.

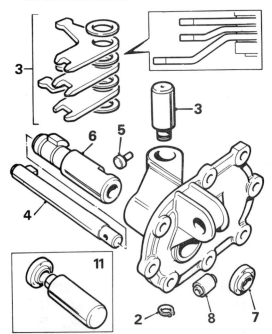

FIG 6 : 4 Dismantling the gear selector mechanism. The bell crank levers and interleaving washers are shown at the top. Tool 18G.1190 is used to fit the selector shaft oil seal (bottom left). The numbers are used in the text

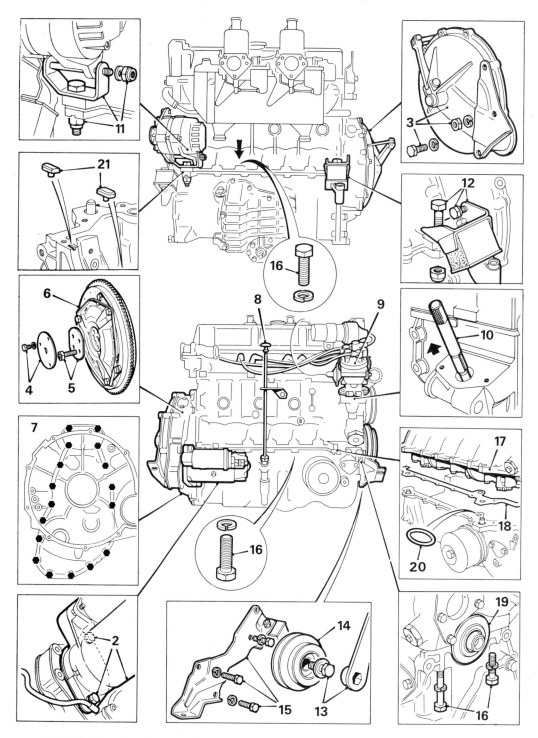

FIG 6:5 Operations for removing and refitting the gearbox. The numbers are used in the text

2 Release oil pump pick-up pipe 7. Extract the pipe. Remove bolts and lift out pump 8. Remove the final drive assembly (see **Section 6 : 12**). Unscrew speedometer drive pinion 10.

3 Remove circlip 11 and roll pin retaining cap 12. Pull off speedometer drive gear 13 without removing the roll pin. Unlock tabs of washer under pinion nut. Move selector forks to lock first and reverse gears together to stop third motion shaft from moving. Unscrew the nut with tool 16 (18G.1022A). **The nut has a lefthand thread.** Pull off the gear and move the forks to unlock the gears.

4 Refer to **FIG 6 : 7** and unlock tabs of washer 19. Remove bearing retainer 20. Check end float of laygear at the front end (see feeler gauge 21). The small thrust washer is at the front. Make a note if adjustment is needed during reassembling.

5 Drive out layshaft 22, leaving the laygear in position. Drive out reverse idler gear shaft 23. Remove selector rod retaining plate 24.

6 Cover the gearbox with a cloth to avoid losing the interlocking balls. Drive out first/second selector rod 25. Drive out third/top selector rod 26. Remove first/second fork 27 and third/top fork 28. Drive out reverse selector rod 29 and remove the fork. Remove reverse idler gear.

7 Refer to **FIG 6 : 8**. Unlock and remove locating bolt 31. Fit impulse extractor 18G.284 to third motion shaft 33 using adaptor 18G.284.AAD (see 32). Pull out the shaft (see arrow).

8 Remove nut, lockwasher and first motion shaft gear 34. Remove circlip 35 and drive out the shaft 36 in the direction of the arrow, using a soft-faced hammer.

9 Lift out the laygear and thrust washers. Extract circlips 38. Drive out first motion shaft needle-roller bearing with tool 39 (18G.1216).

10 Refer to **FIG 6 : 9**. Drive out inner bush 40 using tool 18G.1160 inserted through the idler gear needle roller bearing. Remove the bearing circlip (see 41). Use adaptor 18G.284.AO and impact tool 18G.284 (see 42) to extract the bearing in the direction of the arrow. The bearing will be complete with outer circlip 43.

6 : 7 Overhauling first motion shaft

Dismantling :

Refer to **FIG 6 : 10**. Unlock and remove the bearing nut, using tool 18G.1215 (see 8 and 9). Use soft jaws when holding the shaft in a vice. Using a press (10), push the shaft out of the bearing.

Inspecting :

After cleaning, check the gear teeth and the synchromesh cone for undue wear. Renew ball and needle roller bearings if worn, or if rough in action when turned without lubricant.

Reassembling :

Refit the bearing and tighten the nut to 120 lbf ft (16.6 kgf m). Turn up a tab of the locking washer. Drive the shaft into the gearbox casing with tool 18G.1157 using the needle roller bearing as an alignment guide (see lower view in **FIG 6 : 11**).

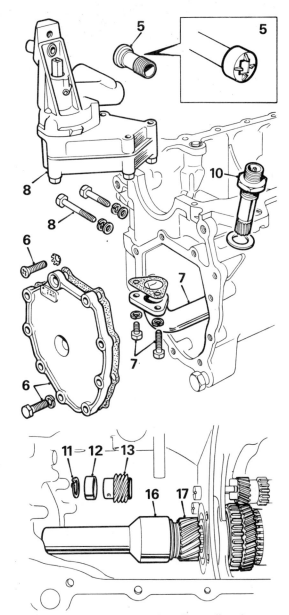

FIG 6 : 6 First operations when dismantling the gearbox. The bottom view shows removal of the pinion nut with tool 16 (18G. 1022A). The numbers are used in the text

Select and fit a circlip of the maximum thickness that will fit in the groove. Circlips are available as follows:

Size	Colour	Part No.
.060 to .061 inch (1.54 to 1.57 mm)	Black	42B.198
.062 to .063 inch (1.59 to 1.62 mm)	Orange	42B.199
.064 to .065 inch (1.64 to 1.67 mm)	Blue	42B.200

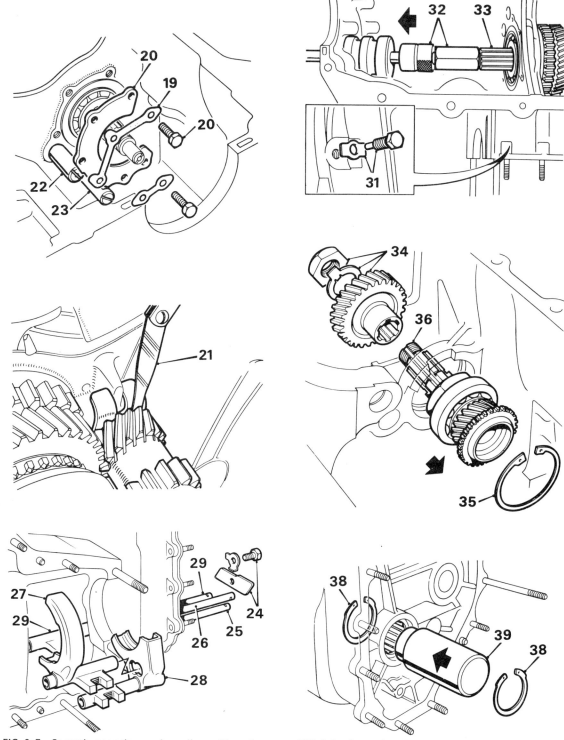

FIG 6:7 Second operations when dismantling the gearbox. Laygear end float is checked with feelers 21. The numbers are used in the text

FIG 6:8 Extracting the third motion shaft (top), first motion shaft (centre) and first motion shaft bearing (bottom). The numbers are used in the text

6:8 Overhauling laygear and reverse idler gear

The gears are shown in the top view of **FIG 6:11**. Check the bearing surfaces of both shafts for wear and renew if necessary. Renew the bearings if worn. Check the gear teeth for wear, cracks or chipping.

The laygear end float was checked before dismantling (see **Section 6:6**). Before reassembling, select a thrust washer to give the correct float of .002 to .003 inch (.05 to .08 mm). Thrust washers are available in the following thicknesses:

> .123 to .125 inch (3.12 to 3.17 mm)
> .126 to .128 inch (3.21 to 3.26 mm)
> .130 to .132 inch (3.30 to 3.35 mm)
> .133 to .135 inch (3.38 to 3.43 mm)

6:9 Overhauling third motion shaft

Dismantling:

Refer to **FIG 6:12**. Use soft jaws in the vice to hold the shaft at the lefthand end. Withdraw third and fourth synchronizer assembly 5. Unlock and unscrew nut 6 using tool 18G.1024 (see inset, bottom right).

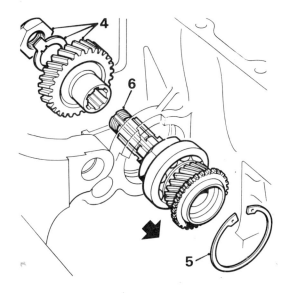

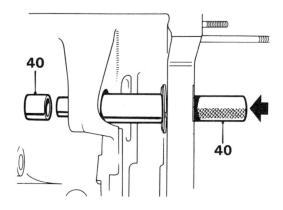

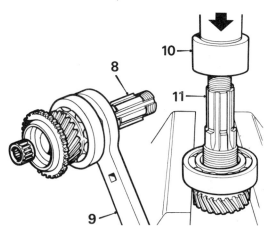

FIG 6:10 Dismantling the first motion shaft 6. Tool 9 is 18G.1215 and is used to remove the bearing nut. The numbers are used in the text

Withdraw sleeve, third speed gear and interlocking thrust washer (see parts 7). Withdraw second speed gear and thrust washer 8. Remove first and second speed synchronizer (parts 9). Use a press to force the shaft out of the bearing housing and then remove the reverse and first speed gears (see 11). If the bearing is worn, press it out of the housing.

Remove the baulk rings (see outer parts of assemblies 5 and 9). After wrapping assemblies in a cloth, push out the hubs from the sliding couplings (see centre parts of the same assemblies). The balls and springs will be retained in the cloth.

Inspecting:

Clean all the parts and check for wear. The bearing should be checked when unlubricated. It must be tight in its housing and be free from side play, pitting or worn cages.

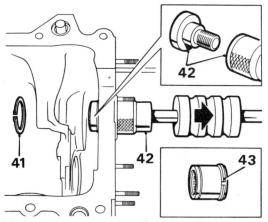

FIG 6:9 Removing idler gear bush 40 with tool 18G1160 (top). Impulse tool 18G284 with adaptor 18G284A0 (see 42) is used to extract idler gear needle roller bearing 43. Circlip 41 is the bearing retainer

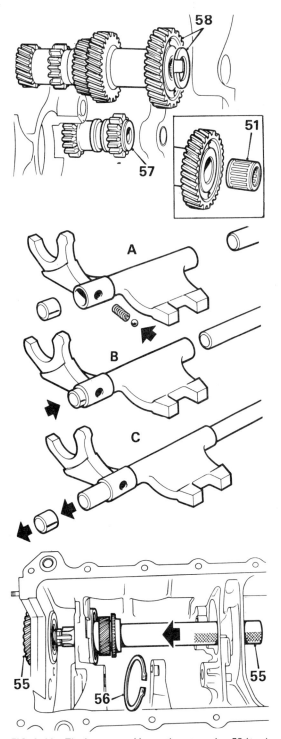

Check the gear teeth for wear, cracks or chipping. Renew thrust washers if worn. Fit baulk rings to mating cones on gears. If the cones do not engage before the rings contact the edge of the gear the worn parts must be renewed. This type of wear will give rise to noisy gearchanging due to the lack of synchronization.

Check all splines for wear and renew synchronizer balls and springs if unsatisfactory. Compare the springs with new ones.

Reassembling:

The correct assembly of the bearing in its housing is shown in the central view of **FIG 6:13**. Note projecting boss and cutaway at 16.

Hold tool 18G.1026 in a vice (see bottom left in **FIG 6:13**). Fit a synchronizer hub and align the loading hole in the tool with one of the holes in the hub (see 17). Insert a spring and ball and turn the hub while pressing on the ball. This will retain the ball and spring. Move on to the next hole. **Make sure to turn always in the same direction or a ball and spring may fly out.** Place the sliding coupling of the synchronizer on a flat surface (see bottom left). Fit the hub and tool assembly with the cutouts aligned (see 18). Using a hammer shaft, give the hub a sharp tap to knock it into the coupling.

Continue reassembling in the reverse order of dismantling. Note that the first/second synchronizer is smaller in diameter than the third/fourth one. Insert sleeve 7 into the third speed gear, fit the thrust washer with sleeve tongues located in slots and fit assembly to shaft (see **FIG 6:12**).

Use a new lockwasher and tap it into the recesses in the nut after tightening (see 6). Lubricate all parts.

6:10 Reassembling gearbox

Refer to **FIG 6:9** and refit the idler gear needle roller bearing 43. Use the impact tool in the reverse direction to the arrow (see 42). Refit the inner retaining circlip. Drive a new idler gear bearing bush into place until it is flush with the casing web (see 40). Lubricate all running parts.

Refer to **FIG 6:8**, refit the inner circlip, followed by the needle roller bearing and second circlip (see 38).

Refer to views A, B and C in **FIG 6:11**. Use new springs and insert them, followed by the balls into the selector forks. Hold in place with tool 18G.1029 or $\frac{1}{2}$ inch (13 mm) lengths of rod (view B). The method is the same for all forks.

Drive the first motion shaft into place with tool 18G.1157, using the gear on the left as a guide (see bottom view). Fit the circlip 56 as selected at the end of **Section 6:7**. Fit reverse idler and laygears into casing without shafts, the laygear having its large thrust washer fitted (see top view in **FIG 6:11**).

Refer to the top view in **FIG 6:8**. Align the groove in the third motion shaft bearing housing (see lefthand 11 in **FIG 6:12**) with the dowel bolt locating hole in the gearbox casing and drive the bearing into place with tool 18G.1197 (see **FIG 6:19**). Fit dowel bolt and new lockwasher 31. Tighten to 6 lbf ft (.8 kgf m) and turn up a tab to lock.

FIG 6:11 The laygear and large thrust washer 58 (top). The inset shows a laygear bearing. Operations A, B and C show how the selector rod balls and springs are fitted. Fitting the first motion shaft with tool 18G.1157 (bottom). The numbers are used in the text

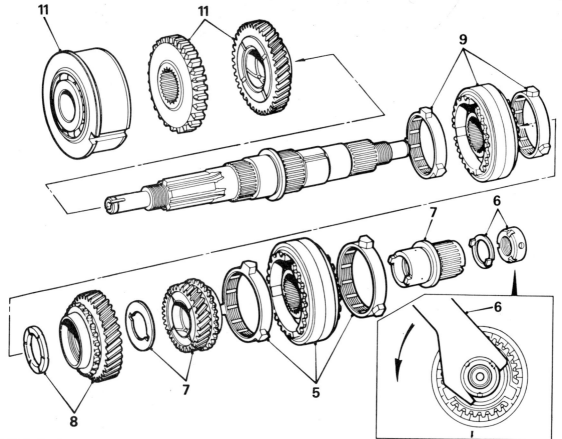

FIG 6:12 Components of the third motion shaft. Inset (bottom right) shows tool 18G.1024 being used to tighten the locking nut. The numbers are used in the text

Refit the layshaft and check the end float (see **Section 6:8**). Fit the reverse idler shaft. Refer to **FIG 6:7** and fit the bearing retainer 20. Use new locking plates, tighten the screws to 18 lbf ft (2.5 kgf m) and lock with tabs.

Refer to **FIG 6:7** (lowest view). Fit reverse fork 29, pushing the shaft into place so that it displaces the loading device (see C in **FIG 6:11**). Fit forks 27 and 28, holding them in place while the rods are fitted. Retrieve the loading devices. Fit plate 24, tighten the bolt to 16 lbf ft (2.2 kgf m) and tap up a locking tab. Move the forks until two gears are locked.

Refit the final drive pinion (see lower view in **FIG 6:6**) with a new lockwasher. Tighten the nut to 150 lbf ft (20.7 kgf m) and tap up three tabs of the lockwasher.

Refit the first motion shaft gear (see 34 in **FIG 6:8**). Tighten the nut to 120 lbf ft (16.6 kgf m) and tap up the lockwasher. Move the forks to select neutral. Refit speedometer drive gear parts 11, 12 and 13 (see **FIG 6:6**). Refit the drive pinion 10 to the casing, noting the copper sealing washer. Tighten to 20 lbf ft (2.8 kgf m).

Refit the final drive assembly (see **Section 6:12**). Continue to reassemble in the reverse order of dismantling.

6:11 Servicing the primary drive gear train

Removing:

Refer to **FIG 6:14** and do the following:
1 Remove the clutch release bearing and cover (see **Chapter 5**). Remove the flywheel housing (see **Section 6:5** and **FIG 6:5**).
2 Make up the tool shown in the top view, using mild steel bar 12 inch x 1 inch x $\frac{1}{4}$ inch. The dimensions are as follows:

A	$9\frac{1}{2}$ inch (241 mm)	B	1 inch (25.4 mm)
C	$\frac{1}{4}$ inch (6.35 mm)	D	5 inch (127 mm)
E	1 inch (25.4 mm)	F	$\frac{5}{8}$ inch (15.87 mm)
G	$\frac{3}{8}$ inch (9.52 mm)	H	$3\frac{7}{8}$ inch (98.43 mm)
J	$1\frac{3}{4}$ inch (44.45 mm)	K	$1\frac{11}{16}$ inch (42.86 mm)
L	$3\frac{7}{16}$ inch (87.31 mm)	M	$\frac{1}{2}$ inch (12.7 mm)

This is used to hold the idler gear into the casing, thus locking the gear train while the first motion gear retaining nut is slackened.
3 Withdraw idler gear 9 and insert two $\frac{5}{16}$ inch (8 mm) bolts into the two holes in the gear from the back. Refit the gear. Fit the tool to the gear and the casing (see 6).

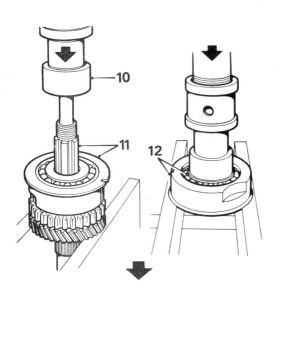

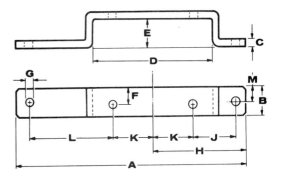

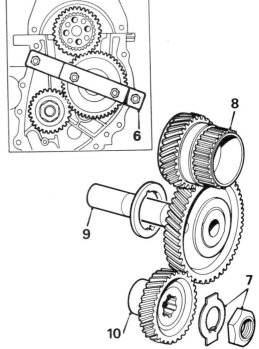

FIG 6:14 Special tool (top). This holds the primary drive idler gear 9 while nut 7 is unscrewed (see central view)

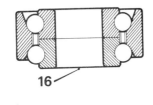

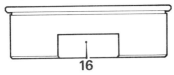

4 Unlock and remove nut and lockwasher 7. Remove primary gear 8 and idler gear 9. Remove first motion shaft gear 10. Idler gear end float should be .003 to .008 inch (.08 to .20 mm).

Refitting:
After checking all parts for wear or damage, reassemble as follows:
1 Reverse the dismantling procedure, lubricating all bearing surfaces and thrust washers with engine oil. Tighten the first motion shaft nut to 120 lbf ft (16.6 kgf m).
2 Refit the flywheel housing, the clutch assembly and the clutch release bearing with cover.

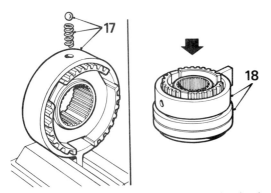

FIG 6:13 Removing third motion shaft bearing (top). Correct reassembly of bearing in housing (centre). Bottom view shows tool 18G.1026 being used to re-assemble the synchronizer balls and springs

6:12 Servicing the final drive gear

Removing:

Refer to **FIG 6:15** and do the following:

1 Remove the power unit (see **Section 1:10** in **Chapter 1**). Remove the end covers (see 2). Note any adjustment shims 18 under the cover on the crownwheel side. On cars with manual gearchange, remove nut 3 which also secures the changespeed housing.

2 Remove housing nuts 4. Lift off bracket 5. Pull off final drive housing (see 6).

3 Lift out the differential assembly (see 6). Clean all joint faces free from old joint washers and check faces for burrs.

Fitting new bearings:

1 Refer to **FIG 6:16**. Mark the crownwheel and differential cage for correct reassembly (see 3). Unlock and remove bolts 4. Lift off crownwheel 5.

2 Pull off bearings 6 with tool 18G.47C with adaptor 18G.47AL (see **FIG 6:19**). Note bearing on crownwheel side is marked 'THRUST' on its outer face.

3 Fit new bearings using tool 18G.134 with adaptor 18G.134P (see **FIG 6:19**). Refit crownwheel in its original position. Fit new lockplates and tighten bolts in diagonal sequence to 55 to 60 lbf ft (7.6 to 8.3 kgf m). Tap up the locking tabs.

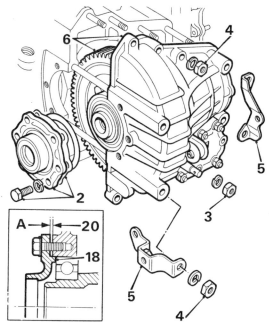

FIG 6:15 Removing the final drive crownwheel and housing 6. Shims for bearing preload are determined by feeler gauge check of gap A (bottom left). The numbers are used in the text

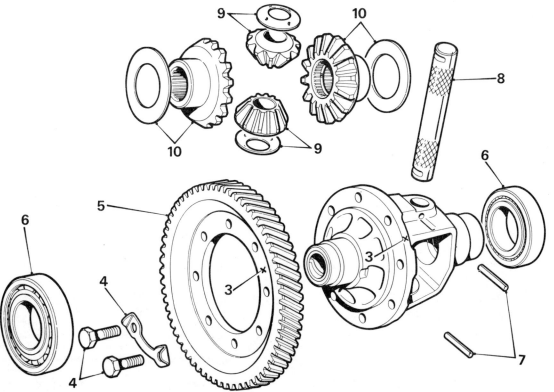

FIG 6:16 The components of the crownwheel and differential assembly. The numbers are used in the text

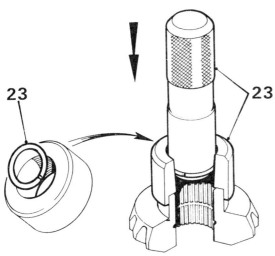

FIG 6:17 Fitting circlips into the differential gears using tool 18G.1217

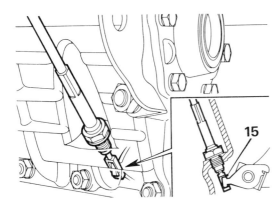

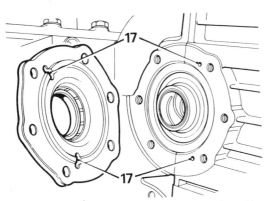

FIG 6:18 Top view shows engagement of parking pawl control cable with lever at 15 (automatic transmission). Oil holes 17 must be aligned when fitting the final drive end covers and joint washers (bottom)

Overhauling the differential assembly:

1 Refer to **FIG 6:16**. Drive out the two roll pins 7. Drive out the pinion pin 8.

2 Lift out the pinions and thrust washers 9 and the differential gears and washers 10.

3 Renew worn gears and pinion pin. Fit new thrust washers. The gears must be renewed as a complete set. If new differential gears are being fitted, drift new circlips into the retaining grooves with tool 18G.1217 (see **FIG 6:17**). Finish assembling in the reverse order of dismantling, lubricating all running parts.

Fitting new crownwheel and pinion:

These **must be renewed as a matched pair.** After the final drive assembly has been removed from the gearbox casing proceed as follows:

1 Note that the following instructions apply exclusively to cars with manual gearchange. Expert attention is needed to remove the final drive pinion on cars with automatic transmission.

2 Remove the front cover, the oil pump, the speedometer drive pinion and gear and the final drive pinion (see **Section 6:6**).

3 Remove the crownwheel as described under 'Fitting new bearings'.

4 Reverse the dismantling procedure when reassembling.

Fitting new oil seals:

Refer to **FIG 6:18**. If the power unit has not been removed it is possible to renew the seals after draining the engine/transmission oil or automatic transmission fluid. Do the following:

1 Remove the road wheel and swivel hub/drive shaft assembly (see **Chapter 7**). Clean the joint edges of the cover to be removed. Remove the bolts and cover. If on the crownwheel side (see **FIG 6:15**), remove the exhaust steady bracket from the final drive housing before removing the end cover. Note any adjustment shims 18 under the cover.

2 Lever out the old seal. Clean up all joint faces and remove burrs.

3 Drive in a new seal with tool 18G.134 and adaptor 18G.134P (see **FIG 6:19**). If adjustment shims were fitted on the crownwheel side, smear them with grease and stick them to the face of the bearing.

4 Fit a new joint washer with the cutouts lined up (see 17). Refit the cover so that the cutouts and the holes are in line. Tighten the bolts to 18 lbf ft (2.5 kgf m). Smear the lip of the seal with grease.

5 Refit the remaining parts and refill the engine/transmission with oil.

Reassembling and adjusting the final drive gear:

If no parts of the differential assembly such as cage, covers, housing or bearings have been renewed, the operation of reassembling can proceed without adjustment. The following instructions assume the need for adjustment because new parts have been fitted:

1 Fit the differential unit to the transmission casing, pressing it towards the flywheel end of the engine. Refit the final drive housing, making sure that the

selectors engage with the fork assemblies in the gearbox. With automatic transmission, engage the parking pawl control cable with its operating lever before pushing the housing home (see 15 in **FIG 6 : 18**).

2 Tighten all nuts just enough to hold the unit firmly in place and yet allow the differential to displace sideways when the flywheel-end cover is fitted.

3 Fit the cover at the flywheel end, lining up the joint washer correctly (see operation 4 under 'Fitting new seals'). Tighten the bolts evenly and note that the differential unit will be displaced away from the flywheel end.

4 Adjust for bearing preload by fitting the opposite cover, without joint washer or shims. Tighten the bolts diagonally and evenly until the cover just nips the bearing outer race. Do not overtighten.

5 Refer to **FIG 6 : 15** and use feeler gauges to measure the gap at A (see inset). Take measurements at several places round the cover flange. If there are variations, adjust the bolt tightness until the same figure is obtained all round. If there is no gap at all, fit some shims of known thickness between the cover and the bearing at 18. This thickness must be included in preload calculations.

6 Any gap must be taken up by a new joint washer with a compressed thickness of .008 inch (.20 mm), plus shims 18 required to give the necessary preload. For example, if the gap is .007 inch (.18 mm) and the joint washer is .008 inch (.20 mm) thick there will be an end float of .001 inch (.025 mm). If this is added to the required preload of .004 inch (.102 mm), the result of .005 inch (.13 mm) is the thickness of shims required. Do not forget to add the thickness of shims already fitted if that was necessary (see end of preceding operation 5).

7 Smear the shims with grease and stick them to the thrust face of the bearing. Fit the new joint washer, followed by the cover and tighten the bolts evenly to 18 lbf ft (2.5 kgf m).

8 Refit the exhaust mounting and tie-rod brackets and tighten $\frac{5}{16}$ inch nuts to 18 lbf ft (2.5 kgf m). Tighten $\frac{3}{8}$ inch nuts to 25 lbf ft (3.4 kgf m) and studs to 6 lbf ft (.8 kgf m).

9 The actual bearing preload required is between .003 and .005 inch (.08 to .13 mm), the figure .004 inch (.102 mm) being taken as the mean.

6 : 13 Fault diagnosis

(a) Jumping out of gear

1 Broken spring behind selector rod ball
2 Worn groove in selector rod
3 Worn synchromesh coupling dogs
4 Worn selector fork
5 Excessive backlash in gearchange mechanism
6 Worn synchromesh sleeve

(b) Noisy transmission

1 Insufficient oil
2 Excessive end float of laygear
3 Incorrect end float of idler and mainshaft gears

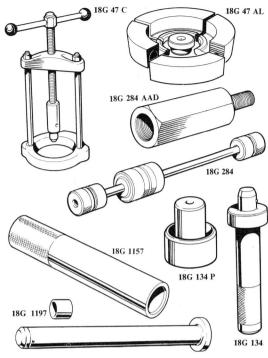

FIG 6 : 19   Some special tools needed when working on the gearbox

Key to Fig 6 : 19   18G.47C, basic tool   18G.47AL, adaptor for differential bearing removal   18G.284, impulse extractor   18G.284AAD, third motion shaft remover   18G.1157, final drive pinion replacer   18G.1197, mainshaft bearing and speedometer gear replacer   18G.134, basic tool for bearing and oil seal replacing   18G.134P, bearing and oil seal adaptor

4 Incorrect preload on differential bearings
5 Worn or damaged bearings
6 Worn bushes on third motion shaft
7 Worn or damaged gear teeth
8 Worn splines on drive shafts and gears

(c) Difficulty in engaging gear

1 Faulty clutch or clutch withdrawal mechanism
2 Worn synchromesh cones
3 Backlash or incorrect adjustment of gearchange mechanism
4 Worn selector forks and couplings

(d) Oil leaks

1 Faulty joint washers or joint faces
2 Worn or damaged oil seals or running surfaces

(e) Steering pulls to one side

1 Check for stiffness of one differential shaft

NOTES

CHAPTER 6a

AUTOMATIC TRANSMISSION

6a:1 Description

This Borg Warner transmission incorporates a fluid torque converter coupled by chain and sprockets to a hydraulically operated gearbox which gives three forward ratios and reverse. The forward ratios are automatically engaged according to accelerator position and the speed of the vehicle.

The layout of the system is shown diagrammatically in **FIG 6a:1**. The hydraulic torque converter is a casing filled with fluid and carrying impeller vanes 5. The casing is bolted to the crankshaft 1. As the casing revolves, fluid is impelled against the vanes of stator 3 and turbine 4. As the stator is virtually stationary at starting, the effect is of torque multiplication. At first this multiplication is about 2 to 1 but as the stator picks up speed this gradually falls to 1 to 1 when it is turning at the same speed as the impeller and turbine. The converter is then turning as a unit and transmitting engine torque to input shaft 8 by way of chain 7.

Front clutch 9 connects the converter to the gears for forward ratios. Rear clutch 11 is for reverse. Bands 12 and 14 are operated by hydraulic pressure and hold elements of the gear set stationary for the ratios required. In '1',

band 14 holds the pinion carrier stationary for first ratio. Band 12 holds reverse sun gear 15 stationary for second ratio.

One-way clutch 13 operates in the first ratio to stop pinion carrier from turning in opposite direction to engine. This allows the gear set to freewheel and ensures smooth changes from first to second and back.

Power flow:

Refer to diagrams in **FIG 6a:2**.

'1' selected (first ratio):

Front clutch applied, converter connected to forward sun gear. Rear band is applied. Pinion carrier gives reaction on drive and overrun to provide engine braking. Reverse sun gear turns in opposite direction. Ratio 2.39 to 1.

'2' or 'D' selected (first ratio):

Front clutch applied. One-way clutch operates to hold carrier stationary. Freewheel on the overrun. Ratio 2.39 to 1.

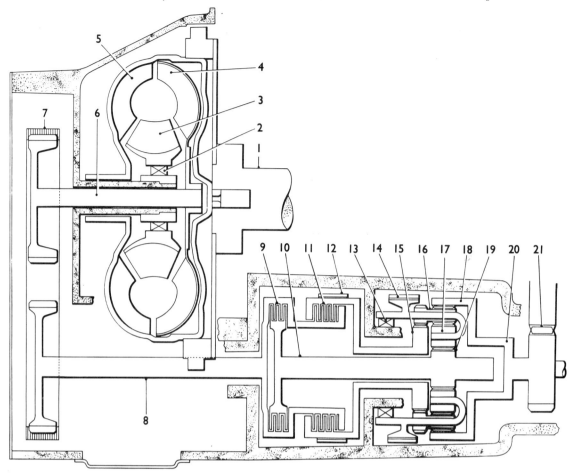

FIG 6a:1 A diagram of the transmission system showing the torque converter (top left) driving the gearbox (bottom right) through chain and sprockets 7

Key to Fig 6a:1 1 Engine crankshaft 2 One-way clutch—stator 3 Stator 4 Turbine 5 Impeller 6 Turbine shaft 7 Primary drive chain 8 Input shaft 9 Front clutch 10 Forward sun gear shaft 11 Rear clutch 12 Front brake band 13 One-way clutch 14 Rear brake band 15 Reverse sun gear 16 Long pinion 17 Short pinion 18 Ring gear 19 Forward sun gear 20 Output shaft 21 Final drive pinion

'2' or 'D' selected (second ratio):

Front clutch and front band applied. Reverse sun gear provides reaction on drive and overrun, giving engine braking. Ratio 1.45 to 1.

'D' selected (third ratio):

Front and rear clutches applied. Both sun gears are locked together, the gear set turning as a unit. This provides drive and engine braking. Ratio 1 to 1.

Reverse:

Rear clutch and rear band applied. Pinion carrier provides reaction on drive and overrun, giving engine braking. Ratio 2.09 to 1.

Hydraulic control:

Automatic control of the gearbox is achieved by using hydraulic fluid pressure directed by valves under the influence of the selector lever, throttle pedal position and a built-in governor that is sensitive to road speed. A pump supplies the hydraulic and lubrication needs of the converter and the transmission.

The clutches and bands shown in **FIGS 6a:1** and **6a:2** are hydraulically operated, the fluid being directed to the required circuit by a valve that is coupled to the selector lever.

A cam inside the gearbox is connected by cable to the carburetter throttle control and operates a valve that controls hydraulic pressure in relation to engine torque and road speed (see **FIG 6a:11**). This affects downshifting, but if the throttle pedal is pressed right down through the 'kickdown' position it will give a down-change at speeds just below the maximum according to governor pressure and an upchange at preset maximum road speeds. The governor regulates hydraulic pressure according to road speed, the pressure deciding the points at which ratio changes will occur.

6a : 2 Routine maintenance

Every 6000 miles (10,000 km or six months) check the fluid level in the automatic transmission. The dipstick is located near the expansion tank and the marks are shown in **FIG 6a : 3**.

Set the car on a level surface, apply the handbrake and move the selector lever to 'P'. Run the engine at normal idling speed for at least two minutes after the engine and transmission have reached normal running temperature. With the engine still idling and 'P' selected, withdraw the dipstick and wipe it on paper or non-fluffy rag.

Reinsert the dipstick and withdraw it again immediately. If necessary, top-up with recommended automatic transmission fluid to the upper mark. It takes 1 pint (1.2 US pints or .6 litre) to span the dipstick marks. **During this operation, observe absolute cleanliness. Do not overfill.**

At the same mileage, check the selector linkage and lubricate any fork connections. Draining and refilling the transmission is covered in **Suction 6a : 8**.

6a : 3 Removing and refitting gearbox :

This Section covers the removal of the gearbox. Due to the complexity of the transmission, further dismantling is not advised, and all rectification of problems is best entrusted to specialists. Those checks and adjustments that are readily made by the normal owner are covered in **Sections 6a : 6** and **6a : 7**. Refer to **FIG 6a : 4**.

Removing :

1 Remove the power unit as instructed in **Chapter 1**. Remove the engine oil filter 2 as instructed in the same chapter. Remove the distributor 3 and the oil pump drive spindle (see **Chapters 1** and **3**).
2 Remove pulley 4 and alternator 5. Remove crossmember 6. Remove rear lefthand engine mounting 7. Remove starter motor 8 to unscrew the four bolts 9 that secure the converter.
3 Remove the bolt between the main casing and the converter housing (see 10). A thin $\frac{9}{16}$ inch AF box spanner or socket will be needed. Remove two bolts 11. Remove ten bolts 12 on the distributor side and eight bolts on the differential side (see inset, top right).
4 Remove two bolts 13. Push converter 14 fully into its housing (see arrow). Take the weight of the engine, clear the converter spigot from the crankshaft bush and lift the engine. Keep it square to clear the drive plate from the converter housing. Remove gasket 16.

Refitting :

1 Fit a new oil pump feed O-ring at 17. Check that the sealing plugs between the front cover and the casing are sound. Fit new ones if necessary. Smear the top face of the casing with Transmission Fluid and fit the gasket.

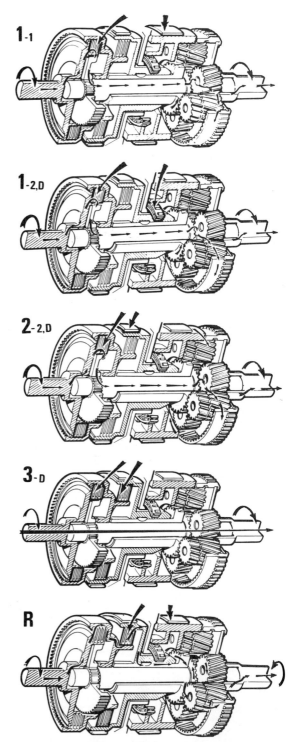

FIG 6a : 2 The power flow through the gearbox in the various ratios. The arrows at the top of each diagram show which clutches and brake bands are applied. The input shaft is on the left

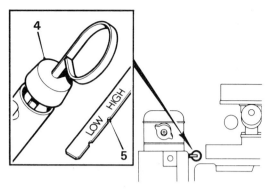

FIG 6a:3 The location of the gearbox dipstick is on the right. The inset shows the dipstick markings

2 Lower the engine until just clear of the casing and engage the converter spigot in the crankshaft. Lower engine fully.

3 Fit bolts and leave them slack. Tighten the converter housing bolts 13 to 8 to 13 lbf ft (1.1 to 1.8 kgf m) and then tighten the casing bolts 10, 11 and 12 to the same torque. Continue reassembling in the reverse order of dismantling.

6a:4 Servicing the primary drive chain

Removing:

Refer to **FIG 6a:5** and do the following:

1 Remove the power unit (see **Chapter 1**). Drain fluid and refit plug 2. Remove cover and gasket 3 (17 bolts).

2 Unlock tab washers 4 then unscrew turbine shaft nut 5. Prevent turning by inserting a wedge between the sprocket and the pump suction boss to be seen behind the chain.

3 Remove input shaft nut 6. Pull sprockets and chain off the shafts (see 7 and 8). The input shaft bearing and spacer should remain in place (lefthand 7).

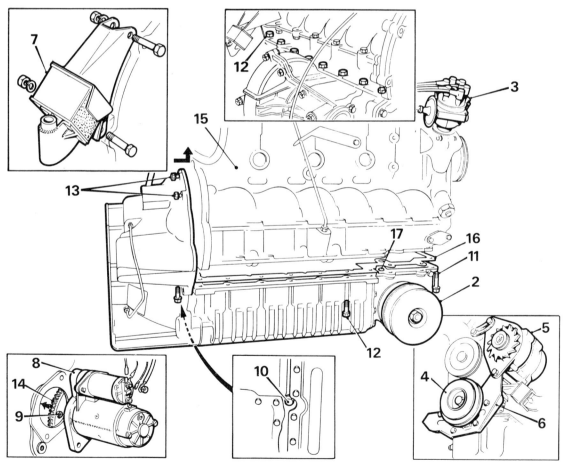

FIG 6a:4 Operations involved when separating the gearbox from the engine. The numbers are used in the text

Refitting:

If chain has been noisy, renew sprockets and chain as required and then reassemble by following the dismantling procedure in reverse. Tighten the turbine shaft nut 5 to 20 to 25 lbf ft (2.8 to 3.8 kgf m) and input shaft nut 6 to 15 to 20 lbf ft (2.1 to 2.8 kgf m). Tighten the cover bolts to 5 to 9 lbf ft (.7 to 1.2 kgf m).

6a:5 Renewing pump oil seal

Removing pump:

The pump can be seen behind the top sprocket in **FIG 6a:5**. Note the inlet pipe leading into the boss. After removing the power unit and the chain drive as described in **Section 6a:4**, remove the six bolts securing the pump flange. Fit an impulse extractor to the splined shaft and use it to withdraw the pump. As it comes away, the inlet pipe must be released from the boss. Note the O-ring on the pipe.

Renewing oil seal:

Refer to **FIG 6a:6** and remove the five bolts 2. Remove locating screw 3. Separate the body from the stator support and turbine shaft assembly and from the pump plate (see 4). Extract the seal 5.

Lubricate a new seal with transmission fluid and press it in until it is flush with the pump face (see 16). The lip faces inwards from the face.

Refitting pump:

Fit new O-rings 6. Reverse the dismantling procedure, tightening the locating screw to 2 to 3 lbf ft (.28 to .42 kgf m) and the pump flange fixings to 17 to 22 lbf ft (2.4 to 3.0 kgf m).

As the pump is introduced into the housing, carefully align the pump driving tangs with the slots in the pump drive gear. Enter the inlet pipe into the pump boss, making sure the O-ring is fitted (see inset, top right in the illustration). The pump unit may need driving home with the impulse tool.

6a:6 Servicing selector lever and switches

Removing:

1 Refer to **FIG 6a:7**. Disconnect battery. Remove clevis pins 2. Remove screws 3 and pull instrument panel out and down. Release speedometer cable 4 if necessary.
2 Unscrew knob 5. Disconnect wires 6. **Ease connectors carefully off the terminals as the switches are fragile.** Alternatively remove the clips, withdraw the pins and extract the switches. The cable colours are WR for white/red, G for green and GN for green/brown.
3 Remove two bolts 7 to release control from panel bracket, noting the spacer for the top bolt. Withdraw the assembly, tilting it rearwards and down.

Overhauling:

1 Refer to **FIG 6a:8** and release the parking control rod 2. Remove clips and extract pins 3. The thin one is nearest the facia. Remove micro-switches 4.

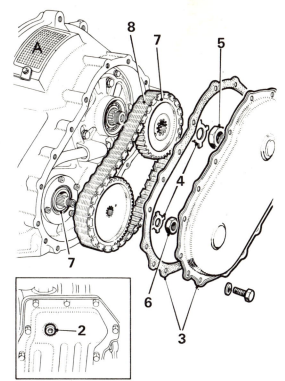

FIG 6a:5 Removing the primary drive chain and sprockets. The numbers are used in the text

2 Remove clips at one end and push out pins 5. Detach the selector rod by removing pin (see 6). Renew worn parts or a broken spring.

The switches are not adjustable. It is a good plan to check the switch circuit and cam operation before removing switches in the event of failure. Note that a high spot on the parking control cam operates the reversing light switch (if fitted) in the 'R' position. High spots on the selector cam operate the starter inhibitor switch in 'P' and 'N' positions.

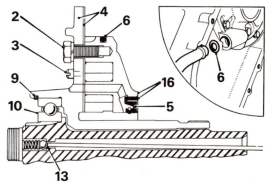

FIG 6a:6 A section of the oil pump showing the location of oil seal 5. Most of the numbers are used in the text

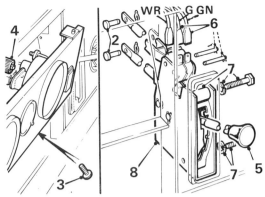

FIG 6a:7 How to remove the selector lever. Note the wiring colours (top right). The numbers are used in the text

Refitting:

1 Refit the levers and rods, taking care that the pivot pin is located by the spring. The spring must press on the lefthand side of the lever (see 7 and 8 in inset, bottom left in **FIG 6a:8**).

2 Continue reassembling in the reverse order of dismantling. Check that the selector lever operates correctly and refit the assembly to the facia. Fit the bottom bolt, then position the spacer and fit the top bolt.

3 Reverse the removal sequence, checking that the bulkhead grommets are correctly fitted. After refitting, check the selector and parking control operations and adjust if necessary (see following Section).

6a:7 Servicing and adjusting cables

Removing and refitting selector cable:

This is the cable indicated at 3 in **FIG 6a:9**. Fitting a new cable entails draining the gearbox, refitting the drain plug and removing the valve bodies cover and gasket shown in the inset to **FIG 6a:5**. A quantity of fluid will be released.

1 Select 'D'. Remove pin 2, release locknut 3 and remove cable.

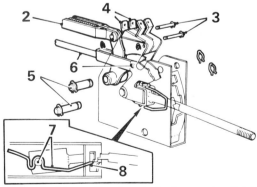

FIG 6a:8 Dismantling the selector lever and switches. The inset shows the correct position for the lever spring. The numbers are used in the text

2 At the gearbox end, release clip 6. Grip the rod to stop it turning and unscrew housing 7. Disengage the rod at 8 and remove cable.

3 Renew O-rings 9 if necessary. Refit the cable assembly and engage it with the manual control valve, which should be in its '2' position (see 8). Reverse the dismantling procedure and check the operation (see later in this Section). Refill the gearbox as detailed in **Section 6a:8**.

Removing and refitting parking brake cable:

Refer to **FIG 6a:10** and do the following:

1 Drain the transmission and refit the drain plug (see **Section 6a:8**). Remove pin 2.

2 Release nut 3 and disengage cable from bracket (see 4). Working under the car, unscrew cable from differential casing at 5. Disengage cable from lever at 6.

3 When refitting, get an assistant to push the inner cable fully down from the top end so that the cable eye may be hooked over the lever.

4 Reverse the dismantling procedure and check the adjustment as described later. Refill with fluid (see **Section 6a:8**).

Removing and refitting downshift cable:

Refer to **FIG 6a:11** and do the following:

1 Remove battery. Withdraw expansion tank and place to one side. Remove dipstick and filler tube.

2 Release the downshift cable from the throttle lever on early models or from the progressive throttle assembly (see 4). Unscrew the cable from the gearbox casing (see 5).

3 Working under the car, drain the gearbox and refit the plug 6. Remove the valve bodies cover and gasket 7 (see inset in **FIG 6a:5**). Turn the downshift cam and release the cable at nipple 8. Remove cable 9.

4 Refit in the reverse order, checking the adjustment as described later and refilling the gearbox (see **Section 6a:8**).

Adjusting selector cable:

Refer to **FIG 6a:9**. Move selector lever to position 'N'. Hold it away from the quadrant and allow it to take up a natural position as dictated by the detent on the manual control valve in the gearbox (see 8). The lever should then enter the quadrant location without strain.

If it does not, slacken and turn nuts at 3 to get the desired result. Tighten the nuts. Select 'N' and check the positioning again. Also check detent and quadrant engagement in 'P', 'R', 'N', 'D', '2' and '1'.

Adjusting parking brake cable:

Refer to **FIG 6a:10**. With car on a level surface, select 'P' and release handbrake. Check that parking pawl engages, by rocking car backwards and forwards. **The pawl must hold.** If it ratchets, adjust by selecting 'N' and slackening cable nut 3. Turn the opposing nut back to decrease the effective length of the outer cable. Tighten the nuts, select 'R' and roll the car forward to check that the pawl is clear.

Select 'P' and check as outlined at the beginning. If there is faulty engagement after adjustment, the mechanism in the gearbox will need expert attention.

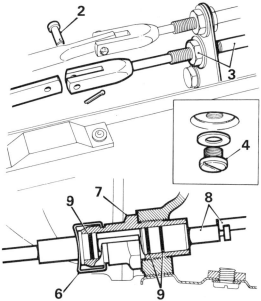

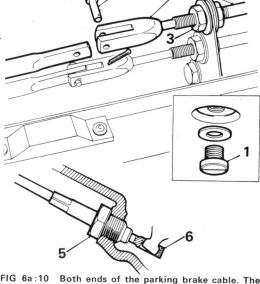

FIG 6a:9 Operations for removing and refitting the selector lever cable. The lowest view is a section at the gearbox casing end. The numbers are used in the text

FIG 6a:10 Both ends of the parking brake cable. The lowest view shows how the cable is hooked onto a lever inside the gearbox

Adjusting downshift cable:

Chock the wheels and apply the handbrake. Refer to **FIG 6a:11** and check that inner cable 4 is not disconnected inside the gearbox. When pulled, it should return under the influence of the cam spring. If faulty, check at the gearbox end.

Connect a tachometer (revolution indicator) and let the engine idle at 600 to 700 rev/min in 'P'. Check that the crimped stop on the inner cable is $\frac{1}{16}$ inch (1.5 mm) from the outer cable collar at the point indicated by the lefthand arrow. The cable trunnion must be free to swivel.

To arrive at the correct cable setting adjust the cable stop below the trunnion. **After adjustment it will be necessary for the gearbox to be pressure tested by automatic transmission specialists.**

6a:8 Draining and refilling gearbox

Select 'P' and apply the handbrake. Remove the drain plug (see 2 in **FIG 6a:5**). **Beware of scalding if the transmission has just been used, as the fluid becomes extremely hot.** Apply 'Loctite' to the plug and tighten securely.

Wipe around the dipstick handle and filler tube and remove the dipstick (see **FIG 6a:3**). Refill with genuine Automatic Transmission Fluid. As the converter remains full, the quantity required will be 8 pints (9.6 US pints or 4.5 litres).

Run the engine up to normal temperature. Stand car on a level surface, select 'P' and apply the handbrake. With engine idling, withdraw dipstick and wipe clean on paper or non-fluffy rag. Reinsert and withdraw it again immediately to check fluid level. Top-up to the upper mark. **Do not overfill. At all times observe scrupulous cleanliness.**

6a:9 Servicing speedometer drive

Refer to **FIG 6a:12** and do the following:
1 Drain fluid and refit plug 1. Release cable at 2. Remove bolts 3 and pull off housing 4, releasing the tube from its seal (see 7).
2 The speedometer drive gear 5 must be removed with a nut-splitter. It is important to place no side load on the shaft or damage the spigot.
3 Fit a new gear with its shoulder to the shaft and tap gently into place with a soft-faced hammer. Refit the housing on a sound gasket, taking care to register the tube in its seal. Continue reassembling, tightening the bolts to 8 to 18 lbf ft (1.1 to 2.5 kgf m). Refill the transmission (see **Section 6a:8**).

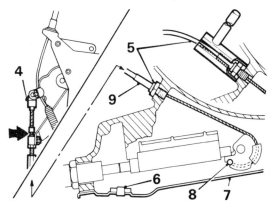

FIG 6a:11 How to remove and refit the downshift cable. The arrow on the left shows the point where correct adjustment is checked. The numbers are used in the text

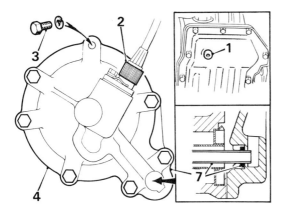

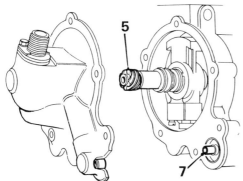

FIG 6a:12 Removing the housing to service the speedometer drive gear. The numbers are used in the text

4 If the cable seal or drive gear need attention, remove the screw to the side of knurled nut 2 and pull out the parts. When refitting them, make sure that the slots at the top of the pinion shaft bush engage with the lugs on the underside of the screwed bush.

6a:10 Tests for faulty operation

The following are carried out on the road. **The speeds are true and may not be those recorded by the speedometer.**

Do not select '1' from 'D' at speeds above 55 mile/hr (88 km/hr) or the engine may be over-revved.

'Kick-down' is obtained by depressing accelerator pedal fully until it touches the carpet. A slight resistance will be felt as the pedal passes through the point of normal full travel.

1 Select 'D', use 'kick-down' acceleration and check that 1 to 2 shift occurs between 37 and 43 mile/hr (60 to 70 km/hr). 2 to 3 shift should occur between 62 and 68 mile/hr (100 to 110 km/hr). If no drive in 'D' (1st ratio not operating), select '1', accelerate to 20 mile/hr (30 km/hr) and select 'D' to verify drive in 2nd and 3rd ratios.

2 Between 53 and 56 mile/hr (85 to 90 km/hr) in 3rd ratio (D3), 'kick-down' and check downshift to 2nd ratio (D2).

3 Between 30 and 35 mile/hr (48 to 56 km/hr) in 3rd ratio (D3), 'kick-down' and check downshift to 1st ratio (D1).

Stall tests:

Although these tests are not completed without hydraulic pressure testing by automatic transmission specialists, it is possible to get some idea of possible faults by the use of a revolution indicator (tachometer) alone.

It is essential that a stall test should not exceed ten seconds in duration. Stall speed is the maximum attainable in 'kick-down' while the converter turbine is held stationary, giving rise to a great deal of heat. The condition of the engine must be taken into account when interpreting a low stall speed. Proceed as follows:

1 Engine and gearbox must be at normal operating temperature. Check fluid level (see **Section 6a:2**).

2 Connect a revolution indicator (tachometer) so that it can be seen from the driving seat. Chock wheels and apply handbrake.

3 Apply footbrake, select '1' or 'R' and press accelerator pedal through the 'kickdown' position for not more than 10 seconds.

4 If the rev/min are below 1300 the indication is of stator slip in the converter. Engine power is down if the reading is 1800 to 1900 rev/min. 2000 to 2300 rev/min indicates normal performance, but over 2300 rev/min indicates gearbox slip.

5 Other indications of converter trouble are as follows:

Slipping stator (freewheel slipping):

Inability to pull away on steep hills, poor acceleration from rest and a low stall test reading.

Seized stator (unusual fault):

Reduced maximum speed in all gears, but pronounced in top ratio. Severe overheating of transmission. Stall test reading normal.

6 If transmission slip is apparent in both '1' and 'R' it is usually due to low hydraulic pressure. If fault in one position only, a faulty transmission component is most likely. These faults will give a high stall test reading.

6a:11 Fault diagnosis

It is impossible to give a detailed fault analysis because most of the innumerable tests for faults and their cure are matters for a service station. Those that are given may be rectified with the help of instructions in this chapter.

(a) Starter will not operate in 'P' or 'N' or operates in all positions

1 Test inhibitor switch(es), circuit(s) and check cam action

(b) Faulty operation of reversing light (when fitted)

1 See 1 in (a)

(c) Excessive bump on engagement of 'D', '1', '2' or 'R'

1 Reduce idling speed of engine (see **Chapter 2**)
2 If no cure, consult experts

(d) Stall test speed less than 1300 rev/min (slipping stator)

1 Renew torque converter (see experts)

(e) Parking pawl does not hold vehicle

1 Adjust/examine parking cable
2 If no cure, consult experts

(f) 'P' operates, but no drive in 'D', '1', '2' or 'R'

1 Check fluid level
2 Check manual cable selector cable/adjustment
3 If no cure, consult experts

(g) Reduced maximum speed in all ratios, converter overheats

1 Fit new torque converter (see experts)

NOTES

CHAPTER 7

DRIVE SHAFTS AND SUSPENSION

7:1 Description of drive shafts

The output gears of the transmission are connected to the front wheels by Hardy Spicer drive shafts fitted with constant velocity universal joints at the outer ends and plunge joints at the inner end (see **FIGS 7:3** and **7:4**). The outer member of each plunge joint carries a splined shaft that engages with the final drive gears in the transmission. The splined shaft of each constant velocity joint runs in bearings in the front hub and swivel axle assembly and carries the brake disc and front wheel (see **FIG 7:1**). The sliding action of the plunge joints accommodates changes in the distance between the transmission and the front hubs due to suspension movements.

7:2 Routine maintenance

The rubber boots enclosing the joints are packed with grease and no routine maintenance is necessary. It is, however, advisable to make an occasional visual check of the condition of the boots. Cracking through damage or deterioration may allow dirt to enter the joint, leading to rapid wear.

7:3 Removing and refitting drive shafts

Removing:

Refer to **FIG 7:1** and do the following:

1 Fit a packing piece $\frac{5}{8}$ inch (16 mm) thick and $1\frac{1}{2}$ inch (39 mm) wide between upper arm and rebound rubber (see 1). Remove brake disc dust shield (see **Chapter 9**).

2 Disconnect steering tie-rod ball joint 3. Do not hammer on the pin but use a proper extractor (see 18G.1063 in **FIG 7:12**). Tool 4 is used to lever out the plunge joint shaft by hammering at the point indicated by the arrow. The tool is shown in **FIG 7:12**. **Do not pull on the drive shaft or the plunge joint will separate.**

3 Using tool 18G.1063, extract the ball pins from the suspension arm and swivel axle (see 5). Withdraw the swivel axle and hub assembly complete with drive shaft.

4 Press the shaft out of the hub and if necessary withdraw the hub inner bearing race from the drive shaft.

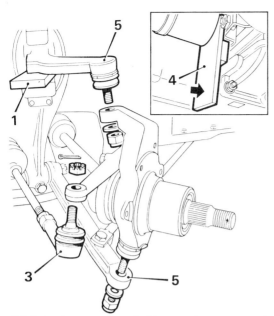

FIG 7:1 Operations entailed in removing a drive shaft

Key to Fig 7:1   1 Packing piece   3 Steering ball joint
4 Special tool 18G.1146   5 Upper and lower suspension
arms

Refitting:

1 Fit the bearings and spacer into the hub (see **Section 7:8**). Use tool 18G.1104 to pull the shaft into the hub (see **FIG 7:12**).

2 Fully compress the plunge or inner joint and offer up the assembly to the transmission. Push the shaft smartly home to lock it into the final drive differential gear.

3 Pull on the **outer member** of the plunge joint to check that it is correctly locked in the final drive. Reverse the rest of the dismantling procedure, tightening the swivel axle ball pin nuts to 45 lbf ft (6.22 kgf m) and the tie-rod ballpin nuts to 35 lbf ft (4.84 kgf m).

4 On automatic transmission models top up the transmission fluid level. On manual gearbox models top up the engine and transmission oil.

FIG 7:2 Fitting clip to rubber boot for constant velocity joint. Pulling tight (left), folding down front tabs (centre) and securing end of clip (right)

The drive shafts differ in length as follows:
Manual gearbox righthand 31 inch (78.8 cm), lefthand 30 inch (76.2 cm). Automatic transmission righthand 30 inch (76.2 cm), lefthand 31 inch (78.8 cm). To check the lengths drive the plunge (inner) joint into the fully-compressed position.

7:4 Overhauling the constant velocity joint
Removing:

With drive shaft removed, take off and discard the clip securing the boot (see **FIG 7:2**). Holding shaft as in **FIG 7:3**, use a soft-faced hammer to strike the edge of the joint 4 at the point indicated by the arrow in the top view.

Overhauling:

Withdraw the rubber boot. Tilt ball cage and prise out balls (see 6). Turn inner member and ball cage into line with axis of joint. Turn cage until the two large windows coincide with two of the lands in the outer ring of the joint (see 7). Withdraw assembly 8.

Line up inner member with axis of ball cage (see 9 in **FIG 7:4**). Two lands of the inner member must coincide with the two large windows in the ball cage. Withdraw inner member (see 10). Clean all parts and examine for damage and wear. Check rubber boots for splits and deterioration.

Reassembling:

Refer to top view in **FIG 7:4** and all views in **FIG 7:3**. Fit the inner member and ball cage into the outer member of the joint with the chamfered bore side of the cage at the blind end of the outer member and the lugs on the inner member at the open end (see central view in **FIG 7:3**).

Refit the balls and pack the joint and rubber boot with 75 cu cms of Duckhams Bentone Grease Q5795.

Fit the drive shaft to the joint by compressing the spring ring and driving home with a soft-faced hammer. Fit the boot and a new clip. The fold in the clip must face direction of rotation (see righthand view in **FIG 7:2**). Pull free end of clip tight (see left). Close front tabs over free end (centre). Fold end back over front tabs and secure with rear tabs (right).

7:5 Overhauling the plunge joint

With drive shaft removed, withdraw the rubber boot. Remove and discard ring 11 (see **FIG 7:4**). Withdraw drive shaft. Remove spring ring and withdraw ball cage assembly (see 12). Prise out balls 13 and turn inner member until its lands coincide with grooves inside ball cage and withdraw it (see 14). Clean the parts and examine for damage or wear. Check boot for splits or deterioration.

Reassemble by fitting the inner member and ball cage assembly to the shaft with the long tapered end of the cage facing towards the constant velocity (outer) joint of the shaft (see 12). Pack boot and joint with 150 cu cms of Duckhams Bentone Grease Q5795. Continue in the reverse order of dismantling, fitting a new ring to the lip of the outer member. Fit a new clip to the boot as described in the preceding Section.

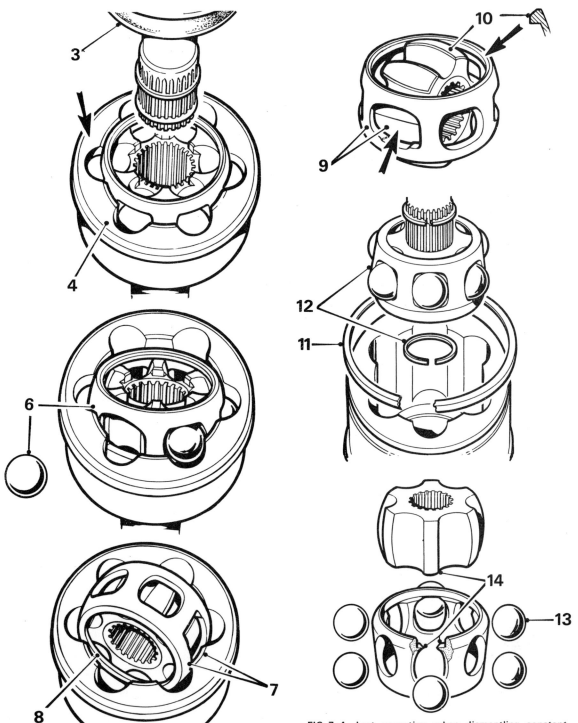

FIG 7:3 Sequence of operations for dismantling a constant velocity joint. The last operation is in FIG 7:4 (top). The numbers are used in the text

FIG 7:4 Last operation when dismantling constant velocity joint (top). Lower views show plunge joint being dismantled. Refer to the text for numbered sequence

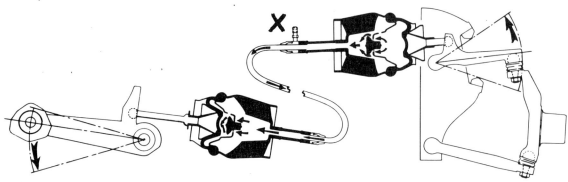

FIG 7:5 How fluid is transferred from front suspension unit (right) to rear unit (left) when Hydrolastic system operates. Upward deflection at front causes downward reaction at rear and vice-versa. Never interfere with valve marked 'X'

7:6 Description of suspension

The Hydrolastic system has front and rear displacer units connected on the same side by a pipe (see **FIG 7:5**). The units incorporate a rubber spring and a diaphragm. Upward movement of the front suspension forces fluid along the pipe and into the rear unit, forcing it downwards, thus raising the rear of the car and keeping the body on an even keel. The same process is reversed when the rear wheels are deflected upwards.

The components of front and rear systems are shown in **FIGS 7:6** and **7:7**. Note the valve marked 'X' in **FIG 7:5**. **As the fluid system is pressurized through these valves it is vital not to interfere with them.** Any work on pressurizing or de-pressurizing must be carried out by agents with the correct equipment. Because many operations on the suspension system call for de-pressurizing we propose to deal only with those that do not need it.

7:7 Servicing front pivot bearings and ball joints

Lower arm pivot bearing:

Flexible bush 23 may need renewal (see **FIG 7:6** and 9 in **FIG 7:8**). Proceed as follows:

1 Hold upper arm 19 in its laden position by inserting a block of wood .75 x 1.5 inch (19 x 40 mm) between the arm and its rebound rubber.
2 Jack up and support the car and remove the road wheel. Disconnect lower ball pin 40 from the arm using tool 18G.1063. Do not hammer on the pin. Remove bolt 4 in **FIG 7:8**.
3 Remove nut 5 (splitpin). Drive the arm free of the pivot pin, using a copper hammer adjacent to the pivot. Ease the pin back, remove nut and washer 8 and extract arm. Remove pin and extract bush (or bushes) with stud or bolt with long thread as shown at 9. The spacer on the right should be 1.3 inch (33 mm) long with a bore of 1.5 inch (38 mm), and washer on left .87 inch (22 mm) in diameter.
4 Fit a new one-piece rubber and metal bush 10, drawing it in as shown at 11. The spacer on the left should be .31 inch (8 mm) long with a bore of 1.37 inch (35 mm). First smear the outside of the bush with geniune rubber grease. **Do not use ordinary grease.** Press bush in from rear until its flange contacts the bracket.
5 Fit plain washer and nut to pivot pin, and holding the lower arm in its normal unladen position, tighten the nut and fit a new splitpin. Now check clearance between arm and bracket at 'A' (see inset). It should be .14 ± .01 inch (3.56 ± .25 mm). If necessary, adjust by altering the location of the bearings.
6 Reverse the rest of the dismantling procedure, tightening the tie-rod bolt to 40 to 50 lbf ft (5.5 to 6.9 kgf m), the swivel axle joint nut to 45 lbf ft (6.2 kgf m) and the wheel nuts to 60 lbf ft (8.3 kgf m).

Upper arm bushes:

As the sleeve is swaged over at each end it is advisable to have the bushes renewed at a service station. The arm is part 19 and the bushes part 46 in **FIG 7:6**.

Upper ball joint:

This is assembly 38 to 44 on the right in **FIG 7:6**. Remove and refit as follows:

1 Repeat preceding operations 1 and 2 but this time remove the top ball pin and do not remove the tie-rod bolt. Knock back tab of lockwasher 39. Remove dust cover 42 and unscrew the ball pin housing.
2 Clean all parts and examine for wear. Renew as necessary. Make sure that the boot is sound or dirt may enter the joint.
3 Press ball pin into socket and locate in housing. Screw housing into arm until the ball pin has no end play but can still be moved in all directions. Measure the gap between the housing flange and the upper arm with feelers. Remove housing and lubricate ball pin and socket liberally with Dextagrease Super GP Lubricant.
4 Fit a new tab washer and shims. From the measured gap subtract .036 inch (.91 mm) for the tab washer and .009 to .013 inch (.23 to .33 mm) for preloading the bearing. Select shims from thicknesses of .002, .003, .005, .01 and .03 inch (.05, .08, .13, .25 and .76 mm).

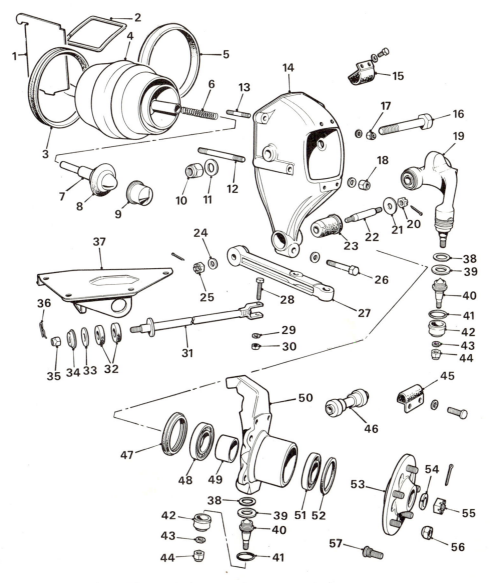

FIG 7:6 Components of front suspension system

Key to Fig 7:6   1 Dividing strip—hose   2 Protection strip—hose   3 Sealing ring   4 Hydrolastic spring unit   5 Anti-rattle sleeve   6 Spring   7 Strut   8 Dust cover   9 Knuckle joint   10 Locknut   11 Plain washer   12 Stud—top   13 Stud—centre   14 Mounting bracket   15 Bump rubber   16 Bolt—upper arm   17 Locknut   18 Locknut   19 Upper support arm   20 Locknut   21 Plain washer   22 Pivot pin—lower arm   23 Pivot bearing—flexible   24 Plain washer—special   25 Locknut   26 Bolt   27 Lower support arm   28 Bolt   29 Spring washer   30 Nut   31 Tie-rod   32 Rubbers   33 Cup washer   34 Plain washer—special   35 Locknut   36 Spring clip   37 Tie-rod mounting and gasket plate   38 Shim(s)   39 Lock washer   40 Ball pin   41 Spring ring   42 Dust cover   43 Plain washer   44 Locknut   45 Rebound rubber   46 Flexible bearing—upper arm   47 Oil seal—inner   48 Bearing—inner   49 Bearing distance tube   50 Swivel hub   51 Bearing—outer   52 Oil seal—outer   53 Drive flange   54 Cone—outer   55 Hub nut   56 Wheel nut   57 Wheel stud

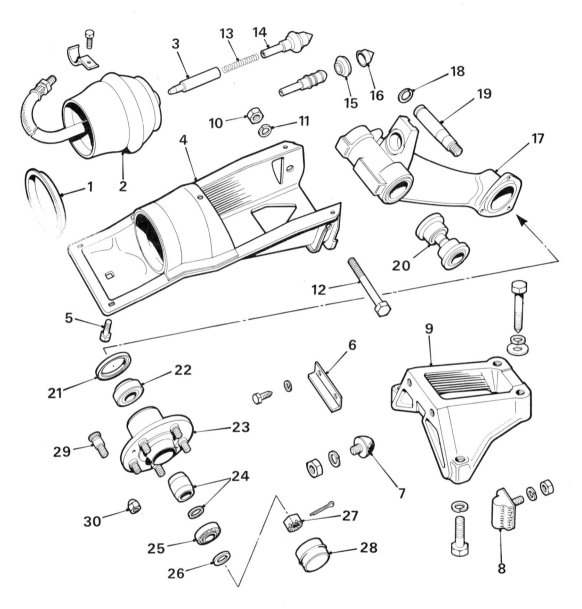

FIG 7:7   Components of rear suspension

Key to Fig 7:7   1 Locating ring   2 Hydrolastic spring unit   3 Pushrod   4 Suspension mounting member   5 Bolt
6 Stiffener channel   7 Bump rubber   8 Rebound rubber   9 Mounting bracket   10 Nut   11 Spring washer   12 Bolt
13 Spring   14 Knuckle joint   15 Dust cover   16 Ball socket   17 Radius arm   18 Circlip   19 Stub shaft   20 Bearing
assembly   21 Oil seal   22 Wheel bearing—inner   23 Rear hub   24 Distance piece and shim   25 Wheel bearing—outer
26 Special plain washer   27 Nut   28 Grease retaining cup   29 Wheel stud   30 Wheel nut

5 Fit housing with shims and washer and tighten to 70 ±5 lbf ft (9.6 ±.06 kgf m). Turn up one locking tab over the end of the arm nearest the brake disc and two over the housing. Fill space between ball and housing with the same grease and fit dust cover.

6 Reverse rest of dismantling procedure, tightening the ball pin nut to 45 lbf ft (6.2 kgf m) and wheel nuts to 60 lbf ft (8.3 kgf m).

Lower ball assembly:

This is assembly 38 to 44, bottom centre in **FIG 7:6**. Remove and refit as follows:

1 Remove the front hub assembly (see **Section 7:8**). Remove the brake disc dust shield. Knock back the tab washer 39, unscrew the ball pin housing and remove the pin assembly.

2 Carry out operations 2 to 5 for the upper ball joint. When refitting the dust shield, tighten the bolt to 20 lbf ft (2.8 kgf m). Refit the front hub (see **Section 7:8**).

7:8 Servicing the front hubs

Removing:

1 Repeat operation 1 in **Section 7:7**. Slacken hub nut and wheel nuts before jacking up and supporting car. Remove road wheel. Disconnect brake hose from bracket (see 4 in **FIG 7:9**).

2 Remove brake caliper 5. Disconnect tie-rod ball joint 6, using tool 18G.1063 (see **FIG 7:12**). Remove hub nut 7, tap the end of the hub with a mallet and extract the outer cone. Pull off disc and flange 9 with a suitable tool or use tool 18G.304 with adaptor bolts 18G.304A. The bolts screw on the wheel studs (see 8).

3 Remove dust shield (one bolt). Remove nuts 11 and break the ball pin tapers free with tool 18G.1063 (see **FIG 7:12**). Drift the inner joint of the drive shaft out of the transmission as described in **Section 7:3**, using tool 18G.1146. Withdraw hub and shaft assembly. **Do not pull on the drive shaft to do this or the plunge or inner joint will be separated.** Press the shaft out of the hub.

Renewing hub bearings and oil seals:

Refer to **FIG 7:10** and remove oil seals 2 and 3. These will be damaged during removal and must be renewed. Use a soft metal drift in the grooves behind them to drive out cones 4. Press the bearings from the shaft.

Clean the parts and check the unlubricated bearings for roughness. Remove all burrs from hub bore and shoulders and assemble parts in perfectly clean state.

Press bearing cones hard against hub shoulders with tool 18G.134CB (see **FIG 7:12**). Drive bearing 9 onto shaft. Pack bearings with recommended lubricant and smear the spacer. Soak inner seal 3 in oil for one hour and dip outer seal 2 in oil. Press in outer seal until flush, using tool 18G.134BN (see **FIG 7:12**). Fit inner seal using tool 18G.134CR.

Pack space between bearings and oil seals with grease. Do not pack grease in space in hub between the bearings.

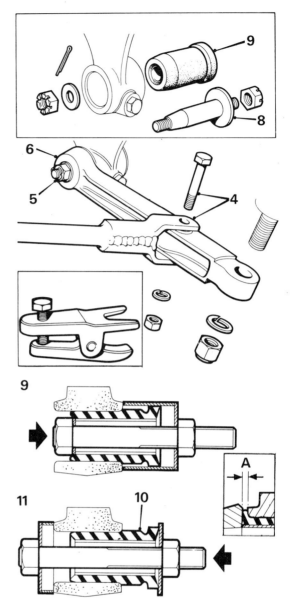

FIG 7:8 How to renew the pivot bearing 9 for the front suspension lower arm. Central inset shows tool 18G.1063 for releasing lower ball pin. The numbers are used in the text

Renewing outer oil seal only:

This can be done by removing the brake disc and flange. Refer to **FIG 7:6** and remove nut 55 and split cone 54. Remove the brake caliper and then withdraw the hub with a suitable puller (see operation 2 under 'Removing').

Prise out the old seal and clean out old grease in front of the bearing. Dip new seal in oil and drive in flush. Pack space between seal and bearing with grease and refit the hub.

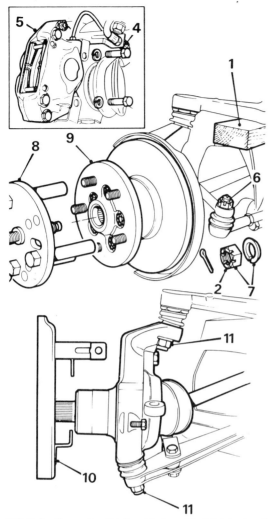

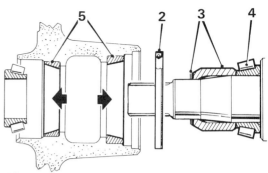

FIG 7:11 Renewing rear hub bearings and oil seal. 2 is the seal, 3 the spacer and shims (if fitted), 4 the inner bearing and 5 the bearing races. Drive out races in direction of arrows

Refitting:

Make sure space between bearings is not packed with grease. Fit shaft and bearings in hub and draw shaft into place with tool 18G.1104 (see **FIG 7:12**). Fit shaft as described in **Section 7:3**. Reverse the rest of the dismantling procedure, tightening swivel axle ball joint nuts to 45 lbf ft (6.2 kgf m), steering ball joint nut to 35 lbf ft (4.8 kgf m), dust shield bolt to 20 lbf ft (2.8 kgf m), caliper bolts to 45 to 50 lbf ft (6.2 to 6.9 kgf m), hub nut (tightening further to next hole) 150 lbf ft (20.7 kgf m) and road wheel nuts to 60 lbf ft (8.3 kgf m). Bleed the brakes as described in **Chapter 9**.

7:9 Servicing the rear hubs

Removing:

Take the weight of the car on a jack. Slacken wheel nuts, remove cup 28 and slacken nut 27 (see **FIG 7:7**). **The lefthand hub has a lefthand thread and the righthand hub a righthand thread.** Jack up car and support on a stand. Remove the wheel.

Slacken off brake adjustment (see **Chapter 9**). Remove drum (two screws). Remove nut 27 and special washer 26. Withdraw hub using a puller or tools 18G.304Z and adaptor bolts 18G.304A.

FIG 7:9 Removing the front hub and ball joints. Inset at top shows removal of brake caliper 5. The numbers are used in the text

Renewing bearings and oil seal:

Refer to **FIG 7:11** and prise out seal 2. It will be damaged so make sure that a new seal is available. Remove distance piece and shims 3 (if fitted). Pull off inner bearing 4. Use a soft metal drift to drive out the cones 5, placing drift in grooves provided.

Clean the parts and check the unlubricated bearings for roughness. Remove burrs or high spots from bores and shoulders. Check bearing lands on axle stub.

Press in new bearing cones hard up to shoulders, using tool 18G.134CC (see **FIG 7:12**). Drift inner bearing onto shaft. Fit standard spacer and enough shims to produce excessive end float. Fit hub with chamfer on washer 26 to bearing. Tighten nut to 40 lbf ft (5.5 kgf m). **Note that original bearing assemblies are made**

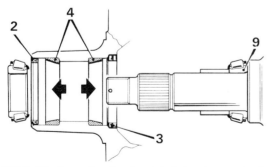

FIG 7:10 Renewing the front hub bearings and oil seals. 2 is the outer seal, 3 the inner seal, 4 the bearing outer races and 9 the inner race and roller assembly. Arrows indicate directions for removal

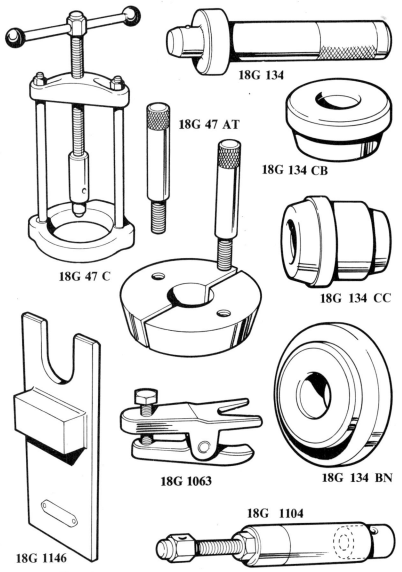

FIG 7:12   Special tools for working on the suspension system

Key to Fig 7:12   18G.47C—Basic press for bearing removal   18G.47AT—Adaptor for drive shaft and bearing removal
18G.134—Basic tool for fitting bearings and oil seals   18G.134CB—Adaptor for fitting front hub bearing   18G.134CC—
Adaptor for fitting suspension arm bearings   18G.134BN—Adaptor for fitting oil seals to hubs   18G.1063—Tool for breaking
out ball joint pins   18G.1104—Tool for fitting front hub assembly   18G.1146—Tool for removing drive shaft assembly

using a specially selected spacer. When renewing
the bearings, use a standard spacer and select the
necessary shims.

Use a dial gauge to check the hub end float by pushing
the hub in and out. Remove the hub and calculate the
shims required to give an end float of zero to .002 inch
(.05 mm). Shims have thicknesses of .003 inch (.08
mm), .005 inch (.13 mm) and .01 inch (.25 mm).

Dip a new seal in oil and fit it, using tool 18G.134BN
(see **FIG 7:12**). Pack bearings with grease and also
recess between inner bearing and seal. Smear spacer with

grease. **Do not pack grease into the hub space
between the bearings and do not put grease in cup
28.**

Fit spacer and correct shims, fit hub and put chamfer
of washer against the bearing. Tighten nut to 40 lbf ft
(5.5 kgf m), tightening still more when aligning splitpin
hole. Fit new pin. Fit drum and wheel, tightening nuts to
60 lbf ft (8.3 kgf m). Adjust brake (see **Chapter 9**).

When fitting a new seal only, clean out old grease
from recess, dip seal in oil and refit as just described and
pack recess between seal and bearing with grease.

Radius arm bearing (part 20 in FIG 7:7):

The bushes are renewable but swaging makes the operation difficult (see 'Upper arm bush' in **Section 7:7**).

Refitting hub:

All the operations needed to refit the hub are covered in the Section devoted to renewing the bearings and oil seal.

7:10 Servicing tie-rods, wheel studs and bump rubbers

Tie-rods:

When removing the tie-rods, support the car and take the weight off the suspension. **Do not let the suspension take the weight of the car while a rod is detached.** Renew perished rubbers and check rod for straightness. Tighten Nyloc nut at bracket end to 27 to 33 lbf ft (3.7 to 4.6 kgf m) and bolt at fork end to 40 to 50 lbf ft (5.5 to 6.9 kgf m).

Wheel studs:

The front drive flange studs are renewable. **If one has failed, always renew all five studs.** To remove the flange, slacken hub nut and wheel nuts, jack up and support car and remove wheel. Remove hub nut and coned washer (see 55 and 54 in **FIG 7:6**). Use a puller to withdraw the flange 53 or use tool 18G.304 and adaptor bolts 18G.304A. Press the studs out.

Check that countersinks are free from burrs. Press in new studs hard up to the heads. Mating faces of flange and disc must be clean. Refit flange and tighten bolts to 40 to 54 lbf ft (5.5 to 6.2 kgf m). Fit coned washer and hub nut, fit wheel, lower car and tighten wheel nuts to 60 lbf ft (8.3 kgf m). Tighten hub nut to 150 lbf ft (20.7 kgf m). If necessary, tighten still more to align split-pin holes. Fit new pin.

Bump rubbers:

Front rubbers are parts 15 and 45 in **FIG 7:6**. When fitting new rubbers, tighten the bolts to 5 lbf ft (.7 kgf m).

Rear bump rubber is part 7 in **FIG 7:7**. After removing the wheel and lifting out the rear seat, remove nut and washer from rear of seat pan. Extract the rubber from inside the suspension mounting member.

Rear rebound rubbers are part 8 in **FIG 7:7**. As it is necessary to depressurize the Hydrolastic system, renewal of these rubbers is a job for a properly-equipped service station.

7:11 Suspension geometry and trim height

With the exception of front wheel alignment (toe-in), the various angles of the suspension system are not adjustable. If the car is damaged or the suspension badly worn, the effect on steering and general handling may be serious. The only cure is a thorough check of the angles and alignment and replacement of defective parts.

Dimensions and angles are given in **Technical Data**. The method of checking and adjusting wheel alignment is given in **Chapter 8**.

Trim height:

Although errors in trim must be rectified by a garage equipped to modify pressure in the Hydrolastic system, the actual checking is a simple job.

Car must be filled with oil, fuel and water, with all wheels standing on a level surface. With tyres at correct pressure, roll car to and fro and bounce the suspension. Measure from the centre of each front wheel cap to the body arch immediately above. The correct figure should be $14\frac{7}{8} \pm \frac{1}{4}$ inch (378 $\pm$ 6 mm).

Damaged suspension:

If fluid in the system is lost through accidental damage, it is permissible to drive the car on metalled roads at speeds not exceeding 30 mile/hr (50 km/hr). The suspension on the damaged side will contact the bump rubbers.

7:12 Fault diagnosis

(a) Wheel wobble

1 Incorrect tracking
2 Worn hub bearings
3 Defective suspension units
4 Worn swivel hub joints
5 Loose wheel fixings

(b) 'Bottoming' of suspension

1 Check 3 in (a)
2 Incorrect pressurizing
3 Bump rubbers worn or missing

(c) Heavy steering

1 Defective swivel hub joints
2 Wrong suspension geometry
3 Tight differential assembly on one side

(d) Excessive tyre wear

1 Check 1 in (a) and 2 in (c)

(e) Rattles

1 Check 1 in (c)
2 Suspension mountings defective
3 Tie-rod mountings loose

(f) Excessive rolling

1 Check 3 in (a) and 2 in (b)

CHAPTER 8

THE STEERING

8:1 Description of manual system

The component parts are shown in **FIG 8:1**. The steering wheel 3 is connected to pinion 36 by column 5 and flexible coupling 6, 7 and 8. The pinion meshes with rack 31 which slides in housing 30, the housing being secured to the underside of the body. The ends of the rack are connected by jointed tie-rods 25 to the steering arms that are bolted to the front wheel swivel hubs.

8:2 Routine maintenance (manual)

No lubrication service is needed on the manual steering gear. Every 6000 miles (10,000 km or 6 months) jack up the front wheels and check all steering joints for security and for backlash. Check the rubber seals or gaiters for splits and deterioration (see parts 20 and 22 in **FIG 8:1**). Check security of bolt for coupling flange 8. Tighten to 12 to 15 lbf ft (1.7 to 2.1 kgf m). **Do not overtighten.**

8:3 Servicing the steering column assembly

Removing and refitting steering wheel:

Refer to **FIG 8:1** and prise out the pad 1. Unscrew the nut and use a puller to draw off the wheel.

When refitting, set the front wheels in the straight-ahead position with steering wheel spokes horizontal. Note correct angle for ends of pad as shown at 11 in **FIG 8:4**. Tighten nut to 35 lbf ft (4.8 kgf m). Press pad into clips 2 (see **FIG 8:1**).

Removing and refitting steering column:

Refer to **FIG 8:2**. Do the following:
1 Disconnect battery. Remove steering wheel. Remove cowl (see 18 and 19 in **FIG 8:1**), by taking out three lower screws first, then single one from upper part. Lift off upper half first.
2 Release combination switch 4 (2 screws). Disconnect multi-plug 5 from below facia. Move floor covering and release clamp plates and bush 7. Push them up column.
3 On manual steering remove bolts 8 from coupling. With power steering remove clamp bolt 9. Remove bolts 10 and withdraw column (manual). With power steering, disengage the inner column from the splines on the rack pinion.
4 When refitting, reverse the procedure, setting the road wheels straight-ahead before connecting the

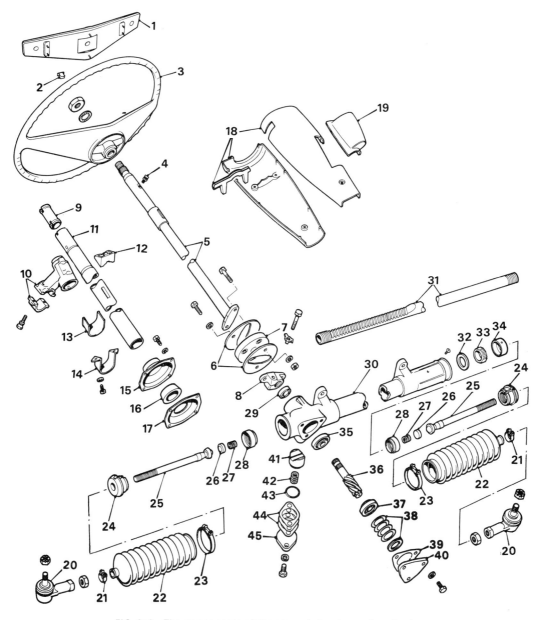

FIG 8:1 The components of the manual steering rack and column

Key to Fig 8:1 1 Steering wheel pad 2 Pad clip 3 Steering wheel 4 Direction indicator switch trip stud 5 Inner column 6 Coupling plate 7 Flexible coupling 8 Pinion coupling 9 Column upper bush 10 Column lock 11 Outer column 12 Column to fascia abutment piece 13 Packing strip 14 Column to fascia clip 15 Bush upper clamp plate 16 Lower bush 17 Bush lower clamp plate 18 Column cowl assembly 19 Steering lock cover 20 Ball joint 21 Seal outer clip 22 Rack housing seal 23 Seal inner clip 24 Ball housing 25 Tie rod 26 Ball seat 27 Thrust spring 28 Locknut 29 Oil seal 30 Rack housing 31 Rack 32 Backing disc 33 Bush 34 Bush housing 35 Pinion bearing 36 Pinion 37 Pinion bearing 38 Shims 39 End cover gasket 40 Pinion end cover 41 Damper yoke 42 Damper spring 43 'O' ring 44 Shims 45 Damper end cover inner column. Note that direction indicator stud (see 2 in **FIG 8:3**) must be midway between the arms on the switch. Lug in bore of switch must locate in slot in outer column. Ensure that peg and slot in packing 15c are properly engaged. Check that lock will engage with inner column, moving outer column axially until it does so. With power steering, tighten clamp bolt 9 and bolts for plates 7 before tightening bracket bolts 10. When refitting upper cowl, align 'X' with 'X' on seating piece (see lefthand part of assembly 18 in **FIG 8:1**).

Overhauling steering column:

To remove inner column, remove trip stud 2 (see **FIG 8:3**). Straighten tongue 3 and extract bush 4 with tool 18G.1191 (see **FIG 8:11**). Withdraw inner column downwards. To release lock, drill out the bolts.

Check bushes, shaft splines and locking bolt and groove for wear. Note that top bush may be renewed without stripping the columns. Repeat operation 1 and remove the combination switch. Remove the trip stud and extract bush as just described. Drive bush into place with drift of tool 18G.1191 making sure slot in lower edge engages with key pressed into bore of outer column. Smear bore with graphited grease.

Reassemble column in reverse order of dismantling. Use new steering lock bolts, tightening them until the heads shear off. Adjust height of trip stud 2 (see inset 11d). Distance 'A' should be 1.182±.005 inch (30±.13 mm).

Flexible coupling (manual):

Refer to parts 6 and 7 in **FIG 8:1**. Do operations 1 and 2 for removing the column, also disconnecting the three multi-plugs from under the facia. Remove bolts 8 and 14 (see **FIG 8:2**).

Before fitting bolts 8 when reassembling, set road wheels straight-ahead with spokes of steering wheel horizontal and ends of pad set as in inset to **FIG 8:4**. Tighten these bolts to 15 lbf ft (2.1 kgf m). Check engagement of lock and of packing piece as described in operation 4 of 'Removing and refitting steering column'.

8:4 Servicing seals and ball joints

Steering rack seals:

These are parts 22 in **FIG 8:1**. Also see **FIG 8:4**. A damaged and leaking seal may allow dirt to enter the rack housing and lubricant will be lost. Renew at once and check condition of rack (see **Section 8:5**).

To renew seals, remove ball joints 20 (see later). Remove clips 21 and 23 and pull off seals. When reassembling, leave off small clip on steering side of car and inject into the seal $\frac{1}{3}$ pint (.4 US pint or .18 litre) of E.P. 90 oil. Use E.P. 80 oil for temperatures below −18°C (0°F).

Ball joints:

With road wheel removed, unlock and slacken nut 8 (see **FIG 8:4**). Break ball pin out of steering arm using tool 18G.1063 (see **FIG 7:12** in preceding chapter).

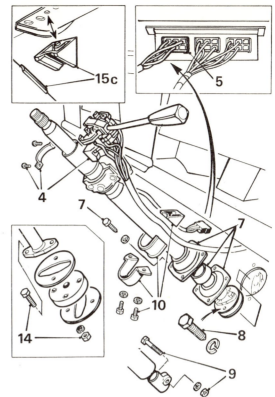

FIG 8:2 Details of the steering column assembly. The power steering clamp for inner column is shown (bottom right). The numbers are used in the text

Do not try to hammer pin out of arm. Unscrew ball joint after releasing locknut. Note number of turns.

Reverse procedure to refit. If joint is rough in action and has backlash, or if rubber boot is damaged, renewal is indicated. Check that tie-rod assemblies on each side of car are equal in length and then check alignment (toe-in) as described in **Section 8:11**.

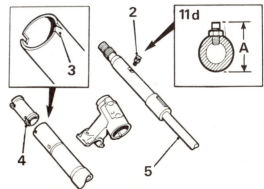

FIG 8:3 Fitting upper bush to outer column (left). Setting direction indicator trip stud (right)

Key to Fig 8:3 2 Trip stud 3 Bush retaining tongue
4 Upper bush 5 Inner column

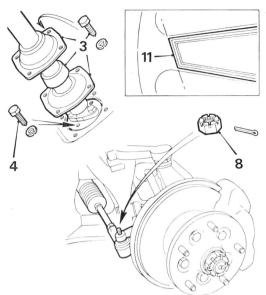

FIG 8:4 Removing and refitting the manual steering rack. Assembly 3 is the lower bush and clamp plates, 4 is a coupling bolt, 8 is a tie-rod ball joint nut and 11 shows the correct inclination for the ends of the steering wheel pad

8:5 Removing and overhauling manual steering rack

Removing:

Refer to **FIG 8:4**. Release clamp plates 3. Remove bolts 4. Chock rear wheels, raise front end and fit supports under front sidemembers. Remove wheel from steering wheel side. Disconnect ball joints (see end of preceding Section). Remove the four bolts securing the steering rack to the body (the lugs can be seen as part of housing 30 in **FIG 8:1**). Withdraw rack from steering side.

Dismantling:

Refer to **FIG 8:1**. Do the following:
1 Remove ball joints and locknuts 20. Remove clips and seals 21, 22 and 23. Drain out oil. Unlock ball housing locknuts 28. Unlock and unscrew ball housings 24 using spanners 18G.1030 (see **FIG 8:11**).
2 Withdraw seats and springs 26 and 27. Unscrew the locknuts 28 from rack 31. Remove clamp bolt and pull off coupling flange 8. Remove damper cover plate 45 and shims 44. Remove parts 41, 42 and 43.
3 Remove pinion cover 40 and joint 39. Withdraw shims 38, bearing 37 and pinion 36. Withdraw rack from pinion end of housing. **Do not withdraw from other end as teeth may damage bush.** Withdraw upper bearing 35.
4 If necessary, remove screw to release bush housing 34, bush 33 and backing disc 32. Withdraw from bush end of housing. Seal 29 may also be removed if in need of renewal.
5 Clean all parts and check for wear or damage. Renew all defective seals.

Reassembling:

Reassemble in the reverse order of dismantling. If a new bush 33 is to be fitted, make sure the three flats on the outside of the bush line up with the three oilways inside the housing. Drill a blind hole $\frac{7}{64}$ inch (2.7 mm) diameter and .29 inch (7.37 mm) deep into the bush. The depth must be measured from the spot facing for the screw head.

Coat underside of screw head with sealer, fit screw and check that inner end of screw has not distorted bore in bush. Oil seal 29 has its sealing lip towards bearing 35 and is fitted flush with housing face.

Preloading pinion bearings:

After fitting the pinion and bearings, preload as follows:
1 Refer to central view in **FIG 8:5**. Fit pinion end cover without gasket but enough shims to produce a gap at 'A'. Tighten bolts lightly and evenly. Measure gap with feelers.
2 Adjust shims until gap is thickness of joint washer less .001 to .003 inch (.03 to .08 mm). With thickest shim against end cover, reassemble using a new gasket.

Tie-rod adjustment:

When assembling tie-rods 25, adjust so that when locknut 28 is tightened the sideways pull required to articulate the tie-rod is 42 ± 10 lbf inch (.48 $\pm$ .11 kgf m) using tool No. 18G.1020.

Flange setting:

Fit flange 8 as shown on left in **FIG 8:5**. Set rack centrally in housing and fit flange so that bolt holes are parallel with rack (see dotted outline). Remove flange, turn it two serrations anticlockwise (see inset) and refit it. The bolt holes will now be at 20 deg. to the rack. Tighten flange bolt to 15 lbf ft (2.1 kgf m). Lock with two tabs over housing and one over bolt head.

Preload damper as follows:

1 Fit damper parts 41, 42 and 45. Centralize rack in housing. Refer to righthand view in **FIG 8:5** and tighten the cover bolts until the clearance between face of yoke and cover is .007 to .011 inch (.18 to .28 mm) as shown at 'A'. Turn pinion half a turn each way, re-centralize rack and again check at 'A', adjusting if necessary. Do not disturb.
2 Measure clearance between cover and housing at 'B'. Remove cover, fit O-ring 43, and shims 44 to the thickness of clearance 'B'. Refit cover.

Finish reassembling, add lubricant as described in **Section 8:4** and fit the rack housing as follows:

Refitting:

Reverse the removal procedure. Ensure, before bolting it into place, that the rack is centralized, the steering wheel spokes are horizontal and the pad ends are inclined as shown at 11 in **FIG 8:4**. If necessary, check and adjust the front wheel alignment as described in **Section 8:11**.

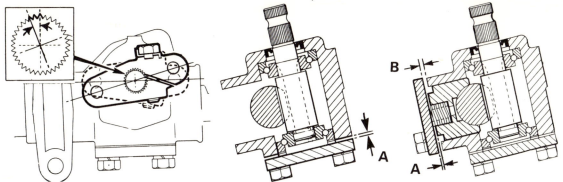

FIG 8:5 Correct setting for coupling flange on manual steering (left). Preloading rack pinion bearings (centre) and preloading the rack damper (right). 'A' and 'B' are measured clearances

Servicing without removal:

It may be helpful to know that the ball joints, rack housing seals, and rack damper may all be serviced without removing the rack assembly from the car.

8:6 Description of power steering system

Power assistance is obtained by fluid under pressure that is provided by a belt-driven pump. This pressure is directed by a control valve 47 to the required side of a piston secured to the rack (see parts 55, 56 and 57 in **FIG 8:8**). At rest, the valve by-passes fluid back to the pump reservoir, but when the steering wheel is moved, pinion housing 27 moves by reaction along the rack tube 38 and also moves the control valve through rod 31. The valve then directs fluid to the appropriate side of the rack piston giving power assistance. As soon as steering wheel and pinion reaction ceases to produce movement of the housing, a strong spring centralizes the valve spool and fluid is again returned to the reservoir.

8:7 Routine maintenance (power steering)

Every 6000 miles (10,000 km or 6 months) carry out the checks outlined in **Section 8:2**. At the same intervals, check fluid level in pump reservoir as shown in

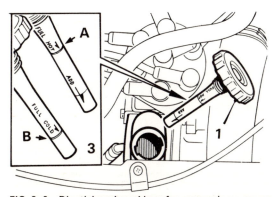

FIG 8:6 Dipstick and markings for reservoir on power steering pump. Use 'A' if fluid is hot and 'B' if it is cold

FIG 8:6. The reservoir is adjacent to the distributor. Wipe filler cap clean and remove anticlockwise. **Make sure dirt cannot fall into reservoir.**

With engine switched off, check fluid level. If system is hot use marks indicated at 'A', topping-up with Automatic Transmission fluid if necessary. Use marks at 'B' if system is cold.

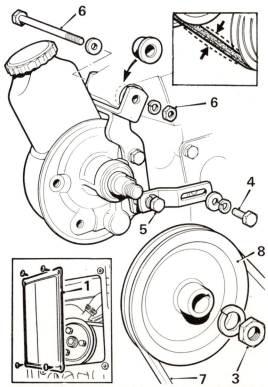

FIG 8:7 The power steering pump mounting and belt adjustment. Checking belt tension (top right). Access panel on cars with automatic transmission (bottom left)

Key to Fig 8:7   1 Access panel   3 Pulley nut   4 and 5 Link bolts   6 Pivot bolt and nut   7 Belt   8 Pulley

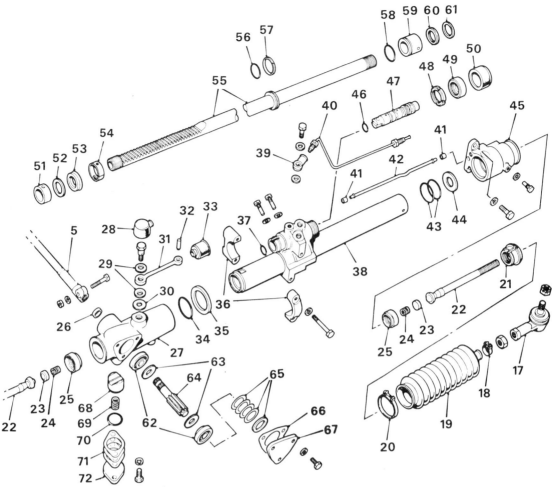

FIG 8:8 Components of the power steering rack that differ from the manual rack shown in FIG 8:1. All other parts in FIG 8:1 are common to both systems

Key to Fig 8:8   5 Inner column   17 Ball joint   18 Clip   19 Rack housing seal   20 Clip   21 Ball housing   22 Tie rod   23 Ball seat   24 Thrust spring   25 Locknut   26 Oil seal   27 Pinion housing   28 Dust seal   29 Belleville washers   30 Lockwasher   31 Operating rod   32 Dowel pin   33 Dust cover   34 O ring   35 Dirt excluder   36 Support bracket and cap   37 O ring   38 Valve body and rack tube   39 Banjo connection   40 Bundy tube   41 Bypass tube seal   42 Lubricating oil bypass tube   43 O rings   44 Backing washer   45 End housing   46 O ring   47 Valve spool   48 Locknut   49 Nut   50 Dust cover   51 Seal abutment   52 Anti-extrusion washer   53 Fluid seal   54 Seal retainer   55 Rack   56 O ring   57 Piston ring   58 O ring   59 Bush   60 Nu-lip ring   61 Anti-extrusion washer   62 Pinion bearing   63 Bearing washer   64 Pinion   65 Shims   66 Gasket   67 Pinion end cover   68 Damper yoke   69 Damper spring   70 O ring   71 Shims   72 Damper end cover

Driving belt adjustment:

Periodically check tension of pump driving belt. Refer to top inset in **FIG 8:7** and check **total deflection** midway between pulleys. Under moderate thumb pressure deflection should be $\frac{1}{2}$ inch (12.7 mm), as indicated by arrows.

To adjust, slacken pivot bolt nut 6 and link bolts 4 and 5. On automatic transmission models it is necessary to remove panel 1 from the lefthand front wing valance for access (see inset, bottom left). Pull pump upwards to increase tension on belt, tighten bolts and nut and check again.

Inner column clamp bolt:

Check periodically for security of bolt 9 in **FIG 8:2**. Tighten to 12 to 15 lbf ft (1.7 to 2.1 kgf m). **Do not overtighten.**

8:8 Servicing power steering rack

Removing:

Disconnect battery and slacken upper bracket bolts 10 (see **FIG 8:2**). Release clamp plates and bush 7. Remove clamp bolt 9 and pull steering wheel upwards to disengage inner column from pinion shaft. Chock rear wheels and lift front end, placing supports under the front sidemembers. Remove road wheel on steering side. Disconnect tie-rod ball joints (see **Section 8:4**). Remove hose banjo bolts from steering rack and drain fluid from the two hoses. Release rack from underside of body (2 short bolts and 2 long bolts with cap and bracket (see 36 in **FIG 8:8**). Withdraw rack from steering side.

Dismantling:

Refer to **FIG 8:8** and do the following:
1 Repeat operations 1 and 2 under 'Dismantling' in **Section 8:5**, noting that there is no flange to remove from the pinion splines. Make allowances for different part numbering of identical parts in **FIGS 8:1** and **8:8**.
2 Remove cover 67, joint 66, shims 65, lower bearing pinion 64 and washers 63. Release operating rod 31 from pinion housing 27. Pull housing off tube 38. Remove pinion upper bearing and seal 26 (if necessary).
3 Remove O-ring 34 and dirt excluder 35. Remove all burrs from tie-rod locking slots at ends of rack 55. Release high-pressure pipe 40 from end housing 45. Remove housing from tube 38 (one dowel bolt). Remove O-rings 43 and washer 44.
4 Withdraw rack 55 and bush 59 from end-housing end. Remove parts 58, 60 and 61 from bush. Remove O-ring 56 and piston ring 57 from rack. Refer to **FIG 8:9** and remove dowel bolts 47. Note sealing washer fitted to bolt at end-housing end. Extract retainer, seal, anti-extrusion ring and seal abutment from bore of rack tube (see 44 in **FIG 8:9**). Remove dust covers from ends of valve body.
5 Remove dowel pin 43 and dust covers from rod. Scribe a line across spool retaining nut 49, locknut 48 and body on tube 38 (see inset, bottom left in **FIG 8:9**). Note position of 48 and 49 on the threads for accurate reassembly. Remove them with tool 18G.-1132 (see **FIG 8:11**). Withdraw valve spool from same end. **Do not alter setting of reaction spring on spool.**
6 Remove O-ring 46 from spool and O-ring 37 from valve body (see **FIG 8:8**). Release banjo 39 and withdraw lubricating oil bypass tube 42 from body. Remove seals 41.

Inspection:

After cleaning, check all parts for wear or damage. Check unlubricated pinion bearings for roughness and pitting. Check seals for splits and deterioration.

Reassembling:

Before assembling, lubricate power steering parts with Automatic Transmission fluid and the rack and pinion parts with SAE 40, 20W/40 or 20W/50 oil. Use the following sequence:
1 Reverse the dismantling procedure in preceding Sections from 'Remove dust covers — ' in operation 4, to 'Release banjo 39 — ' in operation 6, fitting chamfered end of dowel pin 43 first and applying Duckhams LS.1047 grease or equivalent to the areas protected by dust covers at each end (see **FIG 8:9** for dowel pin 43 and following parts).

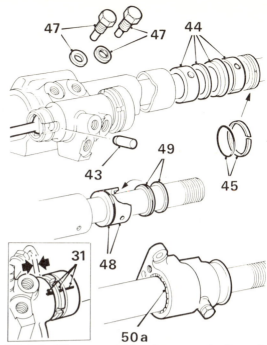

FIG 8:9 When reassembling the power steering rack, these details of the rack seals will be found useful. Note sealer applied at 50a. Inset (bottom left) shows alignment marks made before removing valve spool. The numbers are used in the text

2 Fit seal retainer, seal, anti-extrusion ring and abutment 44 to rack, using tools 18G.1129 and 1130 to pass rack through seal (see **FIG 8:11** for tools). Tools must be burr-free.
3 Fit O-ring and piston ring 45 to rack piston. Fit rack assembly, making sure dowel holes in abutment and retainer (see 44) are in line with dowel bolt holes in valve housing. Fit dowel bolts 47 with sealing washer at end-housing end as shown. Fit O-ring to bush 48 and fit bush with dowel bolt hole in line with hole in rack tube. Fit sealing ring and anti-extrusion ring 49 into bush, using tool 18G.1129 to pass seal over rack threads. Fit tube 42 and seals 41 (see **FIG 8:8**).
4 Reverse operations 1, 2 and 3 under 'Dismantling' noting that Sealastic is applied to the end-housing to rack tube joint (see 50a in **FIG 8:9**). Preload the pinion before fitting a new oil seal and check that the line on the top face of the pinion is vertically at six o'clock when the rack is central in its housing.
5 Preload the pinion bearings and the damper as described under the respective headings in **Section 8:5**. Set tie-rod articulation as described in the same Section. Leave small clip off tie-rod seal at pinion end and inject $\frac{1}{3}$ pint (.4 US pint or .18 litre) of SAE 40, 20W/40 or 20W/50 oil. Fit clip to seal.

Refitting:

Reverse the removal procedure. Before connecting the inner column, set the front wheels straightahead with steering spokes horizontal and pad ends inclined as shown in the inset (top right) in **FIG 8:4**.

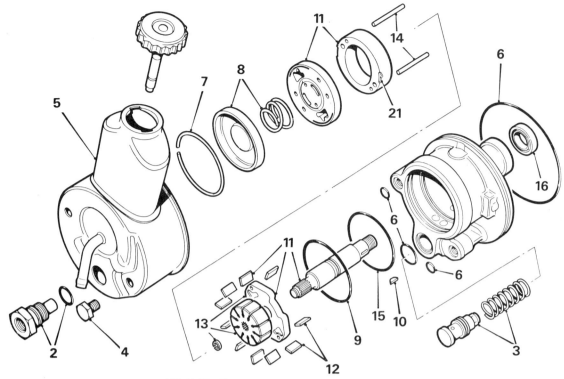

FIG 8:10 Components of power steering pump

Key to Fig 8:10   2 Outlet union and O-ring   3 Control valve and spring   4 Bolt for reservoir   5 Reservoir   6 Reservoir O-ring   7 Retaining ring   8 End plate and spring   9 End plate O-ring   10 Key   11 Pressure plate and pump ring, drive shaft and thrust plate   12 Vanes   13 Retaining ring and pump rotor   14 Dowel pins   15 Pressure plate O-ring   16 Seal for shaft   21 Half arrow

Before tightening the column bracket bolts make sure that the steering lock engages with the inner column. Adjust the outer column up and down if necessary. Bleed the power steering system as described in **Section 8:10**. If necessary, check and adjust the front wheel alignment (see **Section 8:11**). Check power steering. Bias in one direction and loss of self-centring in the other direction may be due to misalignment of the inner column with the steering rack pinion.

Rack housing seals:

These are part 19 in **FIG 8:8**. Service them in the manner described for manual steering in **Section 8:4**. **Note, however that a different lubricant must be injected** (see this Section, just before 'Refitting').

8:9 Servicing power steering pump
Removing and refitting belt:

Refer to **FIG 8:7**. On automatic transmission models remove panel 1 from lefthand front wing valance. Slacken generator pivot and link bolts and nut (see Electrical chapter). Pull top of generator towards engine.

Remove water pump pulley (3 bolts). Slacken steering pump pivot nut 6 and link bolts 4 and 5, push pump towards engine and remove belt, passing it over the water pump belt and withdrawing it from the crankshaft pulley.

Refit in reverse order, tightening water pump pulley bolts to 8 lbf ft (1.11 kgf m). Tension both belts to a total deflection of $\frac{1}{2}$ inch (12.7 mm) under moderate thumb pressure.

Removing pump:

On automatic transmission models, remove oil filter (see **Chapter 1**), and also remove access panel 1 (see **FIG 8:7**). On manual gearbox models remove pulley nut 3, bolt 4 and slacken bolt 5. Remove bolt 6, detach belt 7 and on manual gearbox models, withdraw pulley 8. Release both hose clips from underside of car. Withdraw pump downwards (automatic transmission models). On manual gearbox models, turn pump through 180 deg. and withdraw downwards.

Disconnect hoses from pump after emptying reservoir. Remove pulley (automatic transmission). Remove mounting bracket.

Refitting pump:

Adopt the reverse procedure to removal. Tension drive belt as just described. Bleed the system (see **Section 8:10**).

Dismantling:

Refer to **FIG 8:10** and do the following:

1 Remove union and O-ring 2. From union bore, withdraw control valve and spring 3. Remove screw 4, rock reservoir 5 free from its O-ring and withdraw from housing.

2 Remove four rings 6 from housing. Remove ring 7 by unseating one end with a pin punch inserted through the small hole in the housing. Rock plate 8 until free of O-ring and withdraw plate and spring. Remove O-ring 9 from groove in housing. Remove shaft key 10.

3 Lightly tap pulley end of shaft to free pressure plate from O-ring and withdraw plate, pump ring and drive shaft assembly (see 11). Withdraw vanes 12. Remove retaining ring to release rotor and thrust plate (see 13). Remove dowel pins 14. Remove O-ring 15 from groove in housing. If necessary, prise out seal 16.

Inspecting:

Clean all parts and check for wear or damage. If shaft is pitted where oil seal lip contacts it, polish with crocus cloth (extremely fine emery). Discard the oil seal, the rotor retaining ring and all the O-rings and fit new parts. The outer surface of the control valve assembly and the rotor vanes must be free from burrs and varnish. The control valve is not adjustable and must be renewed if faulty.

Reassembling:

Reverse the dismantling procedure. Lubricate all parts with automatic transmission fluid. Fit thrust plate with cavity side facing towards rotor end of shaft. Fit rotor with countersunk side next to pressure plate (see 13). Fit shaft assembly into housing, making sure that holes in thrust plate engage the dowel pins.

Fit pump ring with half-arrow at end-plate end of housing (see 21). Fit vanes with rounded edge of each one next to the pump ring. Press end-plate into its O-ring just far enough to permit fitting the plate retaining ring.

Fit the control valve with its screened end towards the drive end. Tighten outlet union and reservoir bolt to 35 lbf ft (4.8 kgf m).

Refitting pump:

Reverse the procedure for removal. Tension the belt. Bleed the system as described in **Section 8:10**.

8:10 Bleeding the power system

Refer to **FIG 8:6**. Remove cap from reservoir after cleaning. Top-up with Automatic Transmission Fluid as described in **Section 8:7**. With engine running at idling speed, turn steering wheel slowly from lock to lock. This will bleed air from the system. Top-up level as described in **Section 8:7**. Total power steering fluid capacity is 2 pint (2½ US pint or 1.1 litre). System is bled when fluid level is steady and there is no frothing or bubbling. Carry out the operation with the front wheels jacked up.

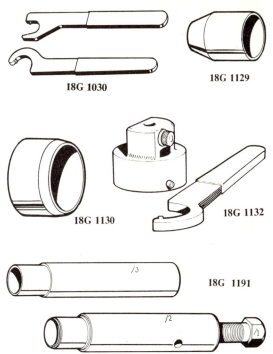

FIG 8:11 Special tools used when working on the steering gear

Key to Fig 8:11   18G.1030 Rack ball joint spanners 18G.1129 Rack oil seal assembly sleeve   18G.1130 Circlip assembly sleeve   18G.1132 Valve setting tool and locknut spanner   18G.1191 Remover and replacer for steering column top bush

8:11 Front wheel alignment

When correctly set the front wheels are not parallel but toe-in by $\frac{1}{8}$ inch (3.2 mm). The angle equivalent is 22 minutes.

Check the alignment every 6000 miles (10,000 km or 6 months). Car must be unladen but provided with oil, fuel and water. Front tyres must be inflated to 30 lb/sq in (2.1 kg/sq cm) and rear tyres to 24 lb/sq in (1.7 kg/sq cm). Front wheels must be set straightahead, and car must be on level ground.

Measure distance between rims at wheel centre height in front and behind the hubs. Mark these positions with chalk then roll car forward by half a turn of the wheels. Take a second set of measurements at the chalk marks. Measurements at the front must be an average of $\frac{1}{8}$ inch (3.2 mm) less than those at the back.

To adjust, slacken gaiter clips 21 and locknuts of ball joints 20 (see **FIG 8:1**). Turn each tie-rod by an equal amount, noting that both rods have righthand threads. The tie-rod threads behind each locknut should be equal in length. If this is not so, screw one rod in and the other out by equal amounts until correct. **This is essential if the rack is to be central and the steering geometry correct.**

Hold outer ball joints square with their ball pins (in steering arms) and tighten locknuts to 35 to 40 lbf ft (4.8 to 5.5 kgf m) Tighten clips and recheck alignment.

8:12 Fault diagnosis

(a) Heavy steering (power)

1 Steering linkage binding. Adjust and lubricate
2 Pump output low. Check flow control valve (see **Section 8:9**)
3 Pump hub wrongly assembled (see **Section 8:9**)

(b) Poor self-centring (power)

1 Steering linkage binding. Adjust and lubricate
2 Excessive friction. Check alignment of inner column and upper bush. Check rack with tie rods detached. Check pinion housing and rack seals

(c) Steering pulls to one side (power)

1 Operating rod damaged or out of adjustment
2 Control valve spool out of centre. Replace assembly

(d) Excessive free play in steering wheel (power)

1 Incorrect yoke adjustment
2 Pinion coupling loose
3 Tie rod joint(s) loose
4 Spool reaction spring out of adjustment. Replace assembly

(e) Lack of power assistance (power)

1 Pump output low. Check flow control valve
2 Hub incorrectly assembled (see **Section 8:9**)
3 Pinion housing seized on rack
4 Assistance in one direction only. Operating rod damaged or out of adjustment. Control valve spool out of centre. Replace assembly

(f) Intermittent assistance when turning (power)

1 Engine idling too slowly
2 Air in system. Bleed as in **Section 8:10**
3 Pump output low. Check flow control valve
4 Internal fault. Check oil seals

(g) Excessive noise (power)

1 Leak in system
2 Air in system. Bleed system (see **Section 8:10**)
3 Hose fouling or damaged
4 Yoke wrongly adjusted
5 Worn pump. Check as in **Section 8:9**

(h) Wheel wobble

1 Unbalanced wheels and tyres
2 Slack steering ball joints
3 Incorrect steering geometry
4 Excessive play in steering gear
5 Faulty suspension
6 Worn hub bearings

(i) Wander

1 Check 2, 3 and 4 in (h) and check (k)
2 Uneven tyre pressures
3 Uneven tyre wear

(j) Heavy steering

1 Check 3 in (h)
2 Very low tyre pressures
3 Neglected lubrication (damaged dust covers)
4 Wheels out of track
5 Rack damper too tight
6 Excessive pinion bearing preload
7 Steering column bent or misaligned
8 Column bushes tight

(k) Lost motion

1 Loose steering wheel, worn splines
2 Defective column coupling
3 Worn rack and pinion teeth
4 Worn ball joints
5 Worn swivel hub joints
6 Slack pinion bearings

CHAPTER 9

THE BRAKING SYSTEM

9:1 Description

Hydraulically-operated disc brakes are fitted to the front wheels and drum brakes to the rear. The friction pad on one side of a front disc is pressed into braking contact by two pistons and the pad on the other side by a single piston. Rear brake shoes are operated by a single hydraulic piston, and a cylinder that is free to slide in the brake backplate, reaction causing simultaneous pressure on both shoes. The handbrake is connected by cables to the rear brakes only.

Hydraulic pressure may be provided by a single master cylinder or a tandem cylinder, the latter ensuring that failure of the front wheel system does not prevent operation of the rear brakes and vice-versa. A vacuum servo unit connected to the inlet manifold boosts pedal pressure to increase braking power. In one system the brake master cylinder is separate from the servo unit and in another system the pedal operates directly on the servo cylinder.

A pressure-reducing valve is fitted near the rear brakes to regulate the braking effort on the rear wheels to prevent them from locking during heavy application. When a tandem master cylinder is fitted there is a pressure differential warning actuator in the circuit that gives visual warning of a failure in either front or rear systems.

9:2 Routine maintenance

Topping-up:

Every 3000 miles (5000 km or 3 months) check the fluid level in the master cylinder reservoir (see 1 in **FIG 9:1**). Single master cylinders have the level marked on the outside. The level on tandem cylinders must be up to the top of the baffle inside.

Clean area round cap before unscrewing. Check that vent hole 3 is clear. If necessary, top-up with UNIPART 550 or a fluid conforming to Specification SAE.J.1703a. **Do not use any other type of fluid. Take great care to keep out dirt and do not let the fluid contact paintwork as it is a solvent.** If there is a marked drop in level at any time, check the whole system for leaks that may eventually lead to brake failure.

Adjusting rear brakes:

Every 6000 miles (10,000 km or 6 months) or if brake pedal travel is excessive, adjust the rear brakes. Chock front wheels, release handbrake and jack up each rear wheel in turn. Behind the brake is a squared adjuster (see **FIG 9:2**). Turn clockwise until solid, then turn back until wheel can be turned without brake linings rubbing. When applied, the pedal should feel solid and the handbrake should pull on effectively. If defective in either case, refer to **Sections 9:8** and **9:9**.

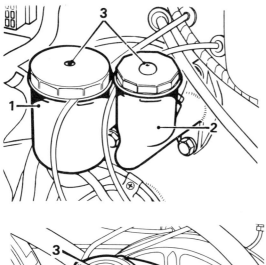

FIG 9:3 Check thickness of pad material at 4 on front disc brakes

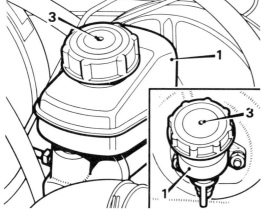

FIG 9:1 Master cylinder reservoirs for braking system 1, for clutch 2, vent holes in caps 3. Single cylinder (top), tandem cylinder (bottom left) and cylinder incorporated in servo unit (bottom right)

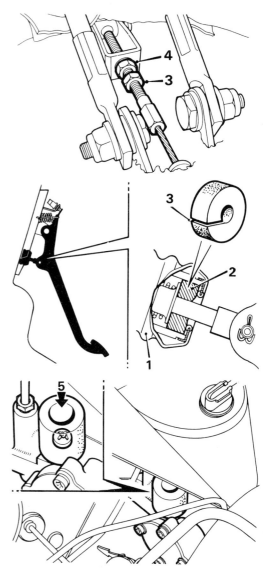

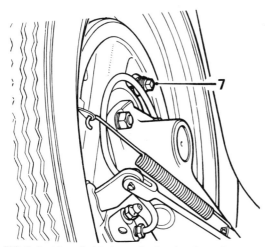

FIG 9:2 View behind rear brake showing adjuster 7. Note bleed screw and handbrake operating fork and lever below

FIG 9:4 Locknut 3 and adjuster nut 4 for handbrake cables (top). Servo unit dust cover 1, filter 2 and assembling slit 3 when pedal operates direct (centre). Servo filter 5 when unit is hydraulically operated (bottom)

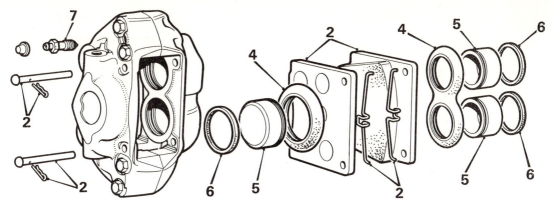

FIG 9:5   The components of a front brake caliper unit

Key to Fig 9:5   2 Spring clips and retaining pins (left), anti-rattle springs and friction pads (centre)   4 Piston dust covers
5 Pistons   6 Piston seals   7 Bleed screw

Handbrake lubrication:

While the rear brakes are being adjusted, lubricate the handbrake linkage and cables (see **Section 9:9**).

Inspecting rear brake drums:

Every 12,000 miles (20,000 km or 12 months) jack up and remove the rear wheels. With front wheels chocked, remove rear wheels, turn adjusters anticlockwise (see **FIG 9:2**) and remove drums (2 screws). Clean out dust, examine cylinder for leaks and check thickness of linings. Renew if down to rivet heads or if linings will be excessively worn by the time of the next inspection.

When reassembled, adjust as described in preceding instructions under that heading. Tighten road wheel nuts diagonally to 60 lbf ft (8.3 kgf m).

Checking front brake pads and discs:

Every 6000 miles (10,000 km or 6 months) check thickness of friction material on pads (see 4 in **FIG 9:3**). The material is adjacent to the disc. Renew if down to a thickness of $\frac{1}{16}$ inch (1.6 mm), or if there is not enough to last until the next inspection. Change the pads over if wear is uneven. Check discs for excessive wear, cracking or scoring.

Brake pipe inspection:

Every 6000 miles (10,000 km or 6 months) inspect all pipes and connections for leaks and corrosion. Check all flexible hoses for leaks, chafing or deterioration.

Brake servo filter:

Every 36,000 miles (60,000 km or 3 years) renew the servo filter. Refer to central view of **FIG 9:4** if brake pedal acts directly on servo unit. Pull back servo dust cover 1 from below parcel tray. Prise off the end cap and remove filter 2. Cut new filter tangential to bore (see 3). Fit it over pushrod, refit cap and dust cover.

On hydraulically-operated servo, refer to lower view in **FIG 9:3**. Release centre screw (see 5) and remove cover and element. Clean filter seat and cover, fit new element and refit assembly.

Preventive maintenance:

It is recommended that brake pads and linings, and hydraulic pipes and hoses should be examined at intervals no longer than those laid down in the preceding instructions.

Change all the brake fluid every 18 months or 18,000 miles (30,000 km) whichever is the sooner.

Check all fluid seals and hoses in the hydraulic system every 3 years or 36,000 miles (60,000 km) whichever is the sooner. At the same time check the working surfaces of pistons and bores in the master and wheel cylinders. The brake servo filter element must be renewed at the same mileage.

Always use the recommended fluid and do not leave it in unsealed containers because it absorbs moisture, which can be dangerous. It is best to discard fluid drained from the system or fluid used for bleeding. **At all times observe absolute cleanliness when dealing with brake fluid and the internal parts of hydraulic systems.**

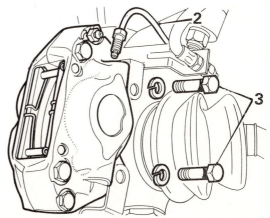

FIG 9:6   Removing caliper unit by unscrewing bolts 3. 2 is the hydraulic feed pipe

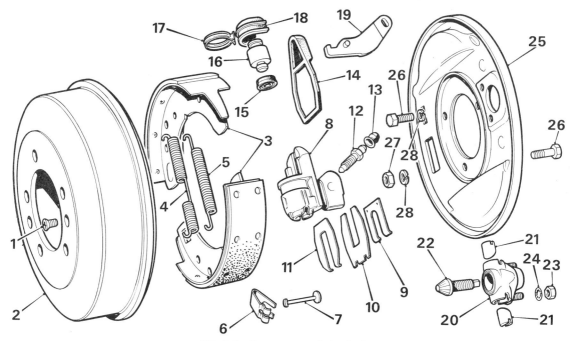

FIG 9:7 Components of rear brake

Key to Fig 9:7   1 Screw—drum   2 Brake drum   3 Brake shoe   4 Spring—shoe return—cylinder end   5 Spring—shoe return—adjuster end   6 Retainer—steady pin   7 Steady pin   8 Wheel cylinder   9 Distance washer   10 Locking plate   11 Retaining spring plate   12 Bleed screw   13 Dust cover   14 Dust cover—wheel cylinder   15 Seal—piston   16 Piston   17 Retaining clip—dust cover   18 Dust cover   19 Handbrake lever   20 Adjuster body   21 Tappets   22 Wedge   23 Nut   24 Shakeproof washer   25 Backplate   26 Bolts—backplate   27 Nut Nut   28 Spring washers

9:3 Servicing the front brakes

Renewing brake pads:

Refer to **FIGS 9:3** and **9:5**. Apply handbrake, jack up car and remove wheel. Remove clips and retaining pins, followed by springs and pads (see 2). Clean recess free from dirt. Check for leakage past pistons.

Use a clamp or tool 18G.590 (see **FIG 9:13**) to press the pistons back in their bores. **This may cause fluid to overflow from master cylinder reservoir.** Check this and if necessary, open a bleed screw to allow surplus to drain out. Tighten the bleed screw and check fluid level (see **Section 9:2**).

Fit the new pads and complete the assembling, taking care to fit the springs so that they cannot rub and puncture the dust seals.

Removing and refitting calipers:

Refer to **FIG 9:6**. Apply handbrake, jack up car and remove wheel. Disconnect pipe 2, remove two bolts 3 and lift away caliper.

Reverse procedure to refit caliper, tightening bolts to 45 to 50 lbf ft 6.2 to 6.9 kgf m). Bleed the system (see **Section 9:8**).

Dismantling caliper:

Remove caliper and pads as just described. Push out the pistons 5 with compressed air, using a wedge of wood in the recess to limit piston travel. After each puff of air, withdraw the wedge a little until the pistons can be extracted by hand after removing dust covers 4. Without compressed air, reconnect the caliper to the hose and eject the pistons by brake pedal pressure, using the wedge to prevent excessive movement.

Remove seals 6 from grooves in bores. Use a blunt tool to avoid damage. **Do not part the caliper into two halves.**

Inspection:

Clean all parts in Girling Cleaning Fluid or methylated spirit. **Use no other type of solvent.** Examine pistons and bores for corrosion, damage or scoring. Renew unit if there is any fault. Renew all seals. These are available in kit form.

Reassembling:

Wet pistons and seals with brake fluid and assemble in that condition. Fit new seals into the bores. Fit each piston squarely into bore. Take great care that piston cannot tilt and press each one into place until about $\frac{5}{16}$ inch (8 mm) protrudes. Fit dust cover lips into piston grooves. Use a clamp or tool 18G.590 to press pistons fully home. Clean bleed screw and blow out with compressed air. Refit screw and brake pads. Refit caliper and bleed the system (see **Section 9:8**).

9:4 Removing and refitting front disc

With handbrake on and wheel removed, unlock and unscrew the drive shaft nut and prise the split inner cone off the shaft. Remove the caliper (see preceding Section). Fit puller 18G.304 and bolts 18G.304A to the wheel studs (see **FIG 9:13** for tools). Withdraw disc assembly and remove tool. Hold disc in a vice with soft jaws and separate the disc from the flange (5 bolts).

Check disc for wear, cracks and excessive scoring. Some slight scoring is normal if it is concentric. A worn disc may be reground to restore the surface.

Refit the disc and tighten the bolts to 40 to 45 lbf ft (5.5 to 6.2 kgf m). Fit to drive shaft and tighten nut to 150 lb ft (20.7 kgf m). Lock with a new splitpin. Check disc for runout. This should not exceed .008 in (.2 mm) at the periphery. If excessive try moving disc to another location on flange and check for burrs. Finish reassembly and bleed the system (see **Section 9:8**).

9:5 Servicing rear brakes

Removing brake shoes:

Refer to **FIG 9:7** and do the following:
1 Chock front wheels, jack up rear of car, remove rear wheels and release handbrake. Slacken off adjusters. Remove screws 1 and pull off drum 2.
2 Depress retainers 6, twist pin 7 to release it and remove. Lever one shoe out of cylinder and adjuster and release it to take the tension off the springs.

Brake shoe linings:

Renew the shoes and linings in complete sets if worn down to rivets. It is best to exchange old parts for shoes already lined. **Do not let oil, grease or paint contact the linings and do not handle with oily fingers.** It is useless to try to clean old linings that are soaked in oil or brake fluid. **Make sure linings are of correct grade and all the same.**

Refitting brake shoes:

Reassemble shoes and springs with two-part spring 4 adjacent to cylinder. Hook one shoe into place, pull on the springs and second shoe and release into cylinder abutment and adjuster. Take care that handbrake lever 19 engages hole in shoe. Refit steady pins and retainers. Fit drum and apply footbrake to centralize shoes. Adjust brakes (see **Section 9:2**). Check that handbrake is satisfactory (if not, see **Section 9:9**).

Overhauling brake:

Remove shoes as just described. Remove adjuster (2 nuts 23). Remove tappets 21. Screw wedge 22 through body 20. If seized, apply penetrating oil, hold squared end of wedge in a vice and turn body to and fro until free. Lubricate with graphite grease, reassemble and refit. Check that tappets move simultaneously when wedge is turned.

With shoes removed, release handbrake pull-off spring from behind brake backplate. Remove clevis pin from fork and lever. Disconnect pipe from cylinder. Remove rubber boot 14. Prise locking and spring plates 9, 10 and 11 apart. Tap locking plate 10 out from between plates. Pull out cylinder 8 complete with lever 19.

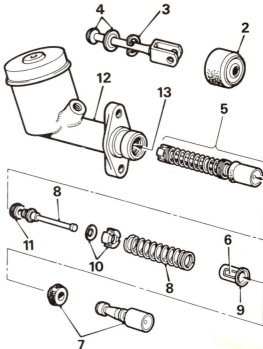

FIG 9:8 Components of single master cylinder

Key to Fig 9:8   2 Dust cover   3 Circlip   4 Pushrod assembly   5 Piston assembly   6 Thimble leaf   7 Piston and seal   8 Spring and valve stem   9 Thimble 10 Curved washer and spacer   11 Valve seal   12 Cylinder and reservoir   13 Bore

To dismantle cylinder, prise off clip 17, remove dust cover 18 and extract piston 16 complete with seal 15. Clean in Girling Cleaning Fluid or methylated spirit and check for wear or damage. Cylinder bore must be polished and free from scores. **Always renew seals.**

Reassemble cylinder with all parts wet with brake fluid. Fit new seal with flat face to piston shoulder. Take care not to trap or turn back the seal when introducing it into the cylinder bore.

When refitting cylinder, grease both sides of aperture in backplate because cylinder must slide. Fit washer 9 and plate 11 to neck of cylinder, insert locking plate 10 and tap it home to engage with spring plate 11.

Finish reassembling by reversing the dismantling procedure, adjust the brakes and bleed the system (see **Section 9:8**). Always remember to slacken off the adjusters, especially when new shoes have been fitted, as this makes it easier to fit the drums. The hub must be removed to remove the backplate (see **Chapter 7**).

If a wheel cylinder is renewed, make sure that it has the correct bore diameter of .70 inch (17.8 mm).

9:6 Servicing master cylinder (single)

Whether the master cylinder is operated directly by the brake pedal or is bolted to the servo unit, the internal parts are the same and the following instructions apply. When the pushrod presses piston and seal 7 down the cylinder bore (see **FIG 9:8**), valve seal 11 closes the

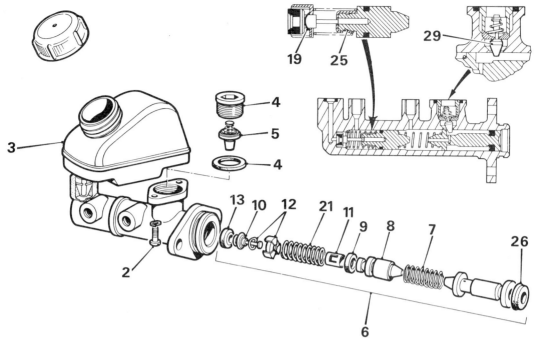

FIG 9:9 Components of tandem master cylinder

Key to Fig 9:9   2 Reservoir screw   3 Reservoir   4 Tipping valve nut   5 Tipping valve   6 Piston assemblies
7 Intermediate spring   8 Secondary plunger   9 Seal   10 Valve stem   11 Thimble   12 Curved washer and spacer
13 Valve seal   19 Curved washer in place   25 Thimble leaf correctly assembled   26 Seal for primary plunger   29 Tipping
valve in situ

port into the reservoir and fluid is forced out under pressure through the outlet port. When the piston returns, the last part of its travel opens the valve. Fluid is then free to flow from the reservoir to replenish any that has been lost by leakage.

Removing:

Remove clevis pin to detach pedal from pushrod fork (see 4 in **FIG 9:8**). Disconnect outlet pipe from cylinder and plug hole and pipe to seal against dirt. **Do not use rag.** Release cylinder flange (one nut and one bolt). Note the packing pieces between flange and bulkhead. These adjust pedal travel and must be refitted.

Overhauling:

Peel back dust cover 2, extract circlip 3 and remove pushrod 4. Withdraw piston assembly 5. Lift leaf 6 of thimble 9 and pull thimble off piston. Compress spring and slide valve stem 8 out of hole in thimble. Remove spacer and curved washer 10 and remove seal 11 from valve head.

Clean all parts in Girling Cleaning Fluid or methylated spirit. Check bore for wear, corrosion, or scoring. Renew unit if there is any fault. **Always renew the seals.** They are available in kit form. Check that inlet and outlet ports are clear.

Dip all parts in brake fluid and assemble wet. Fit valve seal 11 with flat face to valve shoulder. Fit curved washer

with its domed side against shoulder of valve stem then fit the spacer with its legs towards the valve seal (see parts 10 and also 19 in **FIG 9:9**). Fit spring centrally, with thimble inserted. Press thimble to compress spring and engage valve stem through elongated hole in thimble until it is central.

Fit a new seal to piston with its flat face against shoulder of piston. Insert small end of piston in thimble until leaf on thimble engages behind shoulder. Insert piston assembly, taking care that lip of seal is not trapped or turned back. Fit pushrod and circlip. Smear pushrod and sealing areas of dust cover with Girling Rubber grease and fit cover.

Refitting cylinder:

Reverse the removal procedure and then bleed the system as described in **Section 9:8**.

9:7 Servicing master cylinder (tandem)

The components are shown in **FIG 9:9**. The outlet port nearest the mounting flange is connected by pipes to the front brakes, and the other port to the rear brakes. When brake pressure is applied, the servo unit pushrod forces primary plunger and seal 26 up the bore, tipping valve 29 closes and hydraulic pressure is available for the front brakes. The same pressure compresses springs 7 and 21, causing piston and seal 8 and 9 to move down the bore. Valve 13 is closed and fluid under hydraulic pressure

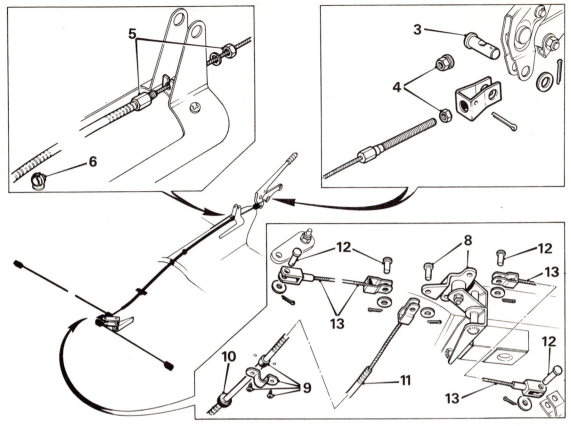

FIG 9:10   Handbrake components and cable assemblies

Key to Fig 9:10   3 Clevis pin   4 Adjusting nut and locknut   5 Cable stop and nut   6 Clip   8 Compensator
10 Grommet   11 Cable   12 Clevis pins   13 Intermediate cables

passes through the outlet part to the rear brakes. Failure of one circuit does not prevent the other from operating. When pistons return, valves 13 and 29 open so that reservoir fluid can replenish the circuits if any has been lost by leakage.

Removing:

Attach bleed tube to bleed screw on a rear wheel cylinder (see **Section 9:8**), open screw one turn and pump brake pedal until reservoir is empty. Do the same at a front wheel bleed screw. Disconnect pipes from cylinder and plug pipes and ports to keep out dirt. **Do not use rag.**

Release cylinder from servo unit (2 nuts). The unit is shown in **FIG 9:12**.

Overhauling:

Refer to **FIG 9:9** and do the following:
1 Release reservoir (2 screws 2) and pivot it to reach nut 4 of tipping valve 5. Remove seal 4. Depress primary plunger (see 26) and remove valve.

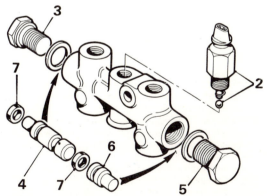

FIG 9:11   Components of pressure differential warning actuator (P.D.W.A.)

Key to Fig 9:11   2 Switch and ball   3 Small plug
4 Long piston   5 Large plug   6 Short piston   7 Seals

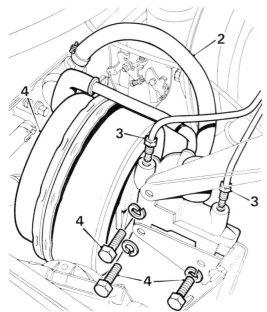

FIG 9:12 Removing a servo unit. 2 is the vacuum hose, 3 the hydraulic outlet pipes and 4 the unit and securing bolts

2 Apply gentle air pressure to the rear outlet to eject the internal parts. Drape in a cloth to prevent loss. Separate plungers from spring. Lift leaf of thimble 11 and pull thimble off secondary plunger 8. Remove seal 9.

3 Compress spring 21 and slide stem of valve 10 out of elongated hole in thimble. Remove spacer and curved washer 12. Remove valve seal 13.

Clean all parts in Girling Cleaning Fluid or methylated spirit. **Do not use any other types of solvent.** Check bore of cylinder. Renew unit if bore is pitted, worn or scored. **Always renew the seals.** These are available in kit form. Check that inlet and outlet ports are clear. Reassemble as follows:

1 Immerse parts in brake fluid and assemble wet. Fit new seal 13 with flat face against valve shoulder. Refit curved washer as shown at 19. Fit spacer with legs towards valve. Insert thimble in spring and locate spring centrally on spacer. Compress spring until valve stem engages elongated hole in thimble. Centralize stem in thimble.

2 Fit new seal to secondary plunger 8 and insert small end of plunger in thimble. Make sure thimble leaf engages behind shoulder on plunger (see 25).

3 Fit seal 26 to primary plunger with flat face against plunger shoulder. Fit intermediate spring 7 and insert complete assembly into bore, taking care not to trap or turn back the seal lips.

4 Refit tipping valve parts 4 and 5, tightening nut to 35 to 45 lbf ft (4.48 to 6.22 kgf m). Refit reservoir.

Refitting:

Refit master cylinder to servo unit and bleed the system as described in **Section 9:8**. Tighten retaining nuts to 17 lbf ft (2.4 kgf m).

9:8 Bleeding hydraulic system

When single master cylinder is fitted:

Provide a supply of new UNIPART 550 Brake Fluid or alternatively a high-boiling point fluid conforming to specification SAE.J1703c (minimum boiling point 260°C or 500°F). **Never use fluid bled from the system, do not let the level in the master cylinder reservoir drop so low that air may enter the system and do not test the brake pedal until the system is fully bled.** Release handbrake and check that all pipe unions are tight.

Start at the rear bleed screw farthest from the master cylinder, move on to the other rear wheel, cross over to the front wheel on the other side and finish at the front brake nearest to the master cylinder.

Attach a rubber or plastic tube to the bleed screw and immerse the free end in a small quantity of clean brake fluid in a glass container. Open the bleed screw about three-quarters of a turn. Make sure the reservoir is full and then ask an assistant to pump the brake pedal in long steady strokes, letting the pedal return freely. Air bubbles may emerge from the immersed end of the tubing at first. When these bubbles cease after further pumping, hold the pedal down at the bottom of a stroke and tighten the bleed screw to 4 to 6 lbf ft (.5 to .8 kgf m). Do not overtighten.

During this operation it is most important to watch the fluid level in the master cylinder reservoir. Keep it topped-up to the level mark (see **Section 9:2**). If the level falls so low that air enters the system it will be necessary to start from the beginning again.

Test the feel of the brake pedal. Travel should be short and the pedal should come up solid. Any sponginess means that there is still air in the system. If pedal travel is excessive, adjust the rear brakes (see **Section 9:2**). Keep brake fluid off paintwork. It is a solvent.

When tandem master cylinder is fitted:

Fill the reservoir with fluid as instructed in the preceding section on the single master cylinder. The grade of fluid must be as specified. Be careful not to spill fluid on the paintwork as it is a solvent.

Start with the pair of brakes on the side of the car on which the master cylinder is mounted. Attach rubber or plastic bleed tubes to the front and rear bleed screws and immerse the free ends in some brake fluid in clean glass containers.

Open both screws half a turn and start with very light strokes of the brake pedal. Do not make complete strokes and let the pedal return unaided. Go on pumping with a slight pause after each stroke. Watch the fluid that emerges from the immersed ends of the tubes and when air bubbles cease, give four more pedal strokes, hold the pedal down and tighten both bleed screws to 4 to 6 lbf ft (.5 to .8 kgf m).

Repeat the procedure on the two brakes on the other side of the car. Keep an eye on the fluid level in the reservoir, topping-up if necessary. The warning about low fluid level given in the single cylinder instructions also applies. When finished, top-up the reservoir to the correct level.

9:9 Handbrake servicing

Adjusting:

If the handbrake is not effective even after rear brake adjustment and it is known that the rear brakes are in perfect order and do not need new linings, it is possible to adjust the cable operation.

Refer to the top view in **FIG 9:4** and to **FIG 9:10**. Set handbrake lever on first ratchet tooth, jack up rear wheels clear of the ground with front wheels chocked and check that moderate hand pressure will turn them. Resistance should be equal and the brake shoes just gripping.

If the wheels are quite free, locate the fork attached to the handbrake lever (see inset, top right in **FIG 9:10**). Slacken locknut 3 (see **FIG 9:4**) and turn adjusting nut 4. Hold the cable with another spanner. After adjustment, pull on handbrake lever by three notches and check that both rear wheels are locked. Release handbrake and check that wheels are free. Tighten locknut.

Look for trouble in the rear brakes if this adjustment fails.

Renewing cables:

Refer to **FIG 9:10**. Remove seat belt centre console and lift rear carpet. Remove pin 3 and unscrew nuts 4. Hold locknut and unscrew cable stop from bracket (see 5). Release cable from clip 6.

Work underneath the car, so jack-up and support securely. Remove pin 8 from rear end of cable 11. Release screws, clip and sleeve 9. Extract rubber grommet 10 from body and pull it along cable. Pull cable out from the rear.

The rear intermediate cables 13 are secured by pins 12. Renew if necessary.

When refitting the cables, lubricate them and all exterior connections with graphite grease. Adjust the rear brake shoes (see **Section 9:2**) and then adjust the handbrake cables as just described.

9:10 Servicing pressure valve and actuator

The pressure reducing valve:

This is a small device located under the car at the rear, adjacent to the suspension arm and having two metal pipes leading into it and the flexible hose to the rear brake leaving it. Its function is to limit the pressure to the rear brakes under heavy braking, to prevent the rear wheels from locking.

If it proves to be faulty it must be renewed as a unit. It is a simple matter to remove it, but release it first before unscrewing it from the flexible hose. Bleed the system after completing the renewal (see **Section 9:8**).

The pressure differential warning actuator (P.D.W.A.):

Refer to **FIG 9:11** which shows that switch and operating ball 2 are fitted into a housing that carries two pistons 4 and 6. These pistons are subject to the two pressures prevailing in the twin circuits of the tandem master cylinder system. One circuit is for the front brakes and the other for the rear. Failure in either circuit causes the pistons to move and operate the switch to complete the warning light circuit. When normally set, the operating

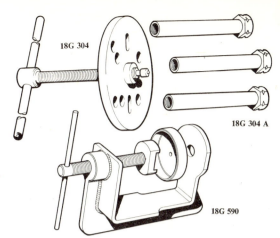

FIG 9:13 Special tools used when servicing the brakes

Key to Fig 9:13 18G.304 Front and rear hub puller 18G.304A Adaptor bolts for puller 18G.590 Clamp for front brake pistons

ball drops into the groove in piston 4. Any imbalance between the pressures on the pistons causes movement to right or to left, the ball is forced out of the groove and it then operates the switch plunger.

The actuator will be found near the tandem master cylinder, at the front of the car and will be recognized by the four metal pipes connected to it, and the electrical cable to the switch.

The actuator is readily removed and dismantled. Discard the copper washers on the end plugs 3 and 5 after removing the switch and ball 2. Extract long piston 4 and then short piston 6. Discard seals 7.

Clean the parts in Girling Cleaning Fluid or methylated spirit, with the exception of the switch. Renew whole unit if pistons or bore show signs of wear, damage or scoring. Reconnect the switch and check that warning lamp lights up when plunger is depressed.

Reassemble with all parts wetted in brake fluid, with the exception of the switch. Fit new piston seals with large diameters facing small-diameter ends of pistons. Fit long piston, groove first and push it in just far enough for the groove to line up with the switch aperture. **Do not let the seal pass the aperture or it will need renewing.** Locate ball in groove in piston, screw in the switch and tighten to 2 to 2.5 lbf ft (.28 to .35 kgf m). Fit small end plug on a new copper washer. Fit the short piston, small-end trailing. Fit large end plug and tighten both plugs to 16 to 20 lbf ft (2.2 to 2.8 kgf m).

Refit the unit and bleed the system (see **Section 9:8**).

9:11 Removing and refitting servo unit

The unit will be recognized from the under-bonnet view in **FIG 9:12**. To remove it, disconnect and remove the windscreen washer bottle. Disconnect vacuum hose 2 from engine intake manifold. Disconnect fluid pipes 3, remove bolts 4 and lift out servo unit.

If the unit is faulty it is best renewed or given to experts for attention. When the unit has been refitted, bleed the system as described in **Section 9:8**. In cases of faulty operation it is wise to check the vacuum hose for collapse or for splits and deterioration before blaming the unit.

9:12 Removing and refitting flexible hoses

Never start to remove a flexible hose by turning the hexagons at each end. First disconnect the metal pipe at the inner or mounting bracket end. Hold the hose hexagon and unscrew the nut securing the hose to the bracket. The hose may now be unscrewed at the other end without strain or twisting. It must be refitted in the reverse manner.

9:13 Handbrake lever and brake pedal

If it is necessary to dismantle the lever, first drive out the small crosspin securing the release button. The pawl and operating rod are carried on a clevis pin secured by a splitpin. The pivot pin for the lever is riveted over. File off the peening and then drive the pin out. When reassembling, grease all working parts.

The brake and clutch pedals are mounted on a common fulcrum pin. To remove the brake pedal, remove the clevis pin securing it to the master cylinder fork. Remove the fulcrum pin, disconnect the return spring and the pedal is free. The clutch pedal can remain in place.

9:14 Fault diagnosis

(a) 'Spongy' brake pedal

1 Leak in hydraulic system
2 Worn master cylinder
3 Leaking wheel cylinder
4 Air in brake fluid
5 Gaps between rear brake linings and shoes

(b) Excessive pedal movement

1 Check 1 and 4 in (a)
2 Rear brakes need adjusting
3 Very low fluid level in reservoir

(c) Brakes grab or pull to one side

1 Distorted or badly worn discs or drums
2 Wet or oily pads or linings
3 Disc loose on hub
4 Worn suspension or steering connections
5 Mixed linings, wrong grade or different thicknesses
6 Unequal tyre pressures
7 Broken shoe return springs
8 Wheel cylinder not sliding on backplate (rear)
9 Seized piston in one brake cylinder
10 Loose caliper or backplate

(d) Excessive pedal pressure needed

1 Check 5 in (c)
2 Leak in vacuum hose to servo unit
3 Defective servo unit
4 Servo filter blocked
5 Brake linings water soaked
6 Linings glazed due to heat
7 Defect in one circuit of dual line system (tandem)

(e) Loss of pedal pressure

1 Defective master cylinder, worn bore, piston or seals
2 Leaking wheel cylinder or servo unit
3 Leaking brake pipes or connections
4 No fluid in master cylinder reservoir

CHAPTER 10

THE ELECTRICAL SYSTEM

10:1 Description

This is a 12-volt system in which the negative terminal of the battery is earthed. A belt-driven alternator provides charging current, the Lucas 17ACR having a higher output than the 16ACR. The starter motor is a Lucas 2M.100 of the pre-engaged type. In this, the pinion is engaged with the flywheel ring gear before the current is switched on automatically. The standard battery is a Lucas A11, but one with a higher capacity may be fitted and this is the A13.

There are wiring diagrams in **Technical Data**. Although servicing instructions are given, we recommend that seriously defective parts be replaced by new ones on an Exchange basis.

10:2 Routine maintenance

Every 3000 miles (5000 km or 3 months) check level of electrolyte (acid) in battery (see **FIG 10:1**). Car must be standing level.

The electrolyte can be seen through the end of the casing (see dotted line). It should be $\frac{1}{4}$ inch (7 mm) below the red top. Alternatively, lift the vent cover vertically and tilt to one side for inspection (see 1). **Do not top-up unless the liquid is below the top of the plate separators. Do not use a naked light to examine the cells, as inflammable gas may be present.**

Top-up with distilled water until the rectangular tubes are full and the bottom of the trough is just covered. Refit the cover and press firmly into place. If weather is cold enough for icing, run the engine immediately after topping up.

At the same intervals, clean off all corrosion with diluted ammonia, dry thoroughly and paint affected parts with anti-sulphuric paint. Smear terminal posts with petroleum jelly and check tightness of connections. Clean mating surfaces of terminals, particularly if the starter does not turn briskly.

Do not leave a battery in a discharged condition. An unused battery should be given a freshening charge every fortnight.

Checking electrolyte for specific gravity:

Every 6000 miles (10,000 km or 6 months), use an hydrometer to check the specific gravity of the electrolyte. Insert the tube into the liquid, squeeze the bulb and

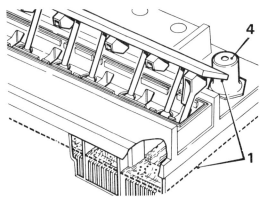

FIG 10:1 Top of battery showing vent cover and electrolyte level 1 and terminal post 4

wait until the float is lifted. Read off the level on the scale of the float. At climates below 27°C (80°F) the readings will indicate conditions as follows:

Cell fully charged	1.270 to 1.290
Cell about half-charged ..	1.190 to 1.210
Cell discharged	1.110 to 1.130

These figures are for an electrolyte temperature of 16°C (60°F). For every 3°C (5°F) above this, add .002 to the specific gravity. Subtract .002 if below. All cells should read about the same. If not, the difference may be due to a defective cell. **Do not try to rectify by adding acid.**

Checking equipment:

Every 3000 miles (5000 km or 3 months), check that all electrical equipment works properly. Check all lights and have the alignment of the head-lamps checked. Operating the switches and brake pedal in a darkened garage will verify the action of the direction indicator and stop lamps.

10:3 Servicing the alternator

Adjusting belt:

Refer to **FIG 10:2**. Check tension midway between pulleys on longest run of belt. Total deflection under normal thumb pressure should be $\frac{1}{2}$ inch (13 mm). To

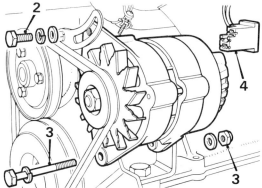

FIG 10:2 Removing alternator, or adjusting belt tension. The link bolt is 2, the pivot bolt and nut 3 and the wiring connector 4

adjust, slacken pivot and link bolts 2 and 3. Move alternator by applying pressure at the mounting bracket **at the driving end only.**

Testing alternator:

Moving coil meters will be required, a voltmeter reading up to 20 volts and an ammeter up to 40 amps.

Before testing ensure that the belt is tensioned correctly, battery is good and connections clean and tight.

First check that battery voltage is reaching the alternator. **Remember the battery must be correctly connected (negative earth).** Remove cable from alternator, connect negative side of voltmeter to earth, switch on ignition and connect voltmeter positive to each of cable connectors in turn.

If no reading at 'IND' connector, check no-charge warning lamp bulb and circuitry. If no reading at main connector, check wiring between battery and alternator. If readings are obtained, do the following:

Reconnect cables. Disconnect brown cable with eyelet, from starter motor solenoid (see **FIG 10:4**). Connect ammeter between brown cable and solenoid terminal. Connect voltmeter across battery. Run engine at alternator revolutions of 6000 and wait for ammeter to settle down.

If no ammeter reading, overhaul alternator. If ammeter reads below 10 amp and voltmeter between 13.6 and 14.4 and battery charge is low, have alternator bench-tested. Correct output is 34 amp at 14 volts at 6000 rev/min.

If ammeter reads below 10 amp and voltmeter below 13.6, renew alternator voltage regulator (see later). If ammeter reads above 10 amp and voltmeter above 14.4 volts, again renew voltage regulator.

Removing alternator:

Refer to **FIG 10:2**, disconnect connector 4, remove pivot and link bolts 2 and 3, disengage the belt and remove the alternator.

Overhauling alternator:

Refer to **FIG 10:3** and do the following:

1 Remove two screws and end cover 2. Detach cable 3. Release brush assemblies (4 screws 4). Release brush holder and regulator (3 screws, see 5).

2 Release regulator (screw 6). Release rectifier earth link (bolt 7). Unsolder stator cables from rectifier (see 8). Hold the diode wires with a pair of pliers to act as a heat sink. This will prevent heat from affecting the diodes. Work quickly to avoid overheating.

3 Release rectifier (nut 9). Mark both end brackets and the stator (11, extreme right) for correct reassembly. Remove bolts 11 and separate the parts. Remove O-ring 12. Remove nut and withdraw pulley and fan (see 13).

4 Remove key and distance piece 14. Press rotor out of end bracket (see 15). Withdraw distance piece 16. Remove circlip to release bearing, cover plates, O-ring and felt washer (see 17).

Inspection:

Check bearings for wear or roughness. If necessary, repack with Shell Alvania RA grease. To renew bearing 18, unsolder connections to slip-ring and pull it off shaft

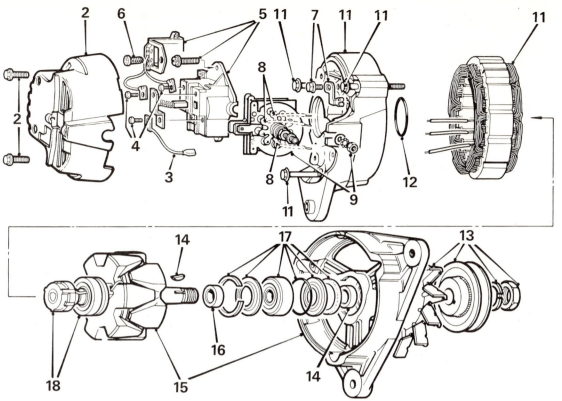

FIG 10:3 Components of the alternator

Key to Fig 10:3 2 End cover and screws   3 Cable to rectifier   4 Brush assembly screws   5 Brush holder and regulator 6 Screw   7 Bolt for earth link   8 Stator cables to rectifier   9 Rectifier nut   11 Slip ring bracket, bolt and stator   12 O-ring 13 Pulley, fan and nut   14 Key and distance piece   15 Rotor and drive-end bracket   16 Distance piece   17 Bearing assembly   18 Rotor bearing and slip ring

(see 18, extreme left). When fitting new bearing make sure shielded side faces the slip-ring. Use Fry's H.T.3 solder to remake the connections.

Clean metal faces of slip-ring with very fine glasspaper. Check field winding insulation by connecting 110-volt A.C. supply and a 15 watt lamp across one of the slip-rings and one of the rotor lobes. Check field windings by connecting an ammeter and then an ohmmeter in series with a 12-volt battery to see whether the current flow is 3 amperes and the resistance is 4.11 to 4.54 ohms. Connect the meter and 12-volt supply across the two slip-rings.

Check stator windings for breaks by using a 12-volt battery and 36-watt lamp. Connect between any two of the cables (see 11, extreme right). Repeat by using the third cable in place of one of the first two.

Check stator winding insulation by using 110-volt A.C. supply and a 15-watt lamp connected between any one of the stator cables and the metal laminations.

Check the nine rectifying diodes (see 8). Connect a 12-volt battery and 1.5-watt lamp between each diode pin and its associated heatsink in the rectifier pack in turn. Reverse the test connections to check that current flows in one direction only. Renew rectifier assembly if a diode is faulty. Check that .20 inch (5 mm) of brush protrudes

beyond brush box. Brush spring should need 9 to 13 oz (255 to 369 g) pressure to bring brush face flush with face of box.

Reassembling:

Reverse the dismantling procedure. Support the inner race of the bearing when refitting the rotor to the bracket at the drive end. Use solder of 'M' grade 45-55 tin-lead to remake the connections to the rectifier pack (see 8). Work quickly and prevent heat flowing to the diodes by gripping their wires with a pair of pliers.

Tighten pulley nut to 25 lbf ft (3.46 kgf m). Have alternator bench-tested for an output of 34 amperes at 14 volts and 6000 rev/min. Refit alternator and tension belt correctly.

10:4 Servicing the starter motor

Removing:

Disconnect the battery, and on cars with automatic transmission, remove the fan and radiator (see **Chapter 4**). Disconnect the four cables, holding the terminal tags stationary while undoing the large nuts. Release starter motor (2 bolts). Note earth cable to one bolt when manual gearbox is fitted.

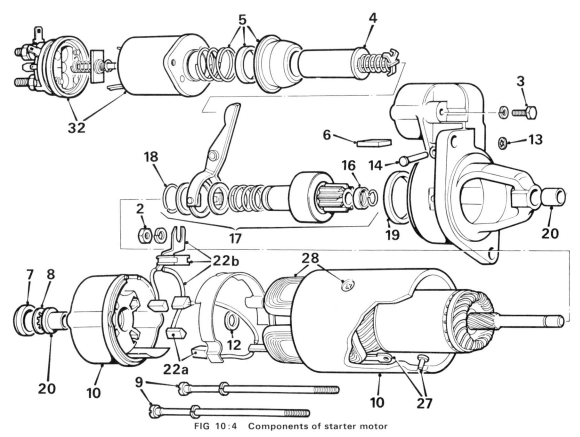

FIG 10:4   Components of starter motor

Key to Fig 10:4 2 Link nut   3 Solenoid bolts   4 Plunger   5 Spring, spring seat and dust excluder   6 Grommet
7 End cap   8 Spire nut   9 Through-bolts   10 End cover and yoke   12 Thrust washer   13 Spire nut   14 Lever pivot pin
16 Thrust collar   17 Pinion drive assembly   18 Spring ring   19 Seal   20 Bushes   22a and 22b Brushes   27 Rivet for
field coil tag   28 Field coils, shoes and screw   32 Solenoid and contacts

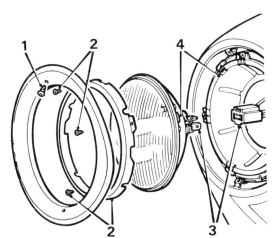

FIG 10:5   How to remove a headlamp sealed-beam
unit. The rim screws are 1, retaining plate screws 2,
cable connections 3 and locating slots and lugs 4

Removing solenoid:

Disconnect the battery. Remove starter (manual gearbox). Disconnect cables (automatic transmission). Slacken nut securing link to solenoid (see 2 in **FIG 10:4**). Remove bolts 3 and withdraw solenoid.

Overhauling starter motor:

Refer to **FIG 10:4** and do the following:

1 Remove solenoid (see preceding instructions). Plunger 4 must be lifted upwards to disengage it from lever. Withdraw parts 5. Withdraw grommet 6. Remove end cap 7. With a cold chisel, remove enough claws from nut 8 to release if from shaft. Remove bolts 9.

2 Withdraw cover and yoke 10 from drive-end bracket. Separate cover from yoke and disengage the brushes (see 22a). Withdraw washer 12.

3 Remove Spire nut 13 and withdraw lever pin 14. Withdraw armature from drive-end bracket. Drive collar 16 off its jump ring, remove ring and remove parts 17. Remove spring ring 18 to release lever, thrust washers and spring from roller clutch drive. Remove seal 19.

Inspection:

Check shaft bushes 20 for wear. When renewing, immerse bushes in engine oil for 24 hours or for 2 hours if oil is at 100°C (212°F). Allow oil to cool before removing bush. **Bushes must not be reamed after fitting.** Press into place with a shouldered mandrel having a diameter to fit in bore of bush of .4377 inch (11.117 mm) at the commutator end of shaft and .4729 inch (12.011 mm) at the driving end.

Check that roller clutch turns freely in one direction and immediately locks when turned in the opposite direction. The drive assembly must move freely on the curved splines on the shaft.

Brushes 22a and 22b must be free in their boxes. Renew if down to a thickness of $\frac{3}{8}$ inch (10 mm). Cut off old field coil brushes, leaving $\frac{1}{4}$ inch (6 mm) of the flexible wire still attached to field coil tag. Solder new brush leads to the old ends. Renew the remaining two brushes complete with terminal and rubber grommet (see 22b). Check brush springs by fitting a new brush which should protrude $\frac{1}{16}$ inch (1.5 mm) under loading of 36 ozf (1.02 kgf). Using 110 volts A.C. and a 15-watt lamp, check the insulation of the brush springs. Lamp must not light when connected between spring and commutator end bracket.

Overheated field coils (see 28) will have tape discoloured by burning. Make sure all field coil connections are sound and then check for continuity by connecting a 12-volt battery and test lamp between either field coil brush and the yoke (the body of the starter motor). Failure under test calls for renewal or repair.

Clean the copper commutator segments that contact the brushes with very fine glasspaper. If badly worn or burned, the commutator may be skimmed in a lathe by mounting the armature between centres. Do not reduce thickness of copper below .14 inch (3.5 mm). After machining, polish with a flat surface of very fine glasspaper. Check windings for earthing by connecting a 15-watt lamp and 110-volt A.C. supply across each commutator segment and the armature shaft. Further tests must be carried out by experts with the necessary equipment.

Check the solenoid windings using a 12-volt battery and an ohmmeter or a moving coil ammeter connected in series across the terminal 'STA' and the solenoid body. Resistance should be 1.01 to 1.07 ohms and current consumption 11.2 to 11.8 amp. If test is satisfactory, solenoid trouble may then be due to faulty contacts. Renew terminal box (see 32, extreme left). Unsolder the winding connectors from the terminal base. Fit new terminal base and contact assembly to solenoid body. Make sure the moving contact registers correctly in the terminal base and that the dowel in the base engages the hole in the solenoid body. Fit the screws and re-solder the winding connections.

Reassembling:

Reverse the dismantling procedure, making sure that the lever is attached to the roller clutch drive in the position shown. Attach solenoid plunger to lever. Lubricate splines on shaft, moving parts of lever, outer surface of roller clutch housing and the lip of seal in drive-end bracket with Shell SB.2628 grease. In very hot climates use Shell Retinax A grease. Fit the spire nut to

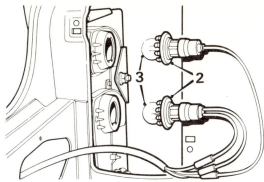

FIG 10:6 Removing tail, stop and flasher bulbs 3. The holders are 2

the armature shaft so that end float measured between nut and flange of bush is .01 inch (.25 mm) maximum.

If it is thought advisable to test the motor while it is removed, connect it across a well-charged battery, using thick cables. The motor should run at high speed, taking about 40 amp at 6000 rev/min.

Refitting:

Reverse the removal sequence. Hold terminal tags of cables while tightening the nuts. Do not overtighten.

10:5 Servicing the lights and switches

Headlamp alignment:

The setting is very critical and is best carried out on optical test equipment. The main beams must be $\frac{1}{2} \pm \frac{1}{4}$ deg. below horizontal and parallel with each other in the straight-ahead position, or in accordance with local regulations. The car must be in normal trim.

Sealed beam unit renewal:

Refer to **FIG 10:5**. Remove rim screws 1, then three retaining-plate screws 2. Pull light unit and plate forward and disconnect cable adaptor 3. When fitting the new unit, make sure the three lugs on the unit engage the slots in the seating (see 4).

Front side and flasher lamps:

Remove the lenses (5 screws). Press bulbs in and turn them anticlockwise to remove. To remove the lamp assembly it is necessary to disconnect the battery and remove the grille.

Tail, stop and flasher lamps:

Refer to **FIG 10:6**. Unclip and fold back the side trim in the luggage compartment. Pull out lampholders 2. Press bulbs in and turn anticlockwise to remove. When refitting holders, note lugs in apertures for correct positioning.

Removing two screws will release the lenses on the 2200. On the Wolseley Six, proceed as for removing the bulbs, release lamp assembly (4 nuts) and then release the lenses (6 screws). Note earthing cable from one nut.

The lamp assembly on the 2200 is held by two nuts inside the body. Note earthing cable under one nut.

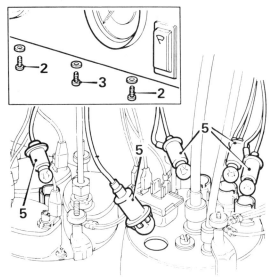

FIG 10:7 Renewing the panel lamp bulbs 5, 2 and 3 are panel fixing screws according to model

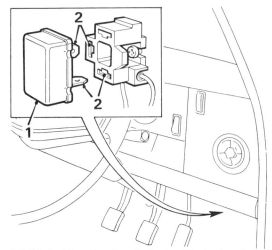

FIG 10:9 The direction indicator (flasher) unit 1 is mounted under the facia. Note contacts 2

Number plate lamps:

Remove lens by pressing in and turning 90 deg. in either direction. Pull bulb out of holder.

To remove lamp assembly, disconnect battery, remove boot lid lock, disconnect cables and release lamp (2 screws). When refitting, make sure cables do not interfere with operation of lock.

Reverse lamp:

Remove cover and lens (2 screws). Lift out festoon bulbs. To remove assembly, disconnect battery, pull cable out of ferrule and release from bumper (2 nuts).

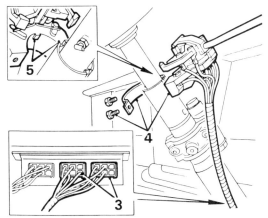

FIG 10:8 Removing the combination switch from the steering column. Wiring connectors are 3, fixing screws 4 and locating lug and slot 5

Roof lamp:

Squeeze the long sides of the lens lightly together to release it. The festoon bulb is removed by pulling it out of the contact clips.

Luggage boot lamp:

Release lamp (2 screws). Detach festoon bulb from contact clips.

Clock bulb:

Disconnect battery. Press clock rim inwards and turn anticlockwise through 30 deg. to release clock. Pull out bulb holder and push and turn bulb in either direction to release it.

Panel lamps:

Refer to **FIG 10:7**. Disconnect battery. On the 2200, remove screws 2 from lower edge of panel. On the Wolseley Six, remove screw 3. Pull lower edge of panel outwards and down. Withdraw bulb holders (see 5), and unscrew bulbs.

Ignition/starter switch:

Remove cowl from steering column (see **Chapter 8**). Remove screw from side of lock housing and withdraw switch from lower end.

Lighting switch:

Release panel from facia (see 'Panel lamps'). On the Six, press inwards the two spring clips behind the panel. On the 2200, press in the four tangs on the switch surround.

Door pillar and boot lamp switches:

These are a simple push-fit and may be pulled out to release them.

116

Stop lamp switch:

This is screwed into its bracket and held by a locknut. When fitting the switch, use a low-voltage lamp and battery across the terminals to check when the contacts open. Screw the switch in another half turn and tighten the locknut.

Combination column switch:

Refer to **FIG 10:8**. To remove the switch, disconnect the battery and remove the cowl (see **Chapter 8**). Disconnect wiring connecters under facia (see 3). Release switch (two screws 4).

When refitting switch make sure that lug in bore of switch registers in slot in top of column (see 5).

Direction indicator (flasher) unit:

Refer to **FIG 10:9**. The unit is a push fit in a socket under the facia on the righthand side panel. When fitting, make sure the contacts engage (see 2).

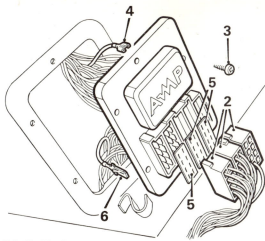

FIG 10:10   Removing the fusebox and connector panel. The multi-connectors are 2, panel screws 3, cables 4, sealing strips 5 and blade with retaining tongue 6

10:6 Fuses and connectors

These are shown in **FIG 10:10**. There are 35 amp fuses under the cover. If a new fuse blows when it is fitted, check all wiring and equipment for faults. Fuses are also fitted in the wiring to some auxiliaries (see, for example, 24 in wiring diagrams). These are always 15 amp unless a different rating is specified by a radio manufacturer. **Always use the correct fuse rating and never substitute with wire or any other metal connector.**

To remove the panel, disconnect the battery and pull off connectors 2. Remove six screws 3. Withdraw cables 4. Remove sealing strips 5. Insert a probe into the rectangular slot at the side of each terminal blade to depress the tongue on the blade (see 6). This will release the blades. Remove the connector panel.

Use the wiring diagram when refitting cables to fusebox (see **Technical Data**). Use the following cable colour code when inserting the blades into the connector panel:

B Black G Green LG Light Green N Brown P Purple R Red U Blue W White Y Yellow

The colour code for the terminals is as follows:

Terminal number		Terminal letters				
		B	C	D	E	F
4	.. ..	RG	GU	W	BLG	
3	.. ..	GW	NLG	WR	G	
2	.. ..	UR	RLG	N	PB	
1	.. ..	UW	GR	N	ULG	NY

Note that N in the lowest row is a short cable that goes to the terminal blade on the fusebox. When a cable has two colour code letters, the first is the main colour and the second the tracer colour.

10 : 7 Electrical instruments

A stabilized voltage is needed for these. The voltage stabilizer is mounted on the speedometer just behind the hole for the foremost bulb in **FIG 10:7**. It is reached by following the instructions under 'Panel lights' in **Section 10:5**.

The coolant temperature gauge is behind the lefthand bulb. The thermal transmitter is screwed into the thermostat housing on the engine and can be traced by the single cable attached to it. Before removing it, partially drain the cooling system (see **Chapter 4**).

The fuel gauge is in front of the lefthand bulb in the illustration. The tank unit is under the floor of the luggage compartment. To remove it, make sure that fuel level is low. Remove floor covering and access plate (4 screws). Disconnect cable. Release unit by turning locking ring by means of lugs. Tool 18G.1001 is made for the job and consists of a short length of thin-walled tubing, slotted to fit the lugs.

When refitting the tank unit, make sure the sealing ring is in good condition.

10:8 Fault diagnosis

(a) Battery discharged

1 Terminals loose or dirty
2 Shorts in lighting circuits
3 Alternator faulty
4 Battery internally defective

(b) Insufficient charging current

1 Check 1 and 3 in (a)
2 Driving belt slipping

(c) Battery will not hold charge

1 Low electrolyte level
2 Battery plates sulphated
3 Electrolyte leaking from cracked case
4 Plate separators defective

(d) Battery overcharged

1 Regulator faulty

(e) Alternator output low or nil

1 Broken or slipping belt
2 Regulator or rectifier faulty
3 Worn bearings, bent shaft
4 Worn, burned or shorted slip rings
5 Brushes sticking, springs weak or broken
6 Battery voltage not reaching alternator

(f) Starter motor lacks power or will not operate

1 Battery discharged, terminals loose or dirty
2 Starter pinion jammed in engagement
3 Starter switch or solenoid faulty
4 Brushes worn or sticking. Leads faulty, springs weak
5 Commutator dirty or worn
6 Armature shaft bent
7 Engine abnormally stiff, perhaps after overhaul
8 Windings faulty

(g) Starter motor runs but will not engage

1 Pinion seized on shaft
2 Defective roller clutch
3 Worn or broken teeth

(h) Starter motor rough or noisy

1 Worn bearings or shaft
2 Worn teeth on pinion or ring gear
3 Mounting bolts loose

(i) Lamps inoperative or erratic

1 Battery low, bulbs burned out
2 Faulty earthing of lamps or battery
3 Switches faulty, connections loose or broken

(j) Wiper motor sluggish

1 Faulty windings
2 Bearings dry
3 Commutator dirty

(k) Fuel or instrument gauges do not work

1 Breaks in wiring
2 Voltage stabilizer faulty
3 Instruments and transmitters at fault

CHAPTER 11

THE BODYWORK

11:1 Bodywork finish

Leave serious body damage to the experts. However, small dents and scratches may be filled and then painted with self-spraying cans of colour in the maker's shades. Remove wax polish with white spirit, but if silicone polish has been used, a very fine abrasive will be needed.

Use primer surfacer or paste stopper according to the amount of filling required. When dry, rub down with 400 grade 'Wet or Dry' paper and plenty of water. Surface must be perfectly smooth and flush to get a good finish. Several light coats of paint are better than a heavy application that may cause runs. When finish is dry, blend it with a cutting compound and then use a liquid polish.

11:2 Fitting seat belts

The various makes are provided with comprehensive fitting instructions. Any owner who doubts his ability to make a first-class job of fitting the type he has chosen, should entrust the work to a competent garage. It is dangerous to take chances.

Renew seat belt assemblies that have been used in a car that has suffered severe impact in an accident.

11:3 Servicing doors

Removing trim pad:

Access to door mechanism is achieved by removing the interior trim pad (see **FIG 11:1**). First open the window and then remove the regulator handle 2. Withdraw the halves of the plastic trim round the lock control, one upwards and the other downwards (see 3).

Remove 2200 arm rest (2 screws 4). On the Six, remove armrest (3 screws) and then remove the bracket (2 screws). On the 2200, release bottom of door pocket (3 screws 5). Lever trim pad away from door. It will need easing upwards to release the upper clips 6.

When refitting, any clips that remained on the door when the pad was removed should be re-located on the trim pad. Note that locating dowel on regulator handle escutcheon must be at the bottom.

Removing glass and regulator:

Remove trim pad plastic sheet from door panel. Wind glass right down and disengage regulator from channel on bottom edge (see 7 in **FIG 11:2**). Turn glass by lifting rear edge and pull upwards so that it passes outside the top frame of the door.

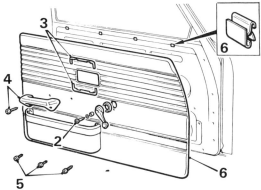

FIG 11:1 Removing the front door trim pad. The numbers are used in the text

Remove screws 3, collapse the regulator assembly and withdraw it through end aperature (see 4). Front door is shown. Principle is the same for rear doors.

Checking and adjusting door locks:

In the case of unsatisfactory operation, do not dismantle any lock parts until the sequence of opening and shutting the door and locking and unlocking it have been tried. Note that the front door locking latch cannot be set in the locked position while the door is open.

To check and adjust the outside pushbutton, refer to **FIG 11:3**. The under side of the head of the plunger screw 9 must project $\frac{1}{4}$ inch (6.4 mm) as shown at 'A'. Close the door or use a screwdriver to close the latch (see outside slot in lefthand view of **FIG 11:4**). Press button which should move noticeably before sliding contactor in latch unit begins to rise, and releases from the striker before full depression of button.

To adjust, disconnect lower end of link rod 12 and lift it to expose the screw.

To check and adjust the remote control, slacken the fixing screws securing it to the door. Move the control towards the latch unit without compressing the rod spring, until the latch release lever touches its stop (see 6 and lever in **FIG 11:4**). Tighten the screws. Close the door or move the latch disc to the latched position and check operation of release lever. It should release striker before completing its full movement. On rear doors, check that children's safety catch can be moved upwards to block release lever when the latch is open.

To check and adjust the lock control rod, refer to central view in **FIG 11:3**. Set latch in locked position (see lefthand view of **FIG 11:4**). The latch is in the slot. Operating rod 20 engages a quadrant. Set this into the locked position, nearest the latch unit. Move latch release lever to locked position (see lever for rod 6 in **FIG 11:4**). Check by releasing rod 20 (spring clip). It should enter hole in locking quadrant without strain. If it does not line up, turn threaded trunnion 21 until aligned and then secure rod with spring clip.

Adjusting striker:

This is shown on the right in **FIG 11:3**. **Do not try to close the door without checking that the latch disc is open.** This will be seen in the slot shown on the left in **FIG 11:4**. If it is closed, operate the pushbutton and draw a screwdriver through the latch disc. **Do not slam the door while making adjustments.**

Slacken screws 22 slightly so that striker plate can move. Shut the door and pull it out or push it in until it lines up with the body. Do not use the pushbutton. Open the door gently with the pushbutton and scribe round the striker plate to establish its horizontal position. Remove the striker plate stop.

Set the striker plate loop at righthangles to the axis of the hinges and tighten the screws. Shut and open the door to check whether it drops or lifts. The striker plate may be moved vertically to correct these defects.

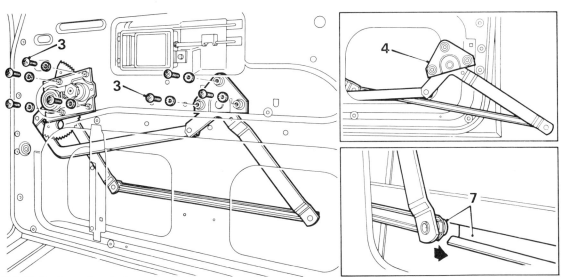

FIG 11:2 Removing the front door window regulator, showing the fixing screws 3, control being withdrawn 4 and arm engaging in channel 7

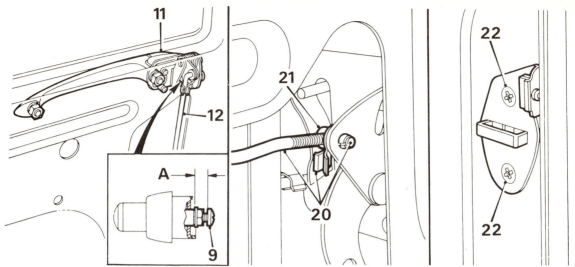

FIG 11:3   Adjusting door locking mechanism. Push button screw 9 and correct dimension at 'A' (left), where 11 is the push button and 12 the link. Locking quadrant adjustment 20 and 21 (centre) and striker plate screws 22 (right)

The position is correct if the door can be closed easily, and without dropping or lifting. When closed, it should be possible to press the door inwards a fraction against its seals. If not, the striker is set too far in.

Renewal of the striker plate is possible by removing the trim over an adjacent hole in the inner panel.

Removing and refitting door lock:

Refer to **FIG 11 : 4**. Remove trim pad and then remove sealing material 2 from hole near latch unit. Ease window channel 3 out of its frame. Disconnect link 4 and upper end of link 5. Disconnect rod 6 from latch release lever. Disconnect rod 7 from latch locking lever. Release latch unit (four screws 8).

In the case of the lock for rear doors, the operation is the same except that there is no rod 5.

Refitting the lock is the reverse of removal.

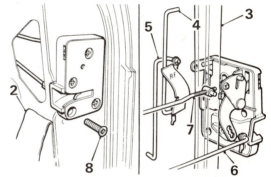

FIG 11 : 4   Removing a front door lock

Key to Fig 11 : 4   2 Plastic seal   3 Glazing channel   4 Link (pushbutton to latch)   5 Link (private lock to latch)   6 Release rod   7 Locking rod   8 Latch unit screw

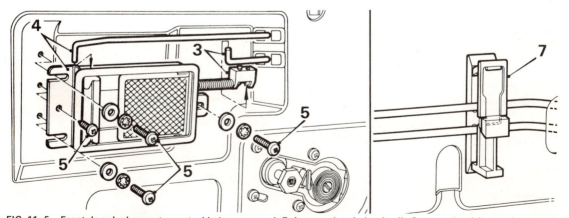

FIG 11 : 5   Front door lock remote control being removed. Release rod and plastic clip 3, control rod 4, securing screws 5 and clip for rods 7 (rear door)

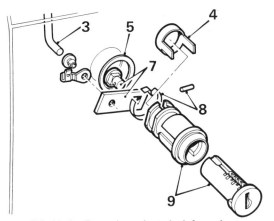

FIG 11:6   Removing private lock from door

Key to Fig 11:6   3 Operating link   4 Spring collar   5 Seal
7 Lever and pivot   8 Spring clip and pin   9 Locking
barrel and body

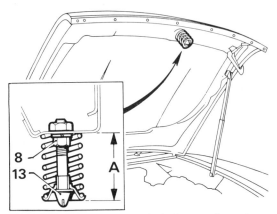

FIG 11:7   Adjusting bonnet lock. Correct dimension at
'A'. Locknut is 8 and locking pin 13

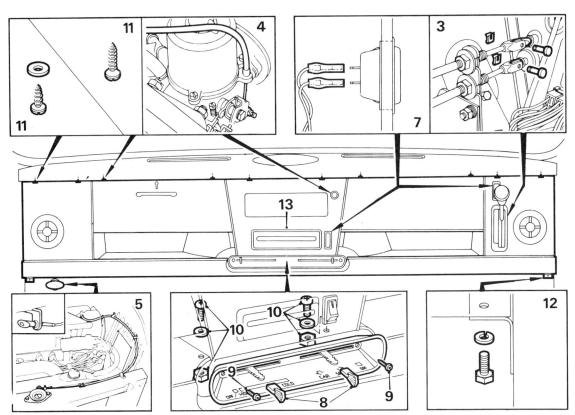

FIG 11:8   Operations involved when removing the facia. The numbers are used in the text

Removing and refitting remote control:

Refer to **FIG 11:5**. Remove trim pad and plastic sealing. Detach release rod from plastic clip (see 3). Detach lock control rod 4. Remove screws 5.

When refitting on rear doors, ensure that rods are located in plastic clip 7. Check and adjust the rods on either door as instructed in 'Checking and adjusting door locks'.

Renewing private lock:

Refer to **FIG 11:6**. Remove trim pad and plastic seal. Disconnect link 3. Prise off spring collar 4 and remove lock 9 and self-adhesive seal 5.

To renew locking barrel, mark fitted position of lever and associated parts (see 7). Remove spring clip and pin 8 and withdraw operating pivot. Insert key and withdraw lock barrel from body (see 9).

Reassemble in the reverse order. Engage legs of spring collar 4 in grooves in body. With seal in place, insert lock in door and give face of locking barrel a sharp blow to force the collar inwards so that the legs engage behind the panel.

Lubrication:

Do not use grease in key lock barrels. Smear linkages inside door panel with grease. Put a few drops of thin oil in key slots or use graphite powder.

11:4 Bonnet and boot lid locks
Bonnet lock:

If bonnet does not lock properly, check locking lever and cable operations. If satisfactory, check dimension 'A' in **FIG 11:7**. It should be about 2.25 inch (57 mm). To adjust, slacken locknut 8 and turn pin 13 as required. Tighten locknut and check.

Boot lid lock:

The striker plate on the rear panel has slotted holes for adjustment. Mark round the plate edges before slackening the two bolts, so that the plate may be restored to its original position if necessary. Mark round the lock for the same reason, if removal is indicated.

The lock and pushbutton are accessible after removing the chrome moulding that carries the number plate lamp. The fixing screws are under the boot lid sealing rubber. Pull this out of its channel. Release the lamp unit (2 screws). Removing a circlip will release the pushbutton assembly.

11:5 Removing and refitting facia
Removing:

Refer to **FIG 11:8**. Disconnect battery. On manual gearchange and power steering models, disconnect electrical connector and remove steering column (see **Chapter 8**). When automatic transmission is fitted, disconnect gear selector linkage inside engine compartment (see 3).

Disconnect choke cables at carburetters (see 4). Disconnect bonnet lock cable at the lock and release from clips (see 5). Disconnect and remove instrument panel complete (see **Chapter 10**). Disconnect wiring from heater blower and windscreen washer switches

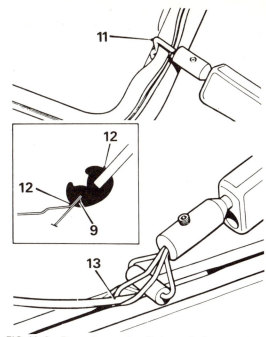

FIG 11:9 Removing and refitting windscreen glass, showing body flange 9, tool lifting rubber lip over glass 11, places to inject sealer 12 and finisher strip 13 being inserted in rubber surround

(see 7). Pull knobs 8 off heater controls. Detach heater indicator panel (two screws 9). Remove heater control (fixings 10).

Remove 10 screws at top of facia (see 11). The four countersunk screws will be found above the instrument panel and the glovebox. Remove bolts 12, pull facia outwards, withdraw the cables and remove facia from car.

Refitting:

Reverse the dismantling procedure. Make sure the cables are routed correctly and securely connected. The air vent hoses must be located on the vents and intakes. Check heater controls.

11:6 Seat fixings
Front seats:

To remove, unscrew bolts holding rear ends of runners to body. Push seat to rear and remove front fixings from runners. The runners are secured to the seat frame by nuts and spring washers.

When refitting, the runner with locking lever goes on the inner member of the seat frame.

Rear seats:

The seat may be lifted out of the seat pan. To remove the squab (back), remove the screws securing the bottom edge, then lift the squab straight up to release it from clips on the back panel.

When refitting, make sure the rod along the top of the squab engages in the clips.

11:7 Renewing windscreen and vents

Removing windscreen:

Refer to **FIG 11:9**. Prise wiper arms off spindles. Lift up the end of the finishing strip and pull it from the channel in the windscreen surround. Working inside the car, press the glass outwards at a top corner and gradually ease it out of the rubber. Pull rubber off body flange.

If glass has broken, make quite sure that all particles are removed from heater and demist ducts and tubes. Disconnect demist ducts and use compressed air. Remove particles from rubber surround and check it for cuts or deterioration. Renew if necessary.

Refitting windscreen:

Clean old sealer from body flange and check flange for damage. Fit sealing rubber to flange (see 9). Wet channel in rubber with a weak solution of soap and water. Working outside the car, place the lower edge of the glass into the channel and use tool 18G.468 to peel the rubber lip carefully over the glass (see 11). The tool is like a shallow 'M' with a long leg that fits into the handle.

Inject glazing compound (Dunlop DP. 421/2G) into channels between glass and flange (see 12). Use tool 18G.468B to fit the finisher strip 13. The eye of the tool runs in a groove and the roller presses the strip into place. Rock the tool when rounding the corners. Clean off surplus sealer.

Removing and refitting rear screen:

Use the same methods are described for the front windscreen, but remember the supply and earthing cables to the heating element. Connect these when inserting the lower edge of the glass during refitting.

Quarter lights:

To remove, open the window and release the catch from the back panel. Hold the window half open and pull it upwards and to the rear to release the hinges from the locating rubbers in the body.

When refitting, lubricate the slots with rubber grease or liquid soap.

APPENDIX

TECHNICAL DATA

Engine   Fuel system   Ignition system   Cooling system
Clutch   Synchromesh transmission   Automatic transmission
Final drive   Steering   Suspension   Brakes
Electrical equipment   Tyres   Capacities
Weights and dimensions   Torque wrench settings

WIRING DIAGRAMS

HINTS ON MAINTENANCE AND OVERHAUL

GLOSSARY OF TERMS

INDEX

NOTES

TECHNICAL DATA

(Inch sizes are given first, followed by metric sizes in brackets)

Engine:

Type	23H, six cylinder
Capacity	135.8 cu in (2227 cu cm)
Bore	3.00 (76.2)
Stroke	3.20 (81.28)
Compression ratio (h.c.)	9.0 to 1
Firing order	1, 5, 3, 6, 2, 4
Idling speed	600 rev/min
Fast idle speed	1100 rev/min

Crankshaft:

Type	7 main bearings
Main journal diameter	2.2515 to 2.2520 (57.20 to 57.21)
Crankpin journal diameter	1.8759 to 1.8764 (47.62 to 47.64)
Undersizes (main and crankpin)	.010, .020, .030 and .040 (.25, .51, .76 and 1.02)
End float	.002 to .003 (.05 to .07)
End float adjustment	Selective thrust washers on each side of No. 3 main bearing

Main bearings:

Type	Thin wall, steel-backed halves
Length	.811 to .821 (203.47 to 203.73)
Diametrical clearance	.002 to .0035 (.05 to .076)

Connecting rods:

Type	Horizontally split big-ends, plain small-ends
Length between centres	5.828 to 5.832 (148.02 to 148.12)
End float on crankpin	.006 to .010 (.15 to .25)
Small-end diameter	.811 to .8115 (20.59 to 20.61)
Bearings	Thin wall, steel-backed halves
Length of bearings	.660 to.665 (16.75 to 16.89)
Diametrical clearance of bearings	.0015 to .003 (.038 to .076)

Pistons:

Type	Aluminium, solid skirt, slotted
Clearance in cylinder:	
Top (below oil control groove)	.0018 to .0024 (.045 to .061)
Bottom	.001 to .0016 (.025 to .039)
Rings	3 compression, 1 oil control
Width of ring grooves:	
Compression	.064 to .065 (1.64 to 1.66)
Oil control	.1565 to .1575 (4.962 to 4.987)
Gudgeon pin bore	.8126 to .8128 (20.64 to 20.65)
Oversizes	.010 and .020 (.254 and .508)

Piston rings:

Type:	
Top	Plain, chrome-faced sintered alloy
Second and third	Tapered, sintered alloy
Oil control	Two chrome-faced rings with expander
Width:	
Compression	.0615 to .0625 (1.55 to 1.60)
Oil control	.10 to .105 (2.54 to 2.66)
Ring to groove clearance (compression)	.0015 to .0035 (.03 to .08)
Fitted gap:	
Compression	.011 to .022 (.350 to .550)
Oil control	.015 to .045 (.38 to 1.14)

Gudgeon pin:

Type	Press fit in connecting rod
Diameter	.8123 to .8125 (20.63 to 20.64)
Fit in piston	Hand push-fit at 20°C (68°F)
Fit in small-end (interference)	.0008 to .0015 (.02 to .04)

Camshaft:

Type	Four-bearing, chain driven, overhead
Bearings	Direct in aluminium carrier
Journal diameter:	
Front	1.9355 to 1.9365 (49.185 to 49.197)
Second	1.9668 to 1.9678 (49.975 to 49.987)
Third	1.998 to 1.999 (50.762 to 50.775)
Fourth	2.0293 to 2.0303 (51.534 to 51.569)
Diametrical clearance	.002 to .003 (.05 to .09)
End float	.002 to .007 (.05 to .17)
Thrust taken	On locating plate at front end
End float adjustment	Renewal of plate
Valve timing marks	Alignment marks on camshaft sprocket, carrier and flywheel
Drive	Chain and sprockets from crankshaft
Chain	.375 (9.52) pitch x 108 pitches

Tappets:

Type	Bucket, with internal shims for valve adjustment

Valves:

Seat angle	$45\frac{1}{4}$ deg.
Head diameter:	
Inlet..	1.5 (38.1)
Exhaust	1.216 to 1.220 (30.88 to 31.04)
Stem diameter (both)	.3115 to .3120 (7.91 to 7.93)
Stem clearance (both)	.0015 (.038)
Lift (both)	.36 (.91)
Running clearance (adjust only if less than .012 (.31):	
Inlet..	.016 to .018 (.41 to .46)
Exhaust	.020 to .022 (.51 to .56)
Clearance for timing purposes only (both) ..	.021 (.53)

Valve springs (approx):

Free length	1.797 (45.70)
Fitted length	1.38 (35.05)
Load at fitted length	52 lb (23.6 kg)

Valve timing:

Inlet	Opens 9 deg. 4' BTDC, closes 50 deg. 56' ABDC (see following setting)
Exhaust	Opens 48 deg. 56' BBDC, closes 11 deg. 4' ATDC (with clearance set at .021 (.53)
Timing marks	Notch on crankshaft pulley, marks on front cover

Lubrication system:

Type	Wet sump, pressure feed
Oil pump	Concentric, serviced as a unit
Oil filter	Fullflow, paper element
Pressure:	
Running	60 lb/sq in (4.2 kg/sq cm)
Idling	15 to 60 lb/sq in (1.1 to 4.2 kg/sq cm)

FUEL SYSTEM

Carburetters:
Make and type	Twin SU, HS6
Piston springs	Red
Jet size	.100 (2.54)
Needles (standard)	BBD

Fuel pump:
Make and type	Electric SU, AUF.222

Air cleaner:
Type	Two paper elements

IGNITION SYSTEM

Sparking plugs:
Make and type	Champion N-9Y
Gap	.025 (.65)

Coil:
Type	Lucas HA.12

Distributor:
Make and type	Lucas 25.D6
Rotation of rotor	Anticlockwise (from above)
Dwell angle	35 deg. $\pm$ 2 deg.
Contact points gap	.014 to .016 (.35 to .40)
Capacitor (condenser) capacity	.18 to .25 mF
Serial number	41295

Ignition timing:
Stroboscopic at 1000 rev/min with vacuum disconnected	12 deg. BTDC
Advance check at 2000 rev/min with vacuum disconnected	19 to 23 deg. BTDC

COOLING SYSTEM

Type	Pressurized spill return with thermostat. Pump and thermostatically controlled electric fan

Thermostat opens:
Standard	74°C (165°F)
Cold climates	88°C (190°F)
Pressure cap	Releases at 15 lb/sq in (1.05 kg/sq cm)
Driving belt	Tensioned to $\frac{1}{2}$ inch (13 mm) deflection in middle of longest run

CLUTCH

Make and type	Borg and Beck, narrow diaphragm

Clutch plate:
Diameter	8.75 (222)
Damper springs:	
Colour and number	Dark Grey/Orange (2), Pink/Dark Grey (2), Dark Grey/Light Green (1) and Dark Grey/Buff (1)
Release bearing	Ball journal
Master cylinder bore	.625 (15.87)
Slave cylinder bore	.875 (22.2)
Fluid	See 'Brake fluid'

SYNCHROMESH TRANSMISSION

Type .. ..   Four forward speeds and reverse. Synchromesh on forward gears

Ratios:

	Gearbox	Overall
Top	1.00 to 1	3.88 to 1
Third	1.38 to 1	5.37 to 1
Second	2.06 to 1	7.99 to 1
First	3.29 to 1	12.78 to 1
Reverse	3.07 to 1	11.94 to 1

End float:

Idler gear	.003 to .008 (.08 to .20)
1st and 3rd speed gears	.006 to .008 (.15 to .20)
2nd speed gear	.005 to .008 (.13 to .20)
Laygear	.002 to .003 (.05 to .08)

AUTOMATIC TRANSMISSION

Make and type .. ..   Borg-Warner, model 35

Primary drive:

Type	Chain and sprockets
Ratio	1.03 to 1 (38/39)

Ratios:

	Gearbox	Overall (1 to 1)
First	2.39 to 1	9.42 to 1
Second	1.45 to 1	5.71 to 1
Top	1.0 to 1	3.95 to 1
Reverse	2.09 to 1	8.23 to 1

FINAL DRIVE

Type .. ..   Integral with gearbox. Helical gears and differential

Ratios:

Synchromesh gearbox	3.88 to 1 (17/66)
Automatic transmission	3.83 to 1 (18/69)

Differential bearings .. ..   Preload .003 to .005 (.08 to .13)

Road speed at 1000 rev/min in top:

Synchromesh gearbox	18.1 mile/hr (29 km/hr)
Automatic transmission	17.8 mile/hr (28.5 km/hr)

Drive shafts .. ..   Unequal length, solid, Hardy Spicer with constant velocity joints

STEERING

Alignment:

Front wheel toe-in	$\frac{1}{8}$ (3.2)
Angle of inner wheel with outer wheel at 20 deg.	$21\frac{1}{2}$ deg. $\pm$ 1 deg.

Manual steering:

Type	Rack and pinion
Steering wheel turns	3.8 (lock to lock)
Pinion bearing preload	.001 to .003 (.03 to .08)
Damper movement	.001 to .006 (.03 to .15)

Power-assisted steering:

Type	Rack and pinion with integral power assistance
Steering wheel turns	3.56 (lock to lock)
Damper movement	.008 to .011 (.20 to .28)
Belt tension at centre of run	.50 (12.7) total deflection under thumb pressure

SUSPENSION

Trim height (unladen)	$14\frac{7}{8} \pm \frac{1}{4}$ (378 $\pm$ 6) at hub centre to wheel arch
Pressure (unladen)	245 lb/sq in (17.2 kg/sq cm)

Front:

Type	Independent, unequal arms, trailing tie-rods, Hydrolastic displacers
Swivel hub inclination (unladen)	12 deg. $\pm \frac{3}{4}$ deg.
Camber angle (unladen)	$1\frac{1}{2}$ deg. $\pm \frac{3}{4}$ deg. positive
Castor angle	2 deg. $\pm$ 1 deg. positive
Wheel bearing end float	Zero to .004 (.10)

Rear:

Type	Independent with trailing arms and Hydrolastic displacers
Wheel alignment (unladen)	Parallel
Camber (unladen)	$\frac{1}{2}$ deg. positive
Wheel bearing end float	Zero to .002 (.05)

BRAKES

Type:

Front	Girling hydraulic disc
Rear	Girling drum with leading and trailing shoes
Handbrake	Mechanical on rear
Both	Vacuum servo assisted. With single master cylinder, rear brakes have pressure-reducing valve. Tandem master cylinder system has pressure control valve
Fluid	Unipart 550 (or fluid conforming to Specification SAE.J1703a)

Front:

Disc diameter	9.7 (246)
Pad material	Ferodo 2430.F
Minimum pad thickness	$\frac{1}{16}$ (1.6)

Rear:

Drum diameter..	9 (229)
Linings:	
Dimensions	1.75 x 8.687 (44.5 x 220.65)
Material	DON 242.FE
Wheel cylinder bore	.70 (17.8) stamped on body

Servo unit:

Single master cylinder (RH steering)	Girling Powerstop Mk 2B, hydraulically operated
Single or tandem master cylinder (LH steering)	Girling Super Vac, mechanically operated from brake pedal

Master cylinder:

Single:	
Type	C.V. (centre valve)
Bore diameter	.75 (19)
Tandem:	
Type	C.V./T.V. (tipping valve)
Bore diameter	.812 (20.6)

Control valve:

Mounting angle:	
Pressure reducing valve	9 to 11 deg. to the righthand side
Pressure control valve	13 deg. to the rear

ELECTRICAL EQUIPMENT

Battery:

Make and type	Lucas A11 or A13 (both 12-volt)
Capacity at 20-hr rate	50 Ah (A11), 60 Ah (A13)
Earthing	Negative terminal

Alternator:

Type	Lucas 16.ACR or 17.ACR
Output at 14 volts and 6000 rev/min	34 amp (16.ACR), 36 amp (17.ACR)
Rotor winding resistance at 20°C (68°F) ..	4.33 ohm ±5% (16.ACR), 4.165 ohm ±5% (17.ACR)
Brush length (new)	.50 (12.6)
Minimum brush length	.20 (5.0) protruding from box
Spring tension (brush face flush with box) ..	7 to 10 ozf (200 to 280 gf)

Starter motor:

Make and type	Lucas 2M.100 with pre-engaged pinion
Light running current	40 amp at 6000 rev/min
Minimum brush length	.38 (9.5)
Brush spring tension	36 ozf (1.02 kgf)

Wiper motor:

Make and type	Lucas 14.WA
Running current (rack disconnected):	
Low speed	1.5 amp
High speed	2 amp
Wiper speed after 60 seconds:	
Low speed	46 to 52 rev/min
High speed	60 to 70 rev/min
Armature end float	.002 to .008 (.05 to .20)
Brush spring tension	5 to 7 ozf (140 to 200 gf)
Minimum brush length	.18 (4.7)
Maximum pull to move rack in tubes	6 lbf (2.7 kgf)

Horns:

Make and type	Lucas 9H, Clear Hooters F725/N or Lucas 6H
Maximum current consumption	3.5 to 4 amp (Lucas 6H-3 amp)

TYRES

Size and type	165 x 14 tubeless radial (e.g. Dunlop SP.68, 165SR x 14)
Pressures (normal):	
Front (tubeless)	30 lb/sq in (2.1 kg/sq cm)
Rear (tubeless)	24 lb/sq in (1.7 kg/sq cm)

CAPACITIES

Fuel tank	12½ gal (15 U.S. gal or 56.7 litre)
Cooling system (with heater)	17 pint (20.5 U.S. pint or 9.6 litre)
Steering system:	
Manual rack	$\frac{1}{3}$ pint (.50 U.S. pint or .2 litre)
Power rack	$\frac{1}{3}$ pint (.50 U.S. pint or .2 litre)
Power pump system	2 pint (2.5 U.S. pint or 1.1 litre)

Transmission system:

Casing (manual gearchange)	Refill, with filter change, 19 pint (22.8 U.S. pint or 10.8 litre)
Filter only	1 pint (1.2 U.S. pint or .6 litre)
Casing (automatic):	
Refill engine sump	10 pint (12 U.S. pint or 5.7 litre)
Engine filter only	1 pint (1.2 U.S. pint or .6 litre)
Gearbox only	8 pint (9.6 U.S. pint or 4.5 litre)
Gearbox with torque converter	13 pint (15.6 U.S. pint or 7.4 litre)

WEIGHTS AND DIMENSIONS

Weights:

Dry:	
Synchromesh	2511 lb (1139 kg)
Automatic	2560 lb (1161 kg)
Kerbside (to include oil, fuel and water):	
Synchromesh	2617 lb (1187 kg)
Automatic	2663 lb (1204 kg)

Weights (loading):

Vehicle loading with 5 passengers and 125 lb (57 kg) luggage	880 lb (400 kg)
Maximum roof rack load	132 lb (60 kg), but take vehicle loading into account
Towing hitch load	75 to 100 lb (34 to 45 kg)—see preceding note
Maximum weight for towing up 1 in 8 in first gear	2240 lb (1016 kg)—see preceding note

Dimensions:

Overall length	13 ft 10.55 inch (4.20 m)
Overall width	5 ft 6.87 inch (1.70 m)
Overall height unladen	4 ft 8.3 inch (1.43 m)
Wheelbase unladen	8 ft 10 inch (2.69 m)
Ground clearance	6.5 inch (165 mm)

TORQUE WRENCH SETTINGS

These are in lbf ft, or in kgf m in brackets

Engine:

Oil filter bolt	20 (2.8)
Cylinder head bolts	60 (8.3)
Lifting bracket bolts	30 (4.1)
Camshaft carrier to cylinder head:	
$\frac{1}{2}$ AF	25 (3.5)
$\frac{9}{16}$ AF	30 (4.1)
Camshaft sprocket	35 (4.8)
Camshaft cover	6 (.80)
Thermostat housing to cylinder head	10 (1.4)
Manifold to cylinder head:	
Studs	15 (2.1)
Nuts	20 (2.8)
Adaptor plugs	30 (4.1)
Carburetter studs	6 to 8 (.80 to 1.1)
Water pump:	
Bolts	20 (2.8)
Plug (body)	35 (4.8)
Pulley	10 (1.4)

Front cover:
Studs	6 (.80)
Nuts	18 (2.5)

Flywheel housing:
Studs	6 (.80)
Nuts and bolts	18 (2.5)

Crankshaft pulley bolt	60 to 70 (8.3 to 9.7)
Timing cover, chain guide strips and pivot pin	20 (2.8)
Big-end nuts	33 $\pm$ 2 (4.6 $\pm$ .30)
Mainbearing bolts	70 (9.7)
Flywheel bolts..	60 (8.3)
Oil pump bolt	20 (2.8)
Engine mounting locknuts	30 (4.1)

Crankcase lower adaptor (automatic):
Screws	30 (4.1)
Bolts	20 to 25 (2.8 to 3.4)

Clutch:
Cover	15 (2.1)
Clutch to pressure plate	35 (4.8)
Thrust plate bolt	10 (1.4)
Slave cylinder bolts	20 (2.8)

Transmission:
Magnetic drain plug	40 (5.5)

Flywheel housing:
Studs	6 (.80)
Nuts and bolts	18 (2.5)

Casing to block and crankcase extension:
$\frac{5}{16}$ bolts	25 (3.4)
$\frac{3}{8}$ bolts	25 (3.4)
Front cover	10 (1.4)

Detent plug:
Small	20 (2.8)
Large	40 (5.5)
First motion shaft nut	120 (16.6)
Final drive pinion nut	150 (20.7)
Remote control steady-rod nuts	25 (3.5)
Speedometer drive housing	20 (2.8)

Final drive:
Driven gear to differential cage bolts	55 to 60 (7.6 to 8.3)
Final drive pinion nut	150 (20.7)

Differential cover:
Studs	6 (.80)
$\frac{5}{16}$ nuts	18 (2.5)
$\frac{3}{8}$ nuts	25 (3.4)
Differential end cover bolts	18 (2.5)

Automatic transmission:
Converter housing:
Chain cover to housing	5 to 9 (.7 to 1.2)
Turbine shaft nut	20 to 25 (2.8 to 3.5)
Input shaft nut	15 to 20 (2.1 to 2.8)
Pump assembly to housing	5 to 9 (.69 to 1.2)

Pump adaptor to pump housing:
Bolts	17 to 22 (2.3 to 3.0)
Screw	1.7 to 2.5 (.23 to .35)
Bearing retainer—input shaft	5 to 9 (.69 to 1.2)

Main casing:
Speedometer drive housing ..	.. ..	8 to 18 (1.1 to 2.5)
Crankcase to main casing ..	.. ..	20 (2.8)
Main casing to crankcase ..	.. ..	30 (4.1)

Steering:
Steering wheel nut ..	.. ..	35 (4.8)
Lock shear bolts ..	.. ..	14 (1.9)
Coupling flange—Manual ..	.. ..	12 to 15 (1.7 to 2.1)
Pinch-bolt—Power ..	.. ..	12 to 15 (1.7 to 2.1)
Steering lever to hub ..	.. ..	85 (11.7)
Ball pin housing ..	.. ..	70 ± 5 (9.6 ± .70)
Ball joint nut ..	.. ..	35 (4.8)
Tie-rod housing locknut ..	.. ..	35 (4.8)
Pinion and damper cover bolts	.. ..	12 to 15 (1.6 to 2.0)

Suspension:

Front:
Swivel axle ball joint nuts ..	.. ..	45 (6.2)
Lower arm pivot nut ..	.. ..	45 (6.2)
Tie-rod to lower arm ..	.. ..	40 to 50 (5.5 to 6.9)
Housing locknut ..	.. ..	35 (4.8)
Upper arm pivot ..	.. ..	60 (8.3)
Tie-rod to bracket (Nyloc nut)	.. ..	45 to 50 (6.2 to 6.9)
Hub nut (tighten to next hole)	.. ..	150 (20.7)
Drive flange to brake disc bolts	.. ..	40 to 45 (5.5 to 6.2)
Caliper to swivel hub ..	.. ..	45 to 50 (5.5 to 6.9)
Shield to hub ..	.. ..	20 (2.8)
Ball pin housings ..	.. ..	70 ± 5 (9.6 ± .70)
Suspension bracket to body	.. ..	60 to 70 (8.3 to 9.6)

Rear:
Radius arm pivot nut ..	.. ..	60 (8.3)
Stub axle nut ..	.. ..	40 (5.5)
Hydrolastic housing to body	.. ..	45 (6.2)

Road wheels:
Wheel nuts ..	.. .. ..	60 (8.3)

Brakes:
Caliper to hub ..	.. ..	45 to 50 (6.2 to 6.9)
Disc to driving flange ..	.. ..	38 to 45 (5.2 to 6.2)
Shield to hub ..	.. ..	20 (2.8)
Bleed screws ..	.. ..	4 to 6 (.5 to .8)
Adjuster nuts ..	.. ..	4 to 6 (.5 to .8)
Pedal pivot nut ..	.. ..	12 (1.7)

Master cylinder:
Cylinder to servo unit ..	.. ..	17 (2.3)
Reservoir to single cylinder ..	.. ..	20 to 25 (2.7 to 3.4)
Tipping valve nut (tandem) ..	.. ..	35 to 45 (4.8 to 6.2)
Inlet and end plugs—'G' valve	.. ..	25 to 35 (3.4 to 4.8)

Warning light actuator (tandem):
End plugs ..	.. ..	18 (2.5)
Electric switch ..	.. ..	2.5 (.30)

Handbrake:
Lever to floor bracket ..	.. ..	15 (2.1)
Cable sector to floor bracket	.. ..	30 (4.1)

Electrical:
  Distributor:
    Plate retaining screws 8 (1.1)
    Clamp bolt ..   ..   2.5 (.35)
  Alternator:
    Mounting bolts 20 (2.8)
    Pulley nut 25 (3.4)
    Through-bolts   ..   ..   4.5 (.62)
  Starter motor:
    Retaining bolts 30 (4.1)
    Through-bolts 8 (1.1)
    Solenoid fixing nuts   ..   ..   ..   4.5 (.62)
    Solenoid terminal nuts   ..   ..   ..   3 (.41)

Seat belts:
  Bracket fixing bolts 25 (3.36)
  Britax reel locating screw   ..   ..   ..   5 lbf in (.06)

WIRING DIAGRAMS

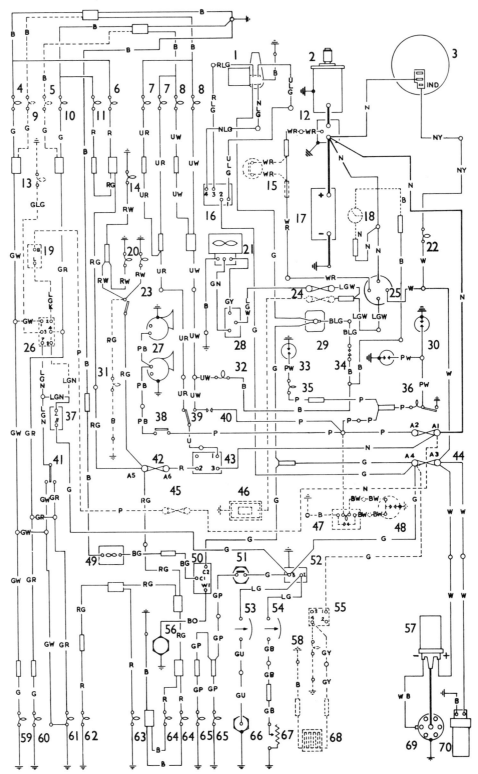

FIG 12:1 Wiring diagram for Austin-Morris 2200

Key to Fig 12:1

1 Windscreen wiper motor 2 Starter motor 3 Alternator 4 R.H. front flasher lamp 5 L.H. front flasher lamp 6 R.H. sidelamp 7 Headlamp—low beam 8 Headlamp—high beam 9 R.H. front flasher repeater lamp 10 L.H. front flasher lamp 11 L.H. sidelamp 12 Starter motor solenoid 13 Hazard warning lamp* 14 Panel lamp 15 Automatic gearbox safety switch* 16 Windscreen wiper switch 17 Battery—12 volt 18 Time clock 19 Hazard warning lamp flasher unit* 20 Panel lamps 21 Heater motor 22 Ignition warning lamp 23 Panel lamp switch 24 Line fuse 25 Ignition/starter motor switch 26 Hazard warning lamp switch* 27 Horns 28 Heater motor switch 29 Windscreen washer pump 30 Interior lamp door pillar switches 31 Automatic gearbox quadrant lamp* 32 Headlamp main beam warning lamp 33 Luggage compartment lamp switch 34 Windscreen washer switch 35 Luggage compartment lamp 36 Interior lamp 37 Flasher unit 38 Horn-push 39 Headlamp dipswitch 40 Headlamp flasher switch 41 Direction indicator switch 42 Fuse unit: 35 amp 43 Lighting switch 44 Fuse unit: 35 amp 45 Line fuse 46 Radio (when fitted) 47 Brake pressure warning lamp and test switch* 48 Brake pressure failure switch* 49 Cooling fan motor 50 Cooling fan motor relay 51 Stop lamp switch 52 Voltage stabilizer 53 Coolant temperature gauge 54 Fuel gauge 55 Heated backlight switch* 56 Cooling fan motor thermostatic switch 57 Ignition coil 58 Heated backlight warning lamp* 59 R.H. rear flasher lamp 60 L.H. rear flasher lamp 61 Direction indicator warning lamp 62 L.H. tail lamp 63 R.H. tail lamp 64 Number plate lamps 65 Stop lamp 66 Coolant temperature transmitter 67 Fuel gauge tank unit 68 Heated backlight unit* 69 Distributor 70 Fuel pump

*Optional or special market fitments, circuits shown dotted

Key to cable colour code B Black G Green K Pink LG Light green N Brown O Orange P Purple R Red U Blue W White Y Yellow

When a cable has two colour code letters the first denotes the main colour and the second denotes the tracer colour

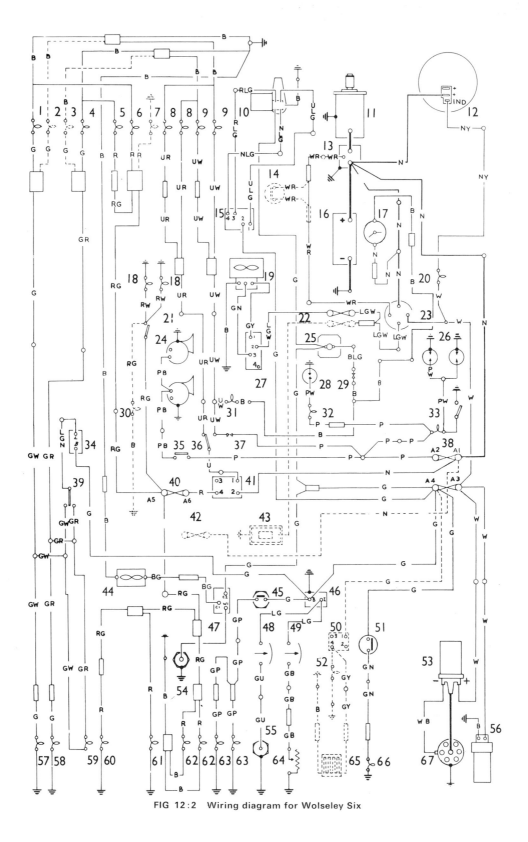

FIG 12:2 Wiring diagram for Wolseley Six

Key to Fig 12:2

1 R.H. front flasher lamp 2 R.H. front flasher repeater lamp 3 L.H. front flasher repeater lamp 4 L.H. front flasher lamp 5 L.H. sidelamp 6 R.H. sidelamp 7 Radiator badge lamp 8 Headlamp—low beam 9 Headlamp—high beam 10 Windscreen wiper motor 11 Starter motor 12 Alternator 13 Starter motor solenoid 14 Automatic transmission safety switch* 15 Windscreen wiper switch 16 Battery—12 volt 17 Time clock 18 Panel lamps 19 Heater motor 20 Ignition warning lamp 21 Panel lamp switch 22 Line fuse 23 Ignition/starter motor switch 24 Horns 25 Windscreen washer pump 26 Interior lamp door pillar switch 27 Heater motor switch 28 Luggage compartment lamp switch 29 Windscreen washer switch 30 Automatic transmission quadrant lamp* 31 Headlamp main beam warning lamp 32 Luggage compartment lamp 33 Interior lamp 34 Flasher unit 35 Horn push 36 Headlamp dip switch 37 Headlamp flasher switch 38 Fuse unit: 35 amp 39 Direction indicator switch 40 Fuse unit: 35 amp 41 Lighting switch 42 Line fuse 43 Radio (when fitted) 44 Cooling fan motor 45 Stop lamp switch 46 Voltage stabilizer 47 Direction indicator switch 48 Coolant temperature gauge 49 Fuel gauge 50 Heated backlight switch* 51 Reverse lamp switch 52 Heated backlight warning lamp* 53 Ignition coil 54 Cooling fan motor thermostatic switch 55 Coolant temperature transmitter 56 Fuel pump 57 R.H. rear flasher lamp 58 L.H. rear flasher lamp 59 Direction indicator warning lamp 60 L.H. tail lamp 61 R.H. tail lamp 62 Number plate lamp 63 Stop lamp 64 Fuel gauge tank unit 65 Heated backlight unit* 66 Reverse lamp 67 Distributor

* Optional or special market fitment, circuits shown dotted

Key to cable colour code B Black G Green K Pink LG Light green N Brown O Orange P Purple R Red U Blue W White Y Yellow

When a cable has two colour code letters the first denotes the main colour and the second denotes the tracer colour

Inches			Decimals	Milli-metres	Inches to Millimetres		Millimetres to Inches	
					Inches	mm	mm	Inches
		1/64	.015625	.3969	.001	.0254	.01	.00039
	1/32		.03125	.7937	.002	.0508	.02	.00079
		3/64	.046875	1.1906	.003	.0762	.03	.00118
1/16			.0625	1.5875	.004	.1016	.04	.00157
		5/64	.078125	1.9844	.005	.1270	.05	.00197
	3/32		.09375	2.3812	.006	.1524	.06	.00236
		7/64	.109375	2.7781	.007	.1778	.07	.00276
1/8			.125	3.1750	.008	.2032	.08	.00315
		9/64	.140625	3.5719	.009	.2286	.09	.00354
	5/32		.15625	3.9687	.01	.254	.1	.00394
		11/64	.171875	4.3656	.02	.508	.2	.00787
3/16			.1875	4.7625	.03	.762	.3	.01181
		13/64	.203125	5.1594	.04	1.016	.4	.01575
	7/32		.21875	5.5562	.05	1.270	.5	.01969
		15/64	.234375	5.9531	.06	1.524	.6	.02362
1/4			.25	6.3500	.07	1.778	.7	.02756
		17/64	.265625	6.7469	.08	2.032	.8	.03150
	9/32		.28125	7.1437	.09	2.286	.9	.03543
		19/64	.296875	7.5406	.1	2.54	1	.03937
5/16			.3125	7.9375	.2	5.08	2	.07874
		21/64	.328125	8.3344	.3	7.62	3	.11811
	11/32		.34375	8.7312	.4	10.16	4	.15748
		23/64	.359375	9.1281	.5	12.70	5	.19685
3/8			.375	9.5250	.6	15.24	6	.23622
		25/64	.390625	9.9219	.7	17.78	7	.27559
	13/32		.40625	10.3187	.8	20.32	8	.31496
		27/64	.421875	10.7156	.9	22.86	9	.35433
7/16			.4375	11.1125	1	25.4	10	.39370
		29/64	.453125	11.5094	2	50.8	11	.43307
	15/32		.46875	11.9062	3	76.2	12	.47244
		31/64	.484375	12.3031	4	101.6	13	.51181
1/2			.5	12.7000	5	127.0	14	.55118
		33/64	.515625	13.0969	6	152.4	15	.59055
	17/32		.53125	13.4937	7	177.8	16	.62992
		35/64	.546875	13.8906	8	203.2	17	.66929
9/16			.5625	14.2875	9	228.6	18	.70866
		37/64	.578125	14.6844	10	254.0	19	.74803
	19/32		.59375	15.0812	11	279.4	20	.78740
		39/64	.609375	15.4781	12	304.8	21	.82677
5/8			.625	15.8750	13	330.2	22	.86614
		41/64	.640625	16.2719	14	355.6	23	.90551
	21/32		.65625	16.6687	15	381.0	24	.94488
		43/64	.671875	17.0656	16	406.4	25	.98425
11/16			.6875	17.4625	17	431.8	26	1.02362
		45/64	.703125	17.8594	18	457.2	27	1.06299
	23/32		.71875	18.2562	19	482.6	28	1.10236
		47/64	.734375	18.6531	20	508.0	29	1.14173
3/4			.75	19.0500	21	533.4	30	1.18110
		49/64	.765625	19.4469	22	558.8	31	1.22047
	25/32		.78125	19.8437	23	584.2	32	1.25984
		51/64	.796875	20.2406	24	609.6	33	1.29921
13/16			.8125	20.6375	25	635.0	34	1.33858
		53/64	.828125	21.0344	26	660.4	35	1.37795
	27/32		.84375	21.4312	27	685.8	36	1.41732
		55/64	.859375	21.8281	28	711.2	37	1.4567
7/8			.875	22.2250	29	736.6	38	1.4961
		57/64	.890625	22.6219	30	762.0	39	1.5354
	29/32		.90625	23.0187	31	787.4	40	1.5748
		59/64	.921875	23.4156	32	812.8	41	1.6142
15/16			.9375	23.8125	33	838.2	42	1.6535
		61/64	.953125	24.2094	34	863.6	43	1.6929
	31/32		.96875	24.6062	35	889.0	44	1.7323
		63/64	.984375	25.0031	36	914.4	45	1.7717

UNITS	Pints to Litres	Gallons to Litres	Litres to Pints	Litres to Gallons	Miles to Kilometres	Kilometres to Miles	Lbs. per sq. In. to Kg. per sq. Cm.	Kg. per sq. Cm. to Lbs. per sq. In.
1	.57	4.55	1.76	.22	1.61	.62	.07	14.22
2	1.14	9.09	3.52	.44	3.22	1.24	.14	28.50
3	1.70	13.64	5.28	.66	4.83	1.86	.21	42.67
4	2.27	18.18	7.04	.88	6.44	2.49	.28	56.89
5	2.84	22.73	8.80	1.10	8.05	3.11	.35	71.12
6	3.41	27.28	10.56	1.32	9.66	3.73	.42	85.34
7	3.98	31.82	12.32	1.54	11.27	4.35	.49	99.56
8	4.55	36.37	14.08	1.76	12.88	4.97	.56	113.79
9		40.91	15.84	1.98	14.48	5.59	.63	128.00
10		45.46	17.60	2.20	16.09	6.21	.70	142.23
20				4.40	32.19	12.43	1.41	284.47
30				6.60	48.28	18.64	2.11	426.70
40				8.80	64.37	24.85		
50					80.47	31.07		
60					96.56	37.28		
70					112.65	43.50		
80					128.75	49.71		
90					144.84	55.92		
100					160.93	62.14		

UNITS	Lb ft to kgm	Kgm to lb ft	UNITS	Lb ft to kgm	Kgm to lb ft
1	.138	7.233	7	.967	50.631
2	.276	14.466	8	1.106	57.864
3	.414	21.699	9	1.244	65.097
4	.553	28.932	10	1.382	72.330
5	.691	36.165	20	2.765	144.660
6	.829	43.398	30	4.147	216.990

HINTS ON MAINTENANCE AND OVERHAUL

There are few things more rewarding than the restoration of a vehicle's original peak of efficiency and smooth performance.

The following notes are intended to help the owner to reach that state of perfection. Providing that he possesses the basic manual skills he should have no difficulty in performing most of the operations detailed in this manual. It must be stressed, however, that where recommended in the manual, highly-skilled operations ought to be entrusted to experts, who have the necessary equipment, to carry out the work satisfactorily.

Quality of workmanship:

The hazardous driving conditions on the roads to-day demand that vehicles should be as nearly perfect, mechanically, as possible. It is therefore most important that amateur work be carried out with care, bearing in mind the often inadequate working conditions, and also the inferior tools which may have to be used. It is easy to counsel perfection in all things, and we recognize that it may be setting an impossibly high standard. We do, however, suggest that every care should be taken to ensure that a vehicle is as safe to take on the road as it is humanly possible to make it.

Safe working conditions:

Even though a vehicle may be stationary, it is still potentially dangerous if certain sensible precautions are not taken when working on it while it is supported on jacks or blocks. It is indeed preferable not to use jacks alone, but to supplement them with carefully placed blocks, so that there will be plenty of support if the car rolls off the jacks during a strenuous manoeuvre. Axle stands are an excellent way of providing a rigid base which is not readily disturbed. Piles of bricks are a dangerous substitute. Be careful not to get under heavy loads on lifting tackle, the load could fall. It is preferable not to work alone when lifting an engine, or when working underneath a vehicle which is supported well off the ground. To be trapped, particularly under the vehicle, may have unpleasant results if help is not quickly forthcoming. Make some provision, however humble, to deal with fires. Always disconnect a battery if there is a likelihood of electrical shorts. These may start a fire if there is leaking fuel about. This applies particularly to leads which can carry a heavy current, like those in the starter circuit. While on the subject of electricity, we must also stress the danger of using equipment which is run off the mains and which has no earth or has faulty wiring or connections. So many workshops have damp floors, and electrical shocks are of such a nature that it is sometimes impossible to let go of a live lead or piece of equipment due to the muscular spasms which take place.

Work demanding special care:

This involves the servicing of braking, steering and suspension systems. On the road, failure of the braking system may be disastrous. Make quite sure that there can be no possibility of failure through the bursting of rusty brake pipes or rotten hoses, nor to a sudden loss of pressure due to defective seals or valves.

Problems:

The chief problems which may face an operator are:
1 External dirt.
2 Difficulty in undoing tight fixings
3 Dismantling unfamiliar mechanisms.
4 Deciding in what respect parts are defective.
5 Confusion about the correct order for reassembly.
6 Adjusting running clearances.
7 Road testing.
8 Final tuning.

Practical suggestion to solve the problems:

1 Preliminary cleaning of large parts—engines, transmissions, steering, suspensions, etc.,—should be carried out before removal from the car. Where road dirt and mud alone are present, wash clean with a high-pressure water jet, brushing to remove stubborn adhesions, and allow to drain and dry. Where oil or grease is also present, wash down with a proprietary compound (Gunk, Teepol etc.,) applying with a stiff brush—an old paint brush is suitable—into all crevices. Cover the distributor and ignition coils with a polythene bag and then apply a strong water jet to clear the loosened deposits. Allow to drain and dry. The assemblies will then be sufficiently clean to remove and transfer to the bench for the next stage.

On the bench, further cleaning can be carried out, first wiping the parts as free as possible from grease with old newspaper. Avoid using rag or cotton waste which can leave clogging fibres behind. Any remaining grease can be removed with a brush dipped in paraffin. If necessary, traces of paraffin can be removed by carbon tetrachloride. Avoid using paraffin or petrol in large quantities for cleaning in enclosed areas, such as garages, on account of the high fire risk.

When all exteriors have been cleaned, and not before, dismantling can be commenced. This ensures that dirt will not enter into interiors and orifices revealed by dismantling. In the next phases, where components have to be cleaned, use carbon tetrachloride in preference to petrol and keep the containers covered except when in use. After the components have been cleaned, plug small holes with tapered hard wood plugs cut to size and blank off larger orifices with grease-proof paper and masking tape. Do not use soft wood plugs or matchsticks as they may break.

2 It is not advisable to hammer on the end of a screw thread, but if it must be done, first screw on a nut to protect the thread, and use a lead hammer. This applies particularly to the removal of tapered cotters. Nuts and bolts seem to 'grow' together, especially in exhaust systems. If penetrating oil does not work, try the judicious application of heat, but be careful of starting a fire. Asbestos sheet or cloth is useful to isolate heat.

Tight bushes or pieces of tail-pipe rusted into a silencer can be removed by splitting them with an open-ended hacksaw. Tight screws can sometimes be started by a tap from a hammer on the end of a suitable screwdriver. Many tight fittings will yield to the judicious use of a hammer, but it must be a soft-faced hammer if damage is to be avoided, use a heavy block on the opposite side to absorb shock. Any parts of the steering system which have been damaged should be renewed, as attempts to repair them may lead to cracking and subsequent failure, and steering ball joints should be disconnected using a recommended tool to prevent damage.

3 If often happens that an owner is baffled when trying to dismantle an unfamiliar piece of equipment. So many modern devices are pressed together or assembled by spinning-over flanges, that they must be sawn apart. The intention is that the whole assembly must be renewed. However, parts which appear to be in one piece to the naked eye, may reveal close-fitting joint lines when inspected with a magnifying glass, and, this may provide the necessary clue to dismantling. Left-handed screw threads are used where rotational forces would tend to unscrew a right-handed screw thread.

Be very careful when dismantling mechanisms which may come apart suddenly. Work in an enclosed space where the parts will be contained, and drape a piece of cloth over the device if springs are likely to fly in all directions. Mark everything which might be reassembled in the wrong position, scratched symbols may be used on unstressed parts, or a sequence of tiny dots from a centre punch can be useful. Stressed parts should never be scratched or centre-popped as this may lead to cracking under working conditions. Store parts which look alike in the correct order for reassembly. Never rely upon memory to assist in the assembly of complicated mechanisms, especially when they will be dismantled for a long time, but make notes, and drawings to supplement the diagrams in the manual, and put labels on detached wires. Rust stains may indicate unlubricated wear. This can sometimes be seen round the outside edge of a bearing cup in a universal joint. Look for bright rubbing marks on parts which normally should not make heavy contact. These might prove that something is bent or running out of truth. For example, there might be bright marks on one side of a piston, at the top near the ring grooves, and others at the bottom of the skirt on the other side. This could well be the clue to a bent connecting rod. Suspected cracks can be proved by heating the component in a light oil to approximately 100°C, removing, drying off, and dusting with french chalk, if a crack is present the oil retained in the crack will stain the french chalk.

4 In determining wear, and the degree, against the permissible limits set in the manual, accurate measurement can only be achieved by the use of a micrometer. In many cases, the wear is given to the fourth place of decimals; that is in ten-thousandths of an inch. This can be read by the vernier scale on the barrel of a good micrometer. Bore diameters are more difficult to determine. If, however, the matching shaft is accurately measured, the degree of play in the bore can be felt as a guide to its suitability. In other cases, the shank of a twist drill of known diameter is a handy check.

Many methods have been devised for determining the clearance between bearing surfaces. To-day the best and simplest is by the use of Plastigage, obtainable from most garages. A thin plastic thread is laid between the two surfaces and the bearing is tightened, flattening the thread. On removal, the width of the thread is compared with a scale supplied with the thread and the clearance is read off directly. Sometimes joint faces leak persistently, even after gasket renewal. The fault will then be traceable to distortion, dirt or burrs. Studs which are screwed into soft metal frequently raise burrs at the point of entry. A quick cure for this is to chamfer the edge of the hole in the part which fits over the stud.

5 **Always check a replacement part with the original one before it is fitted.**

If parts are not marked, and the order for reassembly is not known, a little detective work will help. Look for marks which are due to wear to see if they can be mated. Joint faces may not be identical due to manufacturing errors, and parts which overlap may be stained, giving a clue to the correct position. Most fixings leave identifying marks especially if they were painted over on assembly. It is then easier to decide whether a nut, for instance, has a plain, a spring, or a shakeproof washer under it. All running surfaces become 'bedded' together after long spells of work and tiny imperfections on one part will be found to have left corresponding marks on the other. This is particularly true of shafts and bearings and even a score on a cylinder wall will show on the piston.

6 Checking end float or rocker clearances by feeler gauge may not always give accurate results because of wear. For instance, the rocker tip which bears on a valve stem may be deeply pitted, in which case the feeler will simply be bridging a depression. Thrust washers may also wear depressions in opposing faces to make accurate measurement difficult. End float is then easier to check by using a dial gauge. It is common practice to adjust end play in bearing assemblies, like front hubs with taper rollers, by doing up the axle nut until the hub becomes stiff to turn and then backing it off a little. Do not use this method with ballbearing hubs as the assembly is often preloaded by tightening the axle nut to its fullest extent. If the splitpin hole will not line up, file the base of the nut a little.

Steering assemblies often wear in the straight-ahead position. If any part is adjusted, make sure that it remains free when moved from lock to lock. Do not be surprised if an assembly like a steering gearbox, which is known to be carefully adjusted outside the car, becomes stiff when it is bolted in place. This will be due to distortion of the case by the pull of the mounting bolts, particularly if the mounting points are not all touching together. This problem may be met in other equipment and is cured by careful attention to the alignment of mounting points.

When a spanner is stamped with a size and A/F it means that the dimension is the width between the jaws and has no connection with ANF, which is the designation for the American National Fine thread. Coarse threads like Whitworth are rarely used on cars to-day except for studs which screw into soft aluminium or cast iron. For this reason it might be found that the top end of a cylinder head stud has a fine thread and the lower end a coarse thread to screw into the cylinder block. If the car has mainly UNF threads then it is likely that any coarse threads will be UNC, which are not the same as Whitworth. Small sizes have the same number of threads in Whitworth and UNC, but in the $\frac{1}{2}$ inch size for example, there are twelve threads to the inch in the former and thirteen in the latter.

7 After a major overhaul, particularly if a great deal of work has been done on the braking, steering and suspension systems, it is advisable to approach the problem of testing with care. If the braking system has been overhauled, apply heavy pressure to the brake pedal and get a second operator to check every possible source of leakage. The brakes may work extremely well, but a leak could cause complete failure after a few miles.

Do not fit the hub caps until every wheel nut has been checked for tightness, and make sure the tyre pressures are correct. Check the levels of coolant, lubricants and hydraulic fluids. Being satisfied that all is well, take the car on the road and test the brakes at once. Check the steering and the action of the handbrake. Do all this at moderate speeds on quiet roads, and make sure there is no other vehicle behind you when you try a rapid stop.

Finally, remember that many parts settle down after a time, so check for tightness of all fixings after the car has been on the road for a hundred miles or so.

8 It is useless to tune an engine which has not reached its normal running temperature. In the same way, the tune of an engine which is stiff after a rebore will be different when the engine is again running free. Remember too, that rocker clearances on pushrod operated valve gear will change when the cylinder head nuts are tightened after an initial period of running with a new head gasket.

Trouble may not always be due to what seems the obvious cause. Ignition, carburation and mechanical condition are interdependent and spitting back through the carburetter, which might be attributed to a weak mixture, can be caused by a sticking inlet valve.

For one final hint on tuning, never adjust more than one thing at a time or it will be impossible to tell which adjustment produced the desired result.

NOTES

GLOSSARY OF TERMS

Allen key   Cranked wrench of hexagonal section for use with socket head screws.

Alternator   Electrical generator producing alternating current. Rectified to direct current for battery charging.

Ambient temperature   Surrounding atmospheric temperature.

Annulus   Used in engineering to indicate the outer ring gear of an epicyclic gear train.

Armature   The shaft carrying the windings, which rotates in the magnetic field of a generator or starter motor. That part of a solenoid or relay which is activated by the magnetic field.

Axial   In line with, or pertaining to, an axis.

Backlash   Play in meshing gears.

Balance lever   A bar where force applied at the centre is equally divided between connections at the ends.

Banjo axle   Axle casing with large diameter housing for the crownwheel and differential.

Bendix pinion   A self-engaging and self-disengaging drive on a starter motor shaft.

Bevel pinion   A conical shaped gearwheel, designed to mesh with a similar gear with an axis usually at 90 deg. to its own.

bhp   Brake horse power, measured on a dynamometer.

bmep   Brake mean effective pressure. Average pressure on a piston during the working stroke.

Brake cylinder   Cylinder with hydraulically operated piston(s) acting on brake shoes or pad(s).

Brake regulator   Control valve fitted in hydraulic braking system which limits brake pressure to rear brakes during heavy braking to prevent rear wheel locking.

Camber   Angle at which a wheel is tilted from the vertical.

Capacitor   Modern term for an electrical condenser. Part of distributor assembly, connected across contact breaker points, acts as an interference suppressor.

Castellated   Top face of a nut, slotted across the flats, to take a locking splitpin.

Castor   Angle at which the kingpin or swivel pin is tilted when viewed from the side.

cc   Cubic centimetres. Engine capacity is arrived at by multiplying the area of the bore in sq cm by the stroke in cm by the number of cylinders.

Clevis   U-shaped forked connector used with a clevis pin, usually at handbrake connections.

Collet   A type of collar, usually split and located in a groove in a shaft, and held in place by a retainer. The arrangement used to retain the spring(s) on a valve stem in most cases.

Commutator   Rotating segmented current distributor between armature windings and brushes in generator or motor.

Compression   The ratio, or quantitative relation, of the total volume (piston at bottom of stroke) to the unswept volume (piston at top of stroke) in an engine cylinder.

Condenser   See capacitor.

Core plug   Plug for blanking off a manufacturing hole in a casting.

Crownwheel   Large bevel gear in rear axle, driven by a bevel pinion attached to the propeller shaft. Sometimes called a 'ring gear'.

'C'-spanner   Like a 'C' with a handle. For use on screwed collars without flats, but with slots or holes.

Damper   Modern term for shock-absorber, used in vehicle suspension systems to damp out spring oscillations.

Depression   The lowering of atmospheric pressure as in the inlet manifold and carburetter.

Dowel   Close tolerance pin, peg, tube, or bolt, which accurately locates mating parts.

Drag link   Rod connecting steering box drop arm (pitman arm) to nearest front wheel steering arm in certain types of steering systems.

Dry liner   Thinwall tube pressed into cylinder bore

Dry sump   Lubrication system where all oil is scavenged from the sump, and returned to a separate tank.

Dynamo   See Generator.

Electrode   Terminal, part of an electrical component, such as the points or 'Electrodes' of a sparking plug.

Electrolyte   In lead-acid car batteries a solution of sulphuric acid and distilled water.

End float   The axial movement between associated parts, end play.

EP   Extreme pressure. In lubricants, special grades for heavily loaded bearing surfaces, such as gear teeth in a gearbox, or crownwheel and pinion in a rear axle.

Fade	Of brakes. Reduced efficiency due to overheating.
Field coils	Windings on the polepieces of motors and generators.
Fillets	Narrow finishing strips usually applied to interior bodywork.
First motion shaft	Input shaft from clutch to gearbox.
Fullflow filter	Filters in which all the oil is pumped to the engine. If the element becomes clogged, a bypass valve operates to pass unfiltered oil to the engine.
FWD	Front wheel drive.
Gear pump	Two meshing gears in a close fitting casing. Oil is carried from the inlet round the outside of both gears in the spaces between the gear teeth and casing to the outlet, the meshing gear teeth prevent oil passing back to the inlet, and the oil is forced through the outlet port.
Generator	Modern term for 'Dynamo'. When rotated produces electrical current.
Grommet	A ring of protective or sealing material. Can be used to protect pipes or leads passing through bulkheads.
Grubscrew	Fully threaded headless screw with screwdriver slot. Used for locking, or alignment purposes.
Gudgeon pin	Shaft which connects a piston to its connecting rod. Sometimes called 'wrist pin', or 'piston pin'.
Halfshaft	One of a pair transmitting drive from the differential.
Helical	In spiral form. The teeth of helical gears are cut at a spiral angle to the side faces of the gearwheel.
Hot spot	Hot area that assists vapourisation of fuel on its way to cylinders. Often provided by close contact between inlet and exhaust manifolds.
HT	High Tension. Applied to electrical current produced by the ignition coil for the sparking plugs.
Hydrometer	A device for checking specific gravity of liquids. Used to check specific gravity of electrolyte.
Hypoid bevel gears	A form of bevel gear used in the rear axle drive gears. The bevel pinion meshes below the centre line of the crownwheel, giving a lower propeller shaft line.
Idler	A device for passing on movement. A free running gear between driving and driven gears. A lever transmitting track rod movement to a side rod in steering gear.
Impeller	A centrifugal pumping element. Used in water pumps to stimulate flow.
Journals	Those parts of a shaft that are in contact with the bearings.
Kingpin	The main vertical pin which carries the front wheel spindle, and permits steering movement. May be called 'steering pin' or 'swivel pin'.
Layshaft	The shaft which carries the laygear in the gearbox. The laygear is driven by the first motion shaft and drives the third motion shaft according to the gear selected. Sometimes called the 'countershaft' or 'second motion shaft.'
lb ft	A measure of twist or torque. A pull of 10 lb at a radius of 1 ft is a torque of 10 lb ft.
lb/sq in	Pounds per square inch.
Little-end	The small, or piston end of a connecting rod. Sometimes called the 'small-end'.
LT	Low Tension. The current output from the battery.
Mandrel	Accurately manufactured bar or rod used for test or centring purposes.
Manifold	A pipe, duct, or chamber, with several branches.
Needle rollers	Bearing rollers with a length many times their diameter.
Oil bath	Reservoir which lubricates parts by immersion. In air filters, a separate oil supply for wetting a wire mesh element to hold the dust.
Oil wetted	In air filters, a wire mesh element lightly oiled to trap and hold airborne dust.
Overlap	Period during which inlet and exhaust valves are open together.
Panhard rod	Bar connected between fixed point on chassis and another on axle to control sideways movement.
Pawl	Pivoted catch which engages in the teeth of a ratchet to permit movement in one direction only.
Peg spanner	Tool with pegs, or pins, to engage in holes or slots in the part to be turned.
Pendant pedals	Pedals with levers that are pivoted at the top end.
Phillips screwdriver	A cross-point screwdriver for use with the cross-slotted heads of Phillips screws.
Pinion	A small gear, usually in relation to another gear.
Piston-type damper	Shock absorber in which damping is controlled by a piston working in a closed oil-filled cylinder.
Preloading	Preset static pressure on ball or roller bearings not due to working loads.
Radial	Radiating from a centre, like the spokes of a wheel.

Radius rod	Pivoted arm confining movement of a part to an arc of fixed radius.
Ratchet	Toothed wheel or rack which can move in one direction only, movement in the other being prevented by a pawl.
Ring gear	A gear tooth ring attached to outer periphery of flywheel. Starter pinion engages with it during starting.
Runout	Amount by which rotating part is out of true.
Semi-floating axle	Outer end of rear axle halfshaft is carried on bearing inside axle casing. Wheel hub is secured to end of shaft.
Servo	A hydraulic or pneumatic system for assisting, or, augmenting a physical effort. See 'Vacuum Servo'.
Setscrew	One which is threaded for the full length of the shank.
Shackle	A coupling link, used in the form of two parallel pins connected by side plates to secure the end of the master suspension spring and absorb the effects of deflection.
Shell bearing	Thinwalled steel shell lined with anti-friction metal. Usually semi-circular and used in pairs for main and big-end bearings.
Shock absorber	See 'Damper'.
Silentbloc	Rubber bush bonded to inner and outer metal sleeves.
Socket-head screw	Screw with hexagonal socket for an Allen key.
Solenoid	A coil of wire creating a magnetic field when electric current passes through it. Used with a soft iron core to operate contacts or a mechanical device.
Spur gear	A gear with teeth cut axially across the periphery.
Stub axle	Short axle fixed at one end only.
Tachometer	An instrument for accurate measurement of rotating speed. Usually indicates in revolutions per minute.

TDC	Top Dead Centre. The highest point reached by a piston in a cylinder, with the crank and connecting rod in line.
Thermostat	Automatic device for regulating temperature. Used in vehicle coolant systems to open a valve which restricts circulation at low temperature.
Third motion shaft	Output shaft of gearbox.
Threequarter floating axle	Outer end of rear axle halfshaft flanged and bolted to wheel hub, which runs on bearing mounted on outside of axle casing. Vehicle weight is not carried by the axle shaft.
Thrust bearing or washer	Used to reduce friction in rotating parts subject to axial loads.
Torque	Turning or twisting effort. See 'lb ft'.
Track rod	The bar(s) across the vehicle which connect the steering arms and maintain the front wheels in their correct alignment.
UJ	Universal joint. A coupling between shafts which permits angular movement.
UNF	Unified National Fine screw thread.
Vacuum servo	Device used in brake system, using difference between atmospheric pressure and inlet manifold depression to operate a piston which acts to augment brake pressure as required. See 'Servo'.
Venturi	A restriction or 'choke' in a tube, as in a carburetter, used to increase velocity to obtain a reduction in pressure.
Vernier	A sliding scale for obtaining fractional readings of the graduations of an adjacent scale.
Welch plug	A domed thin metal disc which is partially flattened to lock in a recess. Used to plug core holes in castings.
Wet liner	Removable cylinder barrel, sealed against coolant leakage, where the coolant is in direct contact with the outer surface.
Wet sump	A reservoir attached to the crankcase to hold the lubricating oil.

NOTES

INDEX

THE AUTOBOOK SERIES OF WORKSHOP MANUALS

Alfa Romeo Giulia 1600,
1750, 2000 1962 on
Aston Martin 1921-58
Auto Union Audi 70, 80,
Super 90, 1966-72
Audi 100 1969 on
Austin, Morris etc.
1100 Mk. 1 1962-67
Austin, Morris etc. 1100
Mk. 2, 3, 1300 Mk. 1, 2, 3
America 1968 on
Austin A30, A35, A40
Farina 1951-67
Austin A55 Mk. 2, A60
1958-69
Austin A99, A110 1959-68
Austin J4 1960 on
Austin Maxi 1969 on
Austin, Morris 1800
1964 on
Austin, Morris 2200 1972 on
Austin Kimberley, Tasman
1970 on
Austin, Morris 1300, 1500
Nomad 1969 on
BMC 3 (Austin A50, A55
Mk. 1, Morris Oxford
2, 3 1954-59)
Austin Healey 100/6,
3000 1956-68
Austin Healey, MG
Sprite, Midget 1958 on
Bedford CA Mk2 1964-69
Bedford CF Vans 1969 on
Bedford Beagle HA Vans
1964 on
BMW 1600 1966 on
BMW 1800 1964-71
BMW 2000, 2002 1966 on

Chevrolet Corvair 1960-69
Chevrolet Corvette V8
1957-65
Chevrolet Corvette V8
1965 on
Chevrolet Vega 2300
1970 on
Chrysler Valiant V8
1965 on
Chrysler Valiant Straight
Six 1966-70
Citroen DS 19, ID 19
1955-66
Citroen ID 19, DS 19, 20,
21 1966 on
Citroen Dyane Ami 1964 on

Daf 31, 32, 33, 44, 55
1961 on
Datsun 1000, 1200 1968 on
Datsun 1300, 1400, 1600
1968 on
Datsun 240C 1971 on
Datsun 240Z Sport 1970 on

Fiat 124 1966 on
Fiat 124 Sport 1966 on
Fiat 125 1967-72
Fiat 127 1971 on
Fiat 128 1969 on
Fiat 500 1957 on
Fiat 600, 600D 1955-69
Fiat 850 1964 on
Fiat 1100 1957-69

Fiat 1300 1500 1961-67
Ford Anglia Prefect 100E
1953-62
Ford Anglia 105E, Prefect
107E 1959-67
Ford Capri 1300, 1600 OHV
1968 on
Ford Capri 1300, 1600,
2000 OHC 1972 on
Ford Capri 2000 V4, 3000 V6
1969 on
Ford Classic, Capri
1961-64
Ford Consul, Zephyr,
Zodiac, 1, 2 1950-62
Ford Corsair Straight
Four 1963-65
Ford Corsair V4 1965-68
Ford Corsair V4 2000
1969-70
Ford Cortina 1962-66
Ford Cortina 1967-68
Ford Cortina 1969-70
Ford Cortina Mk. 3
1970 on
Ford Escort 1967 on
Ford Falcon 6 1964-70
Ford Falcon XK, XL
1960-63
Ford Falcon 6 XR/XA
1966 on
Ford Falcon V8 (U.S.A.)
1965-71
Ford Falcon V8 (Aust.)
1966 on
Ford Pinto 1970 on
Ford Maverick 6 1969 on
Ford Maverick V8 1970 on
Ford Mustang 6 1965 on
Ford Mustang V8 1965 on
Ford Thames 10, 12,
15 cwt 1957-65
Ford Transit V4 1965 on
Ford Zephyr Zodiac Mk. 3
1962-66
Ford Zephyr Zodiac V4,
V6, Mk. 4 1966-72
Ford Consul, Granada
1972 on

Hillman Avenger 1970 on
Hillman Hunter 1966 on
Hillman Imp 1963-68
Hillman Imp 1969 on
Hillman Minx 1 to 5
1956-65
Hillman Minx 1965-67
Hillman Minx 1966-70
Hillman Super Minx
1961-65
Holden V8 1968 on
Holden Straight Six
1948-66
Holden Straight Six
1966 on
Holden Torana 4 Series
HB 1967-69

Jaguar XK120, 140, 150,
Mk. 7, 8, 9 1948-61
Jaguar 2.4, 3.4, 3.8 Mk.
1, 2 1955-69
Jaguar 'E' Type 1961 72

Jaguar 'S' Type 420
1963-68
Jaguar XJ6 1968 on
Jowett Javelin Jupiter
1947-53
Landrover 1, 2 1948-61
Landrover 2, 2a, 3 1959 on
Mazda 616 1970 on
Mazda 808, 818 1972 on
Mazda 1200, 1300 1969 on
Mazda 1500, 1800 1967 on
Mercedes-Benz 190b,
190c, 200 1959-68
Mercedes-Benz 220
1959-65
Mercedes-Benz 220/8
1968 on
Mercedes-Benz 230
1963-68
Mercedes-Benz 250
1965-67
Mercedes-Benz 250
1968 on
Mercedes-Benz 280
1968 on
MG TA to TF 1936-55
MGA MGB 1955-68
MGB 1969 on
Mini 1959 on
Mini Cooper 1961-72
Morgan Four 1936-72
Morris Marina 1971 on
Morris (Aust) Marina
1972 on
Morris Minor 2, 1000
1952-71
Morris Oxford 5, 6 1959-71
NSU 1000 1963-72
NSU Prinz 1 to 4 1957-72
Opel Ascona, Manta
1970 on
Opel GT 1900 1968 on
Opel Kadett, Olympia 993cc
1078cc 1962 on
Opel Kadett, Olympia 1492,
1698, 1897cc 1967 on
Opel Rekord C 1966-72
Peugeot 204 1965 on
Peugeot 304 1970 on
Peugeot 404 1960 on
Peugeot 504 1968 on
Porsche 356A, B, C 1957-65
Porsche 911 1964-69
Porsche 912 1965-69
Porsche 914 S 1969 on
Reliant Regal 1952-73
Renault R4, R4L, 4 1961 on
Renault 6 1968 on
Renault 8, 10, 1100 1962-71
Renault 12, 1969 on
Renault R16 1965 on
Renault Dauphine
Floride 1957-67
Renault Caravelle 1962-68
Rover 60 to 110 1953-64
Rover 2000 1963-73
Rover 3 Litre 1958-67
Rover 3500, 3500S 1968 on
Saab 95, 96, Sport
1960-68
Saab 99 1969 on
Saab V4 1966 on

Simca 1000 1961 on
Simca 1100 1967 on
Simca 1300, 1301, 1500,
1501 1963 on
Skoda One (440, 445, 450)
1955-70
Sunbeam Rapier Alpine
1955-65
Toyota Carina, Celica
1971 on
Toyota Corolla 1100,
1200 1967 on
Toyota Corona 1500 Mk. 1
1965-70
Toyota Corona Mk. 2
1969 on
Triumph TR2, TR3, TR3A
1952-62
Triumph TR4, TR4A
1961-67
Triumph TR5, TR250,
TR6 1967 on
Triumph 1300, 1500
1965-73
Triumph 2000 Mk. 1, 2.5 PI
Mk. 1 1963-69
Triumph 2000 Mk. 2, 2.5 PI
Mk. 2 1969 on
Triumph Dolomite 1972 on
Triumph Herald 1959-68
Triumph Herald 1969-71
Triumph Spitfire, Vitesse
1962-68
Triumph Spitfire Mk. 3, 4
1969 on
Triumph GT6, Vitesse
2 Litre 1969 on
Triumph Toledo 1970 on
Vauxhall Velox, Cresta
1957-72
Vauxhall Victor 1, 2, FB
1957-64
Vauxhall Victor 101
1964-67
Vauxhall Victor FD 1600,
2000 1967-72
Vauxhall Victor 3300,
Ventora 1968-72
Vauxhall Victor FE
Ventora 1972 on
Vauxhall Viva HA 1963-66
Vauxhall Viva HB 1966-70
Vauxhall Viva, HC Firenza
1971 on
Volkswagen Beetle 1954-67
Volkswagen Beetle 1968 on
Volkswagen 1500 1961-66
Volkswagen 1600 Fastback
1965-73
Volkswagen Transporter
1954-67
Volkswagen Transporter
1968 on
Volkswagen 411 1968-72
Volvo 120 series 1961-70
Volvo 140 series 1966 on
Volvo 160 series 1968 on
Volvo 1800 1960-73